SOCIAL JUSTICE AND COMMUNICATION SCHOLARSHIP

LEA's COMMUNICATION SERIES
Jennings Bryant and Dolf Zillmann, General Editors

Selected titles include:

For a complete list of titles in LEA's Communication Series please contact Lawrence Erlbaum Associates, Publishers at www.erlbaum.com

SOCIAL JUSTICE AND COMMUNICATION SCHOLARSHIP

Edited by

Omar Swartz
University of Colorado at Denver
and
Health Services Center

LAWRENCE ERLBAUM ASSOCIATES, PUBLISHERS
2006   Mahwah, New Jersey   London

*62282369

Lawrence Erlbaum Associates, Inc., Publishers
10 Industrial Avenue
Mahwah, New Jersey 07430
www.erlbaum.com

Cover design by Kathryn Houghtaling Lacey

Library of Congress Cataloging-in-Publication Data

Social justice and communication scholarship / edited by Omar Swartz.

p. cm. — (LEA's communication series)

Includes bibliographical references and index.

ISBN 0-8058-5482-7 (alk. paper)
ISBN 0-8058-5483-5 (pbk. : alk. paper)

1. Social justice. 2. Social change. 3. Communication and culture.
4. Communication in politics. 5. Communication in the family.
I. Swartz, Omar. II. Series.

HM671.S653 2006
303.3'72—dc22

2005055208
CIP

Books published by Lawrence Erlbaum Associates are printed on acid-
free paper, and their bindings are chosen for strength and durability.

Printed in the United States of America
10 9 8 7 6 5 4 3 2 1

For my wife, Rui Zhao
Whom I love more deeply than ever.

For my son, Avi Zhao Swartz
May your life light the darkness of others.

Contents

Preface

This volume argues for embracing a turn to social justice in communication studies and displays some of the varied ways in which communication scholars have made that turn. Each chapter stipulates (some explicitly, others implicitly) that the relevance of communication scholarship should be tied to its influence in advancing social democratic values through the critique of, and attempt to change, social institutions that promote (or reify) poverty, hierarchy, and other forms of social inequality. For the contributors to this volume, social justice communication research is informed by and contributes to the progressive ideological and political commitments of the individual engaged in research.

The genesis for this edited collection occurred a few years ago as I was in the middle of an extended research project that culminated in my recent book, *In Defense of Partisan Criticism* (Swartz, 2005). In that book, I argued that by embracing a social justice perspective in communication studies, scholars do not cast aside their professional personas but, instead, privilege an academic world in which they take none of their assumptions for granted and evaluate the relative worth of those assumptions in terms of social utility. A fundamental assumption of that text, as well as earlier books of mine, such as *Conducting Socially Responsible Research* (Swartz, 1997), is that there is no worthier end for measuring social utility than the abolishment of social injustice.

In writing *In Defense of Partisan Criticism*, I discussed my ideas with many of the contributors who are included in this volume. As we spoke or exchanged e-mails, we contemplated how social justice is most possible when all people have the maximum freedom to talk about who they are as a society; what they do as citizens, consumers, and workers; and how they envision their future. Fundamental to that freedom is our ability as researchers and teachers to offer the young men and women of the United States an opportunity to rethink their moral identities and realign their political commitments to support policies and practices that advance social justice. Energized by these conversations, I put together a panel for the 2004 Western States Communication Association Convention in Albuquerque, New Mexico, a panel that generated a good deal of interest among the progressive scholars who attended. The time was ripe to take our conversations to the next stage, which is this book. Although the contributors may have different views on contemporary politics or even the definition of social justice, all would agree that an important professional goal of the communication scholar or professor is to offer students options to think about themselves and their society in ways that may be politically challenging but that align themselves with worthwhile political and social causes. The contributors would also agree that an important goal of the communication scholar is the production of research that makes important contributions to progressive social change.

This edited collection is significant because it extends scholarship in the field of social justice studies, articulating new ways for actualizing the goals of applied, engaged, or partisan communication scholarship. Specifically, the book serves the heuristic function of posing new research questions and demonstrating how a wide range of theories and research methods can be employed to study and promote social justice from a communication perspective. Because research oriented to the theme of social justice transcends disciplinary boundaries, the text also has relevance to many departments in the humanities and social sciences beyond the field of communication. Although communication is an organizing motif, the relevance of the collection is not limited to the field from which it emerges.

CHAPTER OVERVIEW

In chapter 1, I discuss the development of my social justice sensibility and how it evolved out of my study of both law and communication. In particular, I focus on C. Wright Mills's notion of the *sociological imagination* and its implication for social justice scholarship in the form of what scholars in our discipline call the *communication imagination*. I articulate my view of social justice as a metamethodology that can be an important element in conceptualizing methodological and professional issues, and I conclude the chapter by discussing how social justice communication scholarship in a democratic society is an essential part of our implicit right and duty as citizens to challenge the normative order so as to continuously construct a society that rejects social stagnation and seeks to reinvent human beings in new and increasingly edifying ways.

In chapter 2, Amardo Rodriguez argues that dominant definitions of communication undermine the ability of communication theory to make meaningful contributions to the creation of a more just and humane world. Rodriguez argues that the institutional absence (or near absence) of social justice matters in the communication field is directly related to the fact that the definitions of communication that guide mainstream communication scholarship and pedagogy are of ontological and epistemological stances that are inherently hostile to social justice concerns. As such, an important task in repositioning communication theory to address social justice issues is to articulate definitions of communication that are more organically amenable to a social justice awareness.

In chapter 3, Lawrence R. Frey examines the reflexive relationship between partisan criticism and applied communicative practices as counterparts for promoting social change and social justice. Frey argues that this reflexive relationship means that the critique of unjust practices is not sufficient in and of itself; partisan critique also must be accompanied by concrete applications and interventions on the part of communication scholars that are directed toward changing those unjust practices. Without intervention—*praxis*—social change, Frey concludes, will remain an unfulfilled promise.

In chapter 4, Phillip K. Tompkins, a 7-year volunteer at a Denver homeless shelter, writes about his struggle to ascertain the causes of homelessness to eliminate it from U.S. society. He reports and analyzes sources of resistance to his abolitionist cause, which he identifies as being political and ontological problems. Adopting aspects of liberation theology, Tompkins explores and critiques the important and underappreciated distinctions between charity and justice, as well as the unfortunate recalcitrance of the "powers and principalities" that enforce *charity* over *justice* in maintaining the social and economic status quo.

In chapter 5, Jennifer Lyn Simpson and Rebecca Brown Adelman use multiple narrative methods to interrogate the construction and performance of knowledge about a wide range of social justice issues. By exploring, reflecting on, and examining the history and process of the Interactive Theatre Project (a model of progressive social change rooted in Augusto Boal's methods of Theatre of the Oppressed) at the University of Colorado at Boulder, Simpson and Adelman demonstrate how performance can invite "otherness" into dialogic space, producing alternative ways of knowing and being, and, thereby, demonstrating the potential of a politically responsive constructionist theory of communication in action.

In chapter 6, Raka Shome interrogates U.S.-centered discourses of multiculturalism and difference against the politics of globalization and postcoloniality. Her chapter addresses limits of the logic of multiculturalism as that concept tends to be engaged in academic and public imaginations. Shome critiques the "American-ness" that informs discourses of diversity in this country in which an American subject position and American understandings of community and justice are taken for granted. She suggests that such a perspective remains limited in not connecting the politics of race in the United States with larger global politics of postcoloniality, especially given that the borders of the United States are themselves implicated in, and produced through, various unfolding relations of globality.

In chapter 7, Philip C. Wander argues that given our modern military weapons of mass destruction and the annual increase in poisons released into land, air, and water around the globe, the survival of life on Earth is in doubt. This condition necessitates a new type of *real politick,* one that calculates not merely bottom-line advantages and disadvantages for a fraction of humanity but one that considers the implications of the decisions made by this fraction for the continuity of life on the planet. Social justice, Wander argues, is not an abstract and unreachable ideal; it is better thought of as a tool for rejecting war, the glorification of war, or the conditions that lead to war.

In chapter 8, Tony Palmeri, writing from the Wisconsin region that produced Senator Joseph McCarthy, describes some of the rhetorical challenges involved in creating space for social justice discourse in a region conditioned to perceiving itself as conservative. Drawing on his experience as a media activist, Palmeri provides practical techniques for communicating socially conscious messages to audiences that initially may be hostile to them. Palmeri demonstrates how the willingness to go beyond "preaching to the choir" to address new audiences, although often a slow and frustrating process, is a crucial element of the process of social change.

In chapter 9, Linda Potter Crumley discusses interpersonal relationships as an integral part of social justice. Although not often framed from the perspective of social justice, interpersonal and family communication theory and research offer a unique and important view of the roots of social justice as it is practiced or subverted in close relationships. Crumley argues that the dialectics and communicative practices that create and are created by the social justice and injustice of close relationships affect individuals' conceptions of and expectations for social justice on a broader societal scale.

In chapter 10, Wenshu Lee searches for theoretically informed ways of transforming college classrooms into social justice communities. In engaging the classroom as a site for bringing up, exploring, and debating socially important issues, Lee struggles to articulate better ways to teach social justice and communication. She describes in detail her effort to re-create the practice of classroom teaching to bring about the social change she hopes to inspire in students. In so doing, she addresses the question of how to engage students with a social justice vision, deal with students who reject the premises of social justice work or question its value, and interact with colleagues and institutions who do not share a commitment to social change.

In chapter 11, W. Barnett Pearce discusses his experience as chairperson in the early 1990s when the Department of Communication at Loyola University Chicago revised its undergraduate curriculum to promote social justice. Although the project was successfully implemented, Barnett and his colleagues were surprised by the number and the intensity of efforts to block or constrain the new curriculum. Pearce recounts what worked and what could have been done better, so that lessons drawn from the experience will be useful to other departments grappling with similar issues.

In chapter 12, Lee Artz concludes this book with observations and questions that arose from being asked to read and comment on the chapters. In particular, he identifies what I consider to be a key criticism with regard to my decision in editing this book to be as inclusive as possible with the term *social justice*. Simply, I chose diversity over specificity so as not to impose my view of social justice on the contributors. The drawback of such a decision, which Artz recognizes, is that the lack of a clear definition for the term across the chapters threatens to problematize the social justice charge that the contributors to this volume assume. In particular, Artz claims that the inclusiveness of the social justice perspective excludes or makes less likely the critique of material practices that places scholars in solidarity with those in struggle.

Artz's point is well taken. However, the benefit of being inclusive is clear: Intellectual diversity on potentially controversial issues always is a virtue. A strength of this collection, therefore, is that the chapters are written by scholars of different races, gender, ethnicities, and religious and political affiliations, who, nevertheless, are all committed to progressive political change. Like our readers, few of us agree about what exactly progressive political change means and involves, but we all agree that communication is consequential and that, in studying and teaching it, we care about its effect on humanity, especially in terms of promoting community health.

—*Omar Swartz*

REFERENCES

Swartz, O. (2005). *In Defense of Partisan Criticism*. New York: Peter Lang.
Swartz, O. (1997). *Conducting Socially Responsible Research*. Thousand Oaks, CA: Sage.

Introduction

Omar Swartz
University of Colorado at Denver
and Health Sciences Center

As I write this introduction in August 2005, the United States is in the midst of a painful—many would even say shameful—occupation of Iraq. More than 2,000 U.S. military personnel have died and the number continues to grow. More than 10,000 American soldiers have been wounded, in many cases seriously. Tens of thousands of Iraqis have been killed and the Iraqi bloodshed shows no sign of abating in the foreseeable future. The President of the United States and others in his administration have been accused of lying about the reasons for invading Iraq and cultivated irrational fears among the U.S. people to justify a policy of global militarism in Afghanistan, Iraq, and probably beyond. Arguably, the world has grown more insecure and essential democratic civil liberties have been eroded in the United States and elsewhere under George W. Bush's leadership.

As President Bush frequently remarks, the defining documents of the U.S. government, such as the *Constitution* and the *Declaration of Independence*, refer to lofty and noble ideas such as equality, democracy, freedom, and the right to pursue happiness. Nobody would oppose any of these goals, as they should be the fundamental reasons for the existence of all political systems. However, this liberal and exciting rhetoric was intended by its authors to be rigidly defined. As is well known (if not underappreciated by U.S. citizens), for most of this country's history political enfranchisement was limited to a minority of the population—White men with property. It was not until the 1960s, more than 150 years after the founding of our Republic, an era that constantly is condemned for its "excesses" by our government elites, that we underwent the widest expansion of political enfranchisement in this country's history. African Americans, women, homosexuals, and politically progressive people began, for the first time, to be accorded a meaningful degree of respect and a place in our political, social, and economic worlds. The 1960s constituted a pivotal period in U.S. history when social justice became, for a time, a normative individual and national goal for many in this country toward which to work.

Although most people understand this history to some extent, what often goes unnoticed is the fact that social justice in the 1960s emerged only after masses of people clamored in the streets and, with great sacrifice, demanded it—and who themselves often were marginalized by the government as "terrorists" and "anti-American." The political progress that we find in the 1960s was just a start, however, and many of the political gains made during that era have eroded, as have many of the more overarching political and economic gains on behalf of workers made by organized labor in the 1930s. These are ill portents for social justice, democracy, and the world our children will inherit.

Although the government does, on occasion, grant suffrage and addresses the needs of the majority of its citizens (in other words, practices social justice on some of the most fundamental levels), it also works to curtail those rights when it can, particularly when those rights conflict with corporate profit. Of all the industrial first-world nations, the United States ranks last (or close to last) on a wide range of political and social rights and freedoms. For example, we have no way of guaranteeing that the poorest among us, roughly a fifth of our population, will have equal political representation, not to mention access to humane levels of shelter, health care, food, and education. Although net wealth in the United States continues to increase, essential public institutions falter for lack of funds. As a result, the overall quality of life for many in the United States is decreasing.

The point I am making in this introduction to an edited collection of essays on communication and social justice is that degrees of freedom, democracy, and openness of communication are to be cultivated through diligence, persistence, and hard work. Social justice never is about absolutes but it is about being able to talk about the pressing problems of the day to articulate, critique, and offer solutions. Doing so, however, is increasingly difficult. Where, for example, are the public venues in this nation for talking about the deleterious effects of corporatism on our society and on the world? How can we talk seriously about getting rid of homelessness and ensuring that all U.S. citizens have decent health care when these and other progressive ideals go against the ideology of corporatism and, more recently, Bush's "war on terror," in which dissent from corporate domination or political plutocracy equals treason? There is little accountability and little freedom of information when the country is geared up for total war against an ideology that has no clear referent and when U.S. citizens have little historical understanding of the factors that contribute to increasing cultures of intolerance and violence.

As communication scholars, we realize that social justice is possible only when all people have the maximum freedom to talk about who they are as a society; what they do as citizens, consumers, and workers; and how they want to envision their future. Fundamental to this freedom is our ability as researchers and teachers to offer the young men and women of the United States an opportunity to rethink their moral identities and realign their political commitments to support policies that advance social justice. The scholars whose work appears in this volume are all committed to social justice. Although the contributors may have differing views on contemporary politics, the Iraq war, or even the definition of social justice, all would agree that an important professional goal of the communication scholar and professor is to offer students options to think about themselves and their society in ways that may be politically challenging but that align themselves with worthwhile political and social causes.

About the Editor

Omar Swartz (PhD, Purdue University, 1995; JD, Duke University, 2001, magna cum laude) is an Assistant Professor in the Department of Communication at the University of Colorado at Denver and Health Sciences Center. His primary areas of research and teaching are persuasion, diversity, philosophy of communication, and mass media law and public policy. His writing focuses on the intersections among the U.S. legal system, the history of social injustice and intellectual intolerance in the United States, and the philosophies of Richard Rorty and Michel Foucault. Dr. Swartz is the author of seven books and more than 60 essays, book chapters, and reviews.

About the Contributors

Rebecca Brown Adelman (MA, New York University, 1994) is the creator and director of the Interactive Theatre Project at the University of Colorado at Boulder. She has worked and trained with Augusto Boal, author, actor, and founder of the Theatre of the Oppressed, and she teaches courses on theatre for social change. Her passion for social justice and community building inspires and informs much of her work in the theater. With an extensive background in theater and improvisation from New York City, she is an actor, director, and writer who performs frequently in Boulder and Denver. She is also a company member of Playback Theatre West, and is co-founder of Theater-13, the in-resident Theatre Troupe of the Boulder Museum of Contemporary Art.

Lee Artz (PhD, University of Iowa) is an Associate Professor in the Department of Communication and Creative Arts and Director of the Center for Instructional Excellence at Purdue University Calumet. He has taught communication at Purdue University Calumet, Loyola University Chicago, the University of Iowa, and Stanford University. In addition to having written numerous articles on cultural diversity, social justice, and democratic communication for leading journals, he has written, coauthored, or edited numerous books, including *Communication Practices & Democratic Society, Of Our Own Making: Marxism and Communication Studies, Bring 'Em On! Media and Politics in the Iraq War, Globalization of Corporate Media Hegemony,* and *Marxism and Communication Studies-The Point is to Change It.*

Linda Potter Crumley (PhD, University of Texas, Austin, 2002) is an Associate Professor in the School of Journalism and Communication at Southern Adventist University. In 2000, she was the recipient (along with cowriter Anita L. Vangelisti) of the Franklin H. Knower Article Award for Scholarship of Exceptional Quality and Influence from the Interpersonal Communication Division of the National Communication Association.

Lawrence R. Frey (PhD, University of Kansas, 1979) is Professor in the Department of Communication at the University of Colorado at Boulder. His research focuses on group communication, particularly the study of natural groups, and on applied communication, with particular emphases on communication and social justice and communication and community building. He is the author or editor of 12 books, three special journal issues, and more than 55 published book chapters and journal articles, and is the recipient of 10 distinguished scholarship awards.

Wenshu Lee (PhD, University of Southern California, 1989) is Professor in the Department of Communication Studies at San José State University. Her primary research and teaching areas include queer/*Kuaer* identities, critical interpersonal communication, critical intercultural communication, and postcolonial gender, feminist, and womanist criticism and methodology. She has served on the review boards of many national and regional journals. Her work has appeared in *Quarterly Journal of Speech, Journal of Applied Communication Research, Western Journal of Communication, Howard Journal of Communications, International and Intercultural Communication Annual,* and *Journal of Homosexuality.*

Tony Palmeri (PhD, Wayne State University, 1987) is an Associate Professor of Communication at the University of Wisconsin Oshkosh. He has published scholarly essays in the *Journal of Communication Inquiry, Speaker and Gavel,* the *Gallatin Review,* and other journals. He publishes and edits a daily alternatives news Web site (tonypalmeri.com) and his monthly column of media criticism, "Media Rants," appears in the northeast Wisconsin *Valley Scene.*

W. Barnett Pearce (PhD, Ohio University, 1969) is Professor of Human and Organization Development at Fielding Graduate University. He is one of the primary developers of the theory of the coordinated management of meaning (CMM). Among his books are *Communication and the Human Condition, Interpersonal Communication: Making Social Worlds,* and, with Stephen Littlejohn, *Moral Conflict: When Social Worlds Collide.* In addition to his scholarly work, he is a practitioner who facilitates, consults, and trains clients through the nonprofit Public Dialogue Consortium and the for-profit Pearce Associates.

Amardo Rodriguez (PhD, Howard University, 1995) is Associate Professor in the Department of Communication and Rhetorical Studies at Syracuse University. His research and teaching interests explore the potentiality of emergent conceptions of communication that foreground moral, existential, and spiritual assumptions about the human condition to redefine and enlarge current understandings of democracy, diversity, and community. His publications include articles in *Journal of Intercultural Communication, Journal of Intergroup Relations, Journal of Religion and Society, Qualitative Report, Journal of Rural Community Psychology, Southern Communication Journal,* and elsewhere. His books include *On Matters of Liberation (I): The Case Against Hierarchy; Diversity as Liberation (II): Introducing a New Understanding of Diversity,* and *Essays on Communication and Spirituality: Contributions to a New Discourse on Communication.*

Raka Shome (PhD, University of Georgia, 1996) is an Assistant Professor at Arizona State University in the Department of Communication. She works in the areas of postcolonial, transnational, feminist, race, and cultural studies. Her work has been published in journals such as *Critical Studies in Media Communication, Communication Theory, Communication Review, International Journal of Cultural Studies,* and *Feminist Media Studies.* She has received numerous awards for her research, including the Karl Wallace Award from the National Communication Association, Outstanding Article Award from Critical and Cultural Studies Division of the National Communication Association, New Investigator Award from the Rhetorical and Communication Theory Division of the National Communication Association, and the Distinguished Scholarship Award (co-winner) from the Intercultural and International Division of the National Communication Association.

Jennifer Lyn Simpson (PhD, University of Colorado at Boulder, 2001) coordinates diversity, dialogue, and community-building efforts at the University of Colorado at Boulder and teaches courses at both the Boulder and Denver campuses of the University of Colorado. Her research interests are in difference matters in organizations, organizational culture, engaged scholarship, and issues of voice, agency, power, and social justice. Her engaged organizational work grew out of, and continues to inform her scholarly work, around creating spaces that foster dialogic engagement around matters of difference and social justice.

Phillip K. Tompkins (PhD, Purdue University, 1962) is Professor Emeritus of Communication and Comparative Literature at University of Colorado at Boulder. A Past President and Fellow of the International Communication Association (NCA), and served as the Editor of *Communcation Monographs.* Tompkins won many research, teaching and service awards, including the Robert J. Kibler Memorial Award from NCA in 1990. He is the author of more than 60 published articles and book chapters in organizational communication and literacy/rhetorical criticism and theory. He is the author of four books and a monograph published by the National Aeronautic and Space Administration (NASA); he is the co-editor (with R. McPhee) of the award-winning volume, *Organizational Communication: Traditional Themes and New Directions* (1985). His most recent book, *Apollo, Challenger, Columbia: The Decline of the Space Program: A Study in Organizational Communication* (2005), was nominated for the Book of the Year Award given by the Organizational Communication Division of NCA. His most recent presentations were presented at an international conference sponsored by NASA in September of 2005 and a keynote address at Embry-Riddle Aeronautic University in January of 2006. Since retiring from teaching in 1998 he has worked as a volunteer at the St. Francis Center, a homeless shelter in Denver, Colorado, and is preparing a book on how charity and justice are relevant to the abolition of homelessness.

Philip C. Wander (PhD, University of Pittsburgh, 1968) is Professor of Communication Studies at San Jose State University. His primary research and teaching areas include argumentation and debate, cultural and rhetorical criticism, and political communication. He has served on review boards for national and regional journals and has published in the *Quarterly Journal of Speech*, *Journal of Communication*, *Journal of Popular Culture*, and various regional journals. He is a coauthor of the book *Cold War Rhetoric*.

1

Reflections of a Social Justice Scholar

Omar Swartz

University of Colorado at Denver and Health Sciences Center

Axiomatic to critical scholarship is the assumption that criticism, even so-called academic criticism, embraces the heuristic and transformative power of praxis. Furthermore, our goal as engaged scholars is not only to generate knowledge but also to have an impact on the democratic society in which we live and to redress the injustices that hurt many of its members (Conquergood, 1995; Rodden, 1993). An important subcategory of critical scholarship is social justice scholarship, a growing area of inquiry in the rhetoric, communication, and composition literatures (see, e.g., Artz, 2001; Cushman, 1996; Frey, 1998; Frey, Pearce, Pollock, Artz, & Murphy, 1996; Swan, 2002; Swartz, 1997a, 2005a). Bradley (1996) defines social justice as

> [T]he directing and shaping of society's laws and institutions (e.g., the economy, medical care, social systems, unemployment insurance, etc) to achieve an equal level of fairness and just treatment for all members of society; a system in which just conduct within a society toward all members of that society is guided by the moral principles of truth, reason, justice and fairness. (p. 373)

Although social justice is an abstract and indefinite political and ideological concept (Cooks, 2000), it is, nevertheless, a powerful and inspiring goal. Animated by this goal, much of the literature in this area argues that the relevance of scholarship should be tied to its influence in advancing social

1

democratic values through the critique of social institutions that promote (or reify) poverty, hierarchy, and social inequality. In the words of Artz (2001), "Our discipline's ongoing concern with democracy, justice, and ethics compels continued reasoned attempts to put communication at the service of humanity" (p. 243).

In this chapter, I synthesize the concept of social justice scholarship and its importance to a democratic society that underlies much of my published work (e.g., Swartz, 1997a, 2004d, 2005a, 2005b). This concept is based on two unorthodox yet highly intuitive notions of rhetoric. First, I seek to understand how *rhetoric*—defined broadly as the sustained social manipulations by cultural and economic elites—affects society in ways that seek to limit thought and cultural and economic opportunity for those outside the ruling classes. Second, I seek to articulate a *liberating rhetoric*—defined broadly as an emancipatory counterdiscourse, the act of speaking truth to power—as a method for creating new potentials for thought, opportunity, and experience. Situating both notions of rhetoric are assumptions of philosophy and human nature as articulated in critical theory and Western Marxism (see Fromm, 1992), as well as in Rorty's (1989, 1998) articulation of the U.S. pragmatist tradition.

This chapter is comprised of three sections. In the first, I discuss the development of my social justice sensibility and how it evolved out of my study of both law and communication. In particular, I focus on Mills's notion of the *sociological imagination* and its implication for social justice scholarship in the form of what Engen (2002) called the *communication imagination*. In the second section, I articulate my view of social justice as a metamethodology that can be an important element in conceptualizing methodological and professional issues. I conclude in the third section by discussing how social justice communication scholarship in a democratic society is an essential part of our implicit right and duty as citizens to challenge the normative order to continuously construct a society that rejects social stagnation and seeks to reinvent human beings in new and increasingly edifying ways.

ASSUMPTIONS BEHIND MY SOCIAL JUSTICE SENSIBILITY

My practice of social justice scholarship is intended to critique U.S. society to enable progressive, inclusive, and fair communities to emerge from within that society. By progressive, I mean a movement toward an egalitarian, sustainable society in which social wealth and opportunity are equitably distributed. Wander (1984b) stated it well when he wrote that to "be progressive, change must progress toward something. That something, oriented around traditional humanist notions of human potential, is grounded in the emancipation of human potential" (p. 205). Human beings have the potential to create a society that is kind, just, healthy, and fair, but often are discouraged from doing so by the rhetorical and legal environments in which our society is situated, compromising many of the admirable values that the United States claims in its normative narratives to represent (e.g., equality, fairness, justice, and commitment to human rights; see Swartz, 2005a).

A scholarship of social justice is not incompatible with more traditional or systemic research—it is merely different (see Kersten, 1986). Unlike traditional scholarship, which tends to serve middle- or upper class interests, social justice scholarship "makes an explicit 'preferential option' for those who are disadvantaged by prevalent social structures or extraordinary social acts" (Frey et al., 1996, p. 115). By privileging the disadvantaged, I have not cast aside my professional persona but, instead, assume an academic world in which scholars take none of their assumptions for granted and evaluate the relative worth of their assumptions in terms of their social utility. My most fundamental assumption is that there is no worthier end for measuring scholarship's social utility than the abolishment of social injustice.

Nevertheless, as part of my engaged persona, I disclaim pretensions to authority in a positivistic sense (i.e., belief in "true" knowledge, essentialist values, and commitment to a disciplinary hierarchy). Similar to how Rorty (1983) frequently positions himself, my self-image is of a privileged North American White man who had the opportunity to progress full time through 12 years of college and four degrees, where I had the freedom to read many books. As an academic, I still have this freedom, which I take very seriously. The more I read—primarily in law, political science, history, and philosophy—the more dedicated I become to social justice, but this bookish habit of mine (a kind of "occupational psychosis" in Burke's terms) does not, in a technocratic sense, make me an authority on anything, although I hope it does enable me to be persuasive as a writer on those topics I study and about which I feel most passionate. I even shy away from claiming that I am a *communication scholar*, although I teach in a communication department and am nominally identified with communication scholarship. I agree with Anderson and Baym (2004) when they wrote that "none of us can lay claim to being *a* communication scholar as each of us must be *some kind* of communication scholar" (p. 610). For me, a critical communication scholar, the value of an academic discipline is that it provides cultural space for writing what are, essentially, noncommercial works of social and political analysis. That, in itself, is an important form of communication scholarship, similar to the text *Permanence and Change* as was originally intended by Burke (1984; Schiappa & Keehner, 1991). There are few independent scholars in this country, people such as Burke, who have the freedom to pursue a research agenda free from the political and ideological boundaries of established academic departments (Jacoby, 1987). Thus, I view traditional academic forms and pretensions as necessary evils. I do not worship them and use them only to the extent that they help me to do what I hope to accomplish as a teacher and scholar.

Social justice criticism helps to bring the systemic manipulations of culture into focus so that they can be judged by the standards of social justice (defined in terms of equity and the wide distribution of wealth and societal resources). In this way, my practice of scholarship does more than merely call attention to the threats to our humanity that exist through the arguments and manipulations of others. It also stems from an urge to perform rhetoric—to articulate a "No" to the falsifications and manipulations of our government and institutions of private economic power and to counter them with texts that inform and influence society in progressive ways.

Having been trained as a lawyer, as well as a rhetorical theorist and critic, my passion for social justice is grounded in my suspicion of normative power that is based in a critique of U.S. constitutional law (via a critical and historical legal perspective). Intellectually, being in law school was enlightening, but on a day-to-day level, I found it excruciatingly difficult to fit in and act as if I believed in the normative values being inculcated (Swartz, 2004b). In fact, I identified not with the judges who were upholding the social order but with those I considered to be the victims of that order. It was not just the social construction of the criminal and the draconian prison sentences that have created the first prison society in U.S. history that offended me, but I felt solidarity for the renters in their struggle against the landlords, people fighting the system for substantive equality; dissenting shareholders who tried to prevent their companies from producing napalm during the Vietnam War; and the thousands of anarchists, socialists, and communists imprisoned under anti-free-speech laws or hunted down and murdered by government agents. These are just some of the victims of the law that come to mind as I reflect on my law school experiences (see Swartz, 2004b, 2005a).

Much of the law, I discovered, is like a coral reef built largely from the calcification of human bodies, lost potential, and sadness over 500 years in the common law tradition (i.e., Swartz, 2004a). I took issue with many, if not most, of the court decisions I read and found a great deal to criticize about the assumptions that the judges brought to the law. I began to suspect that these venerated elites had no privileged philosophical or moral right to judge, that their judgments were violence, that judges serve something other than justice, and that the respect Americans vest in them and in their decisions often is misplaced. Similar to Nietzsche (1995), I "mistrust all in whom the impulse to punish is powerful" (p. 100). Although I did well in law school, graduating *magna cum laude*, I left with a strong anarchist suspicion of professionalism. Now I believe in no authority figure or dogma. As I indicated previously, I judge people, institutions, and cultural artifacts, such as legal proscriptions and scholarship, by the work they accomplish toward social justice and not by their status. In and of itself, status often is a hindrance to progressive thought and social commitment.

Even more fundamental to my development as a social justice scholar is my pre-law-school awareness of what could be called (after Mills) the communication imagination—of the rhetorician's role in helping citizens to name the constraints placed on them by politicians, the exploitative class, and the legal system (Engen, 2002, Kairys, 1993; Swartz, 1997a, 2005a). It is to an explication of this idea that this chapter now turns.

THE COMMUNICATION IMAGINATION

Nearly half a century ago, Mills (1959) warned that what he termed "social scientists" (but what I recognize simply as scholars) were losing what he considered to be the classic commitment to social engagement. Such engagement had existed in the second half of the 19th century, inspired, in part, by the writings of Emile Durkheim, Karl Marx, Sigmund Freud, Thorstein Veblen, and Max Weber. These scholars founded intellectual traditions that informed and inspired the rising public concern with issues of poverty, child labor, public health, and political and corporate corruption. Since World War II, however, Mills observed that this critical public ethos had waned and that scholars have become "less intellectually insurgent and more administratively practical" (p. 96). Such bureaucratic ethos, what Burke (1984) diagnosed as the "bureaucratization of the imaginative," has, as one of its goals, providing "new justifications for corporate business as a system of power" (Mills, 1959, p. 96). The result of this trend, as clear now as it was when Mills first described it, is that "the centers of higher learning tend increasingly to produce seemingly a-political technicians" (p. 98). Mills lamented how higher education in the United States avoids "political education," which involves the ability for students to recognize and understand the power struggles that permeate modern society and to view these struggles as consequential for their lives. Mills's notion of political education can be contrasted with what Burke (1989) once described as "adult education" (p. 269) in the United States; namely, Hollywood and advertising. To Burke's insight, articulated as it was in the 1930s, we can add the more recent "educational" tools of television, public relations, and much political communication.

The prevalence of such adult education and the lack of a political education contribute to what Mills and many others since identify as mass apathy in our society, as well as an insensitivity to progressive social and political ideas and practices. In short, Mills (1959) argued that academics in his day, much like in our more modern academic environment "[n]either raise demands on the powerful for alternative policies, nor set forth such alternatives before publics. They do not try to put responsible content into the politics of the United States; they help to empty politics and to keep it empty" (p. 183). As a result, Mills argued, private uneasiness among citizens and voters often remains private, segmented, and unconnected to the concerns and practices of normative politicians. The collective spirit of the nation, which I assume is kind and progressive, and the heartfelt concerns of most people for a fair and just society, seldom are discussed in terms of impeding structural inequality.

Still, Mills was hopeful that these trends in academia toward corporate and governmental apologetics and political quietism could be curtailed and that scholars could once again cultivate a rational, humanistic, and inspiring approach to social and political engagement. Fundamental to his hope was the ascendance of what he called the sociological imagination. With this phrase, Mills described and advocated a general intellectual ethos—a critical attitude and an engaged academic persona—that easily encompasses the humanities and, more specifically, the field of communication studies (see Engen, 2002). The goal of the social sciences, Mills (1959) contended, is to cultivate a critical ethos so as to help ordinary people to "achieve lucid summations of what is going on in the world and of what may be happening within themselves" (p. 5). An important task of scholarship involved the effort of scholars "to translate personal troubles into public issues, and public issues into terms of their human meaning for a variety of individuals" (Mills, 1959, p. 187). Toward this end, Mills envisioned a social science "as a sort of public intelligence apparatus, concerned with public issues and private troubles and with the structural trends of our time underlying them both" (p. 181).

Mills's vision is attainable, I argue, and is needed now, more than ever, as extreme political and cultural conservatives solidify their control over U.S. society. The widespread adoption of the sociological imagination, or some disciplinary specific form of it, is crucial if academics are to transcend their provincial and insular isolation in U.S. political life. In a passage that reso-nates eerily today, Mills (1959) asked:

> Where is the intelligentsia that is carrying on the big discourse of the West-ern world *and* whose work as intellectuals is influential among parties and publics and relevant to the great decisions of our time? Where are the mass media open to such men? Who among those who are in charge of the two-party state and its ferocious military machines are alert to what goes on in the world of knowledge and reason and sensibility? Why is the free intel-lect so divorced from decisions of power? Why does there now prevail among men of power such a higher and irresponsible ignorance? (p. 183)

Engen's (2002) rearticulation of Mill's sociological imagination as the communication imagination was novel, although I have been using this concept since 1995 to ground my pedagogy and explain to students the sig-nificance of studying communication. Engen wrote that "those with well developed communicative imaginations are morally intelligent in that they recognize their connections to fellow human beings" (p. 45). Such moral in-telligence is essential to social justice scholarship. Now, I redefine Mills's so-ciological imagination and Engen's communication imagination as *partisan criticism*, an important goal of which is to "interrupt moral exclusion" (Leets, 2001, p. 1860). As Leets explains, moral exclusion "is a psychosocial orien-tation toward certain individuals or groups for whom justice principles or considerations of fairness and allocation of resources are not applicable" (p. 1860). In other words, moral exclusion is a normative and social condition (i.e., systemic) in which some people, on the basis of their membership in a disfavored group or their socioeconomic conditions, are rendered morally inconsequential, unimportant as human beings, and undeserving of basic levels of dignity and integrity.

For years, my work has been dismissed by disciplinary gatekeepers as "partisan," as if partisanship is a bad thing. Lately, however, I have begun embracing this label and believe that a partisan stance toward communica-tion and legal scholarship is both a necessary and beneficial part of the criti-cal persona for academics, as well as a vital dynamic within public intellectual culture (Swartz, 2005a). In so doing, I hope to relieve the word *partisan* of its negative connotations and reposition it as an important method or attitude for informed social criticism (see Swartz, 2004c).

The partisan attitude is a relationship that critics construct with their work and audience—both in a professional, as well as in a larger, social sense. Similar to Brummett (1984), who argued that the primary audience for communication scholarship is ordinary people, I maintain that the goal of critical, partisan, or social justice scholarship is, in Brummett's words, less to contribute "to the store of scholarly knowledge possessed by the academic community," and more as a way for "enriching the stack of general knowledge possessed by ordinary people" (p. 99). Scholarship, I believe, should serve the needs of people as opposed to institutions or other reified abstractions (i.e., corporations or bureaucracies).

Essential to this notion of engaged scholarship is the integration of the scholar's life and values with his or her scholarship; such scholarship "emerges from and channels the emotions of the researcher" (Frey et al., 1996, p. 115). We are human beings and our scholarship is an expression of our hopes, dreams, faiths, and passions; therefore, it often is necessary to "embrace our emotionality as a central component of scholarship" (Allen, Orbe, & Olivas, 1999, p. 406). Constraints within the academy, however, often preclude scholars from professionally engaging in the socially transformative work that is fundamental to their personal identities (Bach, Blair, Nothstine, & Pym, 1996; Blair, Brown, & Baxter, 1994; Swartz, 1997b). I take issue with that preclusion and assert that we can be both scholars *and* socially engaged intellectuals. We can be constructively hostile to the political and economic status quo at the same time that we reaffirm our commitments to equality, tolerance, diversity, and community. In the tradition of Mills, I reaffirm Wander's (1983) argument that disciplinary criticism should address public issues and that the academic persona and the persona of the public intellectual are not necessarily in conflict.

I also take as my model for criticism what Rorty (1979) called "edifying scholarship"—it is abnormal; its purpose is "to take us out of our old selves by the power of strangeness, to aid us in becoming new beings" (p. 360). As people tend to resist change, this necessarily generates social controversy. Such controversy is not negative, however, but heuristic, contributing, possibly, to the widening and transformation of disciplinary thought (Mills, 1959). To be controversial is to take a stand against what people in a given context commonly accept as being true. It is to enact a counterdiscourse, which is important on two levels: It helps to remind people that all truths are perspectival (Hawhee, 1999) and that context is contingent and subject to change. More pragmatically, it activates otherwise abstract scholarly thought and places it in the lived world of experience. In McKerrow's (1989) terms, the "act of performing, within the context of our expertise as critics/readers of the social condition, moves the focus from criticism as method to critique as practice" (p. 108). As I see it, an important aim of social justice criticism parallels McKerrow's function for critical rhetoric, which is "to understand the integration of power/knowledge in society—what possibilities for change the integration invites or inhibits and what intervention strategies might be considered appropriate to effect social change" (p. 91). Such criticism has a unique value—a value distinct from, and in some ways incompatible with, the gathering and codification of disciplinary knowledge.

SOCIAL JUSTICE AS A METAMETHODOLOGY

Now that I have discussed some of the subjective experiences that ground my understanding of and commitment to social justice or partisan scholarship, I turn in this section to a more general discussion of social justice as a form of metamethodology. By this, I mean that a social justice approach to scholarship can be an important element in situating methodological and professional issues. In discussing the interconnections among methodology, professionalization, and communication, it is not my purpose in this chapter to explicate one particular methodology. Instead, I want to talk more generally about a metamethodology in communication research, highlighting its social justice elements.

Communication scholars, we all know, are in excellent positions to understand how language contributes to the unhealthy social and economic relationships that plague our society and the world (Black, 1970; Burke, 1973; Solomon, 1985). Many of us chose to study communication precisely because of this awareness. Focused expressions of this view appear throughout the large body of work by Wander (e.g., 1983, 1984a, 1984b, 1990), as well as in the work of others, such as Cloud (1998) and many of the contributors to this volume.

In the early 1980s, as the "new" cold war was beginning and as U.S. intervention in the Third World was accelerating, Wander (1983) argued that "a reconsideration of the purposes of criticism and the study of rhetoric take on meaning" (p. 18). Because rhetoricians, in particular, and communication scholars, in general, can identify abusive uses of language, offer alternatives to preferred readings, and dilute the power of elites to manipulate the public, we are positioned to intervene, to point out different courses of action, and to edify. At the very least, we can show to suffering people that we care. In a classic formulation of what I reposition as partisan or social justice scholarship, Wander (1983) argued explicitly:

Criticism takes an ideological turn when it recognizes the existence of powerful vested interests benefiting from and consistently urging politics and technology that threaten life on this planet, when it realizes that we search for alternatives. The situation is being constructed; it will not be averted either by ignoring it or placing it beyond our province. (p. 18)

As academics, much of this intervention in our discipline takes place through teaching students (Brummett, 1984; Frey et al., 1996). Although such intervention does not preclude direct action in the political realms when the opportunity presents itself (Conquergood, 1995, 2002), it is important to recognize and embrace our occupational roles as educators. Within our professional roles, scholars should write and teach for social influence to advance a radically democratic political agenda (tempered variants of this call appear in Hart, 1993, and Redding, 1985). Common to Frey et al., Wander, Conquergood, Hart, Redding, and myself is the belief that, as communication scholars, we have something to say about the experiences that we share with others as citizens in this society, and that we can articulate criteria to distinguish between acceptable and unacceptable behavior.

Although this view of scholarship and an occupational persona finds its disciplinary expression (e.g., in the National Communication Association) most notably in Wander, it has ties to earlier intellectuals and scholars from outside the field (e.g., Said, 1994). In the last 40 years, the exemplar of this type of scholarship has been Chomsky. In 1966, Chomsky (1966/1987) published his paradigm-defining essay, "The Responsibilities of Intellectuals," which has been recognized as perhaps the "single most influential piece of anti-war literature" in U.S. history (Schalk, 1991, p. 142). Chomsky (1966/1987) argued that:

Intellectuals are in a position to expose the lies of governments, to analyze actions according to their causes and motives and often hidden intentions. In the Western world at least, they have the power that comes from political liberty, from access to information and freedom of expression. For a privileged minority, Western democracy provides the leisure, the facilities, and the training to seek the truth lying hidden behind the veil of distortion and misrepresentation, ideology, and class interest through which the events of current history are presented to us. (p. 60)

Authoring more than 100 books and countless essays and interviews on political and social analysis and criticism, Chomsky continues to fulfill the agenda that he set forth in his early essay. Although many scholars disagree with Chomsky's politics, they should keep in mind that I am not presenting the model for academic scholarship when I hold Chomsky up as an exemplar; rather, I claim Chomsky exemplifies an important commitment in which we can situate some of what we do. This Chomsky-inspired commitment to social justice may very well rank among our discipline's most important contributions to a society that continues to wonder what exactly communication scholars accomplish. As an alternative framework, I think it is useful for students to be exposed to counternormative and critical ideas, as they are unlikely to receive them in other places. Democracy is enriched by critical scholars, such as Chomsky and Zinn (2003), as well as by earlier engaged scholars, such as Mills, Russell (1993), Dewey (1954), and de Beauvoir (1989). Along with others in our field (e.g., Rodden, 1993), I have to wonder when the communication discipline will attract or produce such towering and influential public scholars.

To recognize that language contributes to the unhealthy social and economic relationships that plague our society and the world is simply to say that communication matters. Communication matters because our lives, in various manners, are created, conditioned, helped, accentuated, and positioned by the decisions we make about, and through, our communicative practices. If this is true, then the inverse must also be true: To the extent that communication creates understanding, it also creates misunderstanding and leads to social harm (Richards, 1979). Here, however, many scholars begin to diverge in terms of interests and practices. The question that scholars cannot reach consensus in answering is, "In what ways is communication harmful?" It is obvious now that we are beginning to make the slip into ideology, of which many of our colleagues and students are suspicious. It should be clear, however, that ideology is a specter in human life that is never far away, even in our most "objective" research (Novick, 1988; White, 1987). If it is nothing else, ideology is ideas and their relationships to people. Such a concept is intimately connected to the rhetorical function of "adjusting ideas to people and of people to ideas" (Bryant, 1953, p. 313).

In summary, social justice communication scholars do their work in the same ways that other scholars do theirs: by observing, questioning, arguing, justifying, and applying (Brockriede, 1974). Scholarship is little more than reasoned inquiry; such reasoning does not (and probably cannot) be divorced from politics. Social utility is what makes critical scholarship of such great importance, and why what the scholar has to say carries a significant degree of weight, justifying our interventions in public life. This is not to indicate that what others have to say is unimportant; on the contrary, nothing, as I indicated earlier, separates scholars from others besides a certain commitment, discipline, and opportunity resulting from having spent many years in school and having read a great many books (Mills, 1959; Rorty, 1983). Thus, much of what makes us who we are is attitude. Discipline creates attitude, a scholarly attitude that can be made sharp and relevant by our moral commitments. As Hollihan (1994) noted:

> Critics who ignore the moral implications of rhetoric thus perform support for the mystery that preserves the social order. Those critics, on the other hand, who engage the moral issues in rhetoric act to illuminate the implications of the mystification, peel back the mystery, and thus raise the issues that can lead to social change. The act of criticism involves moral choice, and reveals the moral force of the discourse under study. Critics, merely by doing their work, spark a moral debate, for the very act of rhetorical criticism places the values of the social culture at risk. (p. 230)

This process of moral engagement is inevitable. The language that critics use is itself moralistic; consequently, criticism necessarily enacts a morality (Klumpp & Hollihan, 1989; Weaver, 1964, 1970). This leads some people—administrators and conservative politicians, in particular—to worry about a scholarship that seeks to potentially undermine entrenched institutional values associated with positivistic scholarship or Republican, right-wing worldviews and ideology, and to consider such critical writing an inappropriate form of scholarship. Condit (1993) isolated a poignant form of this fear:

> Among humanists, rhetorical critics face an unusually large problem with charges of political bias. Because the texts and contexts we routinely focus upon are self-evidently political, many of our conclusions will instantly and obviously be of greater service to some political constituencies than to others. To protect our jobs as academics, therefore, rhetorical critics have had to respond to intimations that our efforts are generated *merely* by political interests rather than by any unique academic skills. (p. 182)

Consider the national controversy surrounding the critical writings of ethnic studies professor Ward Churchill in January 2005. Churchill (2003), a tenured professor at the University of Colorado at Boulder, implied in an essay that the actions of some U.S. bureaucrats, technicians, bankers, and soldiers were as morally reprehensible as the actions of Adolf Eichmann, the German bureaucrat who administered the Holocaust. Churchill's observation is not particularly original or different than those offered by many other critical writers, even before 9/11 (see, e.g., Burke, 1982). These writers argue that it is not productive to think of what is now called the "war on terror," and used to be called the "war against communism," in black-and-white terms, and that questions of who is or is not innocent and who is or is not evil often serve a base propagandistic function in promoting blind nationalism, aggression, and war.

Rather than talking in these terms, it would be better to confront how little we care as individuals for the suffering of others and how our way of life deleteriously impacts others around the world. Fromm (1988) once wrote that we, meaning everyone, must never tire of watching out for the Eichmann in us all, the tendency to do our jobs and live our lives as if we were a world unto ourselves without connection or obligation to work for the better of humanity. Arendt (1994) famously defined this issue as the "banality of evil" and Hardin (1968) called it the "tragedy of the commons." Churchhill's (2003) argument strikes me as simply another reminder of that very important point, and reflects the importance of what a liberal arts education should seek to foster in students. Yet, in calling for his resignation, the governor of Colorado, Bill Owens, the man ultimately in charge of the university, wrote that "Mr. Churchill's views are not simply anti-American. They are at odds with simple decency, and antagonistic to the beliefs and conduct of civilized people around the world. His views are far outside the mainstream of civil discourse and useful academic work" (Owens, 2005).

Hollihan (1994), however, suggested a way of being that helps us to respond to the not infrequent charges that critical scholarship is anti-American, indecent, uncivilized, and, most important, unuseful academic work. He argued that the "critic's loss of moral detachment emphasizes the importance of the critic's character in the evaluation of his or her arguments" (p. 231). In short, we are what we write and our writing, to be authentic, must be an expression of our values as they are communicated. As Hollihan argued, evidence is audience-dependent and consists of what seems needed to persuade a given audience of what are a set of "facts." Thus, critics should feel free to make whatever claims they can persuade their readers to accept, challenging their audiences to expand their perspectives. Our various audiences—internal to academia or external—are all the "reality check" we need to stipulate. Some, like Governor Owens, may never appreciate what we do. Others, and I believe this community will continue to grow, can use critical scholarship as an opportunity to rethink their moral identities and realign their political commitments to support policies that advance social justice.

SOCIAL JUSTICE COMMUNICATION SCHOLARSHIP IN A DEMOCRATIC SOCIETY

A scholarship of social justice embraces what Hariman (1989) identified as the "rhetorical perspective," one that "replaces disinterestedness with advocacy, balances specialization with generality, and confronts expertise with an assertion of voice" (p. 213). Repositioned from being a disciplinary agency to an individual agency, the voice that speaks is that of the individual, the person we call a scholar. In my view, this scholar speaks for him or herself, not as a member of a disciplinary community; the disciplinary community simply provides important resources and useful training for the scholar to accomplish his or her work. Scholars, as individuals, citizens, socialists, feminists, humanists, or whatever progressive labels people attach to their identities, provide the moral imperative and ethical sensitivity to take the resources available to them and apply them. This is the essence of *praxis* (Swartz, 1996). Aside from its social utility, this *praxis* approach to scholarship has the potential to transform academic professionalization from a "repressive" to a "productive" power (Hariman, 1989, p. 212) and to reject what Edelman (1988) called "professional imperialism" (p. 119). This change in professional perspective becomes easier once we take seriously the observation that moral violation often assumes literary form (Lang, 1988). Language does support material conditions in which people are seriously mistreated; recognizing this compels us to intervene. When injustice is tangible, as often is the case, and when the materiality of suffering cannot be denied, scholarship is just when it acts as moral critique. Scholarship, as enacted in this chapter and throughout this book, embraces this heuristic and transformative point.

In a democratic society, scholarship is both personal and public (Hollihan, 1994; Klumpp & Hollihan, 1989). As someone trained in rhetoric, I have a difficult time distinguishing between these two arenas. For this, I am unashamed. Like other critical scholars, many of us in the discipline have long known that the personal is public. To acknowledge this point is to embrace an empowering perspective. As far back as Aristotle (1991), public personas were recognized as being intimately tied to private selfhoods. We gain influence through who we are as individuals. Aristotle recognized that who we are is more important than the emotions to which we appeal or the reasoning that we use. In other words, we are the message. We are what we speak and write. The more we believe in ourselves, our tasks, and our visions, the more real these tasks and visions become, and the greater our strength in enlisting the support of others (Bormann, 1972). Eventually, if we are lucky, our visions become communal. With our lives and our work, we help to create something larger than ourselves. To achieve this state is to profoundly affect human beings with our will. This is to make history and to remake it. History is a human phenomenon and exists through the power of those who construct it (White, 1987).

As a social justice scholar, I remind students and readers that, from a rhetorical and critical perspective, nothing is ever complete and no system of control is ever total. Our ability to ask questions can empower, energize, and inspire us. The system of control under which we live is only as real as we allow it to be. As we learn to ask questions, we learn that we have potential of which we were unaware. Grappling with this idea is a form of a liberating rhetoric that my scholarship seeks to enact. A liberating rhetoric is one that can be contrasted with the traditional rhetoric of manipulation and control, and of fragmentation and baseness. A liberating rhetoric is an antidote to hierarchy, bureaucracy, scientism, and the deleterious effects of professionalization (Rodriguez, 2001). It is everything that much professional education is not—it is anticoercion, antiauthority, antitradition, and cooperative rather than competitive. In Mills's (1959) words:

> The industrialization of academic life and the fragmentation of the problems of social science cannot result in a liberating educational role for social scientists. For what these schools of thought take apart they tend to keep apart, in very tiny pieces about which they claim to be very certain. But all they could thus be certain of are abstracted fragments, and it is precisely the job of liberal education, *and* the political role of social science, *and* its intellectual promise, to enable men to transcend such fragmented and abstracted milieux: to become aware of historical structures and of their own place within them. (p. 189)

At Duke University Law School, were I earned my law degree, there is a sculpture of a half-dozen people locked in a cage, their hands reaching through the bars toward freedom. The implication of the sculpture, sitting as it does in a main thoroughfare, is that the law is a force to set hapless people free. What is suppressed in that reading is the fact that it is the law, as an embodiment of hierarchy and bureaucracy, that constructs the bars in the first place and that commands people into the cage. A liberating rhetoric, in contrast, seeks to replace bars with opportunities and to replace cages with educational and cultural enrichment. A liberating rhetoric does not ask if it is just when we imprison a particular person; rather, it asks why we feel the need to imprison. It does not ask if a punishment is just but, rather, what is this impulse to punish. A liberating rhetoric asks: Is there not another way to act justly? There usually is.

In our democracy, at least, scholarship is about words, not silence. Ultimately, it is about deeds, but we have to be able to articulate what deeds need to be done first, before we can act. To disregard social justice, critical, or partisan scholarship on the grounds that it is different from traditional or positivistic scholarship or that it is focused on progressive social values when it "should" be politically neutral, is a great encroachment on democratic and humanistic values. Of course, engaged scholarship is not faultless. At times, it can be irresponsible (e.g., much so-called postmodernist scholarship is intellectually and politically questionable because it promotes solipsism and social disengagement; Rosenau, 1992). Furthermore, critical or engaged scholars can suffer from ideological blindness, and their work can rely on tenuous assumptions, as in the belief that cultural politics in and of itself translates into public sphere significance (Rorty, 1998). Engaged inquiry is not a perfect type of inquiry but it is no worse than any other approach, and it never claims to be the final word. It simply is scholarship that often offers intellectual strength and heuristic insight.

When partisan or social justice scholars engage with the world, this does not mean that readers have to accept their claims. No critical scholar would want his or her ideas to be accepted uncritically. However, the place to demonstrate the validity, wisdom, or ethics of an argument is in print and public argument, and a disciplinary and social commitment to this space, therefore, must be jealously guarded. This social commitment represents, arguably, the highest ideals of the university. According to Rorty (1998):

> All universities worthy of the name have always been centers of social protest. If American universities ever cease to be such centers, they will lose both their self-respect and the respect of the learned world. It is doubtful whether the current critics of the universities who are called "conservative intellectuals" deserve this description. For intellectuals are supposed to be aware of, and speak to, issues of social justice. (p. 82)

Although I suspect that Rorty (1998) was being hyperbolic with this statement, I appreciate his sentiment. I read Rorty's quote as the articulation of a goal to work toward. I firmly believe that U.S. universities can be more than they currently are and that they should be more concerned with social justice. With others, I am working to make this vision a reality. Along the way, I take great joy in the relationships that I cocreate with many of my students (Rawlins, 2000). Through these relationships, we engage with texts to accentuate a moral, loving, joyful relationship with the best minds who have left a record for the wisdom of the past to give us needed strength for the present work of changing the world.

REFERENCES

Allen, B. J., Orbe, M. P., & Olivas, M. R. (1999). The complexity of our tears: Dis/enchantment and (in)difference in the academy. *Communication Theory, 9,* 402–429.

Anderson, J. A., & Baym, G. (2004). Philosophies and philosophic issues in communication, 1995–2004. *Journal of Communication, 54,* 589–615.

Arendt, H. (1994). *Eichmann in Jerusalem: A report of the banality of evil.* New York: Penguin.

Aristotle. (1991). *On rhetoric: A theory of civic discourse* (G. A. Kennedy, Trans). New York: Oxford University Press.

Artz, L. (2001). Critical ethnography for communication studies: Dialogue and social justice in service-learning. *Southern Communication Journal, 66,* 239–250.

Bach, T., Blair, C., Northstine, W., & Pym, A. (1996) "How to Read 'How to Get Published.'" *Communication Quarterly, 44,* 399–422.

Black, E. (1970). The second persona. *Quarterly Journal of Speech, 56,* 109–119.

Blair, C., Brown, J. R. & Baxter, L. A. (1994) "Disciplining the Feminine." *Quarterly Journal of Speech, 80,* 383–409.

Bormann, E. G. (1972). Fantasy and rhetorical vision: The rhetorical criticism of social reality. *Quarterly Journal of Speech, 58,* 393–407.

Bradley, K. (1996). *Worldviews: The challenge of choice.* Toronto: Irwin.

Brockriede, W. E. (1974). Rhetorical criticism as argument. *Quarterly Journal of Speech, 60,* 165–174.

Brummett, B. (1984). Rhetorical theory as heuristic and moral: A pedagogical justification. *Communication Education, 33,* 97–107.

Bryant, D. C. (1953). Rhetoric: Its functions and its scope. *Quarterly Journal of Speech, 39,* 401–424.

Burke, K. (1973). The rhetoric of Hitler's "battle." In *The philosophy of literary form* (pp. 191–220). Berkeley: University of California Press.

Burke, K. (1982). Realisms, occidental style. In G. Amirthanayagam (Ed.), *Asian and Western writers in dialogue: New cultural identities* (pp. 26–47). London: Macmillan.

Burke, K. (1984). *Permanence and change: An anatomy of purpose* (3rd ed.). Berkeley: University of California Press.

Burke, K. (1989). Revolutionary symbolism in America. In H. W. Simons & T. Melia (Eds.), *The legacy of Kenneth Burke* (pp. 267–273). Madison: University of Wisconsin Press.

Chomsky, N. (1987). The responsibilities of intellectuals. In J. Peck (Ed.), *The Chomsky reader* (pp. 59–82). New York: Pantheon Books. (Original work published 1966)

Churchill, W. (2003). *On the justice of roosting chickens: Reflections on the consequences of U.S. imperial arrogance and criminality.* London: AK Press.

Cloud, D. L. (1998). *Control and consolation in American culture and politics: Rhetoric of therapy.* Thousand Oaks, CA: Sage.

Condit, C. (1993). The critic as empath: Moving away from totalizing theory. *Western Journal of Communication, 57,* 178–190.

Conquergood, D. (1995). Between rigor and relevance: Rethinking applied communication. In K. N. Cissna (Ed.), *Applied communication in the 21st century* (pp. 79–96). Mahwah, NJ: Lawrence Erlbaum Associates.

Conquergood, D. (2002). Performance studies: Interventions and radical research. *Drama Review, 46,* 145–156.

Cooks, L. (2000). Toward a practical theory of training in social justice: Participation, identity and power among women's groups in Panama. *World Communication, 29,* 3–24.

Cushman, E. (1996). Rhetorician as agent of social change. *College Composition and Communication, 47,* 7–28.

de Beauvoir, S. (1989). *The second sex.* New York: Vintage Books.

Dewey, J. (1954). *The public and its problems.* Athens, OH: Swallow Press.

Edelman, M. (1988). The political language of the helping professions. In T. Govier (Ed.), *Selected issues in logic and communication* (pp. 111–124). Belmont, CA: Wadsworth.

Engen, D. E. (2002). The communicative imagination and its cultivation. *Communication Quarterly, 50,* 41–57.

Frey, L. R. (Ed.). (1998). Communication and social justice research [Special issue]. *Journal of Applied Communication Research, 26*(2).

Frey, L. R., Pearce, W. B., Pollock, M. A., Artz, L., & Murphy, B. A. O. (1996). Looking for justice in all the wrong places: On a communication approach to social justice. *Communication Studies, 47,* 110–127.

Fromm, E. (1988). Disobedience as a psychological and moral problem. In R. M. Baird & S. Rosenbaum (Eds.), *Morality and the law* (93–99). Buffalo, NY: Prometheus Books.

Fromm, E. (1992). *Marx's concept of man.* New York: Continuum.

Hardin, G. (1968). The tragedy of the commons. *Science, 162,* 1243–1248.

Hariman, R. (1989). The rhetoric of inquiry and the professional scholar. In H. W. Simons (Ed.), *Rhetoric in the human sciences* (pp. 211–232). Newbury Park, CA: Sage.

Hart, R. (1993). Why communication? Why education? Toward a politics of teaching. *Communication Education, 42,* 97–105.

Hawhee, D. (1999). Burke and Nietzsche. *Quarterly Journal of Speech, 85,* 129–145.

Hollihan, T. A. (1994). Evidencing moral claims: The activist rhetorical critic's first task. *Western Journal of Communication, 58,* 229–234.

Jacoby, R. (1987). *The last intellectuals: American culture in the age of academe.* New York: Basic Books.

Kairys, D. (1993). *With liberty and justice for some: A critique of the conservative Supreme Court.* New York: New Press.

Kersten, A. (1986). Philosophical foundations for the construction of critical knowledge. In M. McLaughlin (Ed.), *Communication yearbook* (Vol. 9, pp. 756–774). Beverly Hills, CA: Sage.

Klumpp, J. F., & Hollihan, T. A. (1989). Rhetorical criticism as moral action. *Quarterly Journal of Speech, 75,* 84–97.

Lang, B. (1988). Language and genocide. In A. Rosenberg & G. E. Myers (Eds.), *Echoes from the holocaust: Philosophical reflections on a dark time* (pp. 341–361). Philadelphia: Temple University Press.

Leets, L. (2001). Interrupting the cycle of moral exclusion: A communication contribution to social justice research. *Journal of Applied Social Psychology, 31,* 1859–1891.

McKerrow, R. (1989). Critical rhetoric: Theory and praxis. *Communication Monographs, 56,* 91–111.

Mills, C. W. (1959). *The sociological imagination.* New York: Oxford University Press.

Nietzsche, F. (1995). *Thus spoke Zarathustra* (W. Kaufmann, Trans.). New York: Modern Library.

Novick, P. (1988). *That noble dream.* Cambridge, England: Cambridge University Press.

Owens, B. (2005, February 1). Gov. Owens letter calls for Churchill to step down. *TheDenverChannel.com.* Retrieved February 10, 2005, from http://www.thedenverchannel.com/news/4151452/detail.html

Rawlins, W. K. (2000). Teaching as a mode of friendship. *Communication Theory, 10,* 5–26.

Redding, C. W. (1985). Rocking boats, blowing whistles, and teaching speech communication. *Communication Education, 34,* 245–258.

Richards, I. A. (1979). *The philosophy of rhetoric.* New York: Oxford University Press.

Rodden, J. G. (1993). Field of dreams. *Western Journal of Communication, 57,* 111–138.

Rodriguez, A. (2001). *On matters of liberation: Vol. 1. The case against hierarchy.* Cresskill, NJ: Hampton.

Rorty, R. (1979). *Philosophy and the mirror of nature.* Princeton, NJ: Princeton University Press.

Rorty, R. (1983, September–October). What are philosophers for? *The Center Magazine,* 40–44.

Rorty, R. (1989). *Contingency, irony, and solidarity.* New York: Cambridge University Press.

Rorty, R. (1998). *Achieving our country: Leftist thought in twentieth-century America.* Cambridge, MA: Harvard University Press.

Rosenau, P. M. (1992). *Post-modernism and the social sciences: Insights, inroads, and intrusions.* Princeton, NJ: Princeton University Press.

Russell, B. (1993). *Skeptical essays.* New York: Routledge.

Said, E. W. (1994). *Representations of the intellectual: The 1993 Reith lectures.* New York: Pantheon.

Schalk, D. L. (1991). *War and the ivory tower: Algeria and Vietnam.* New York: Oxford University Press.

Schiappa, E., & Keehner, M. F. (1991). The "lost" passages of Kenneth Burke's *Permanence and Change. Communication Studies, 42,* 191–198.

Solomon, M. (1985). The rhetoric of dehumanization: An analysis of medical reports of the Tuskegee Syphilis Project. *Western Journal of Speech Communication, 49,* 84–93.

Swan, S. (2002). Rhetoric, service, and social justice. *Written Communication, 19,* 76–108.

Swartz, O. (1996). Praxis. In T. Enos (Ed.), *The encyclopedia of rhetoric and composition: Communication from ancient times to the information age* (p. 553). New York: Garland.

Swartz, O. (1997a). *Conducting socially responsible research: Critical theory, neo-pragmatism, and rhetorical inquiry.* Thousand Oaks, CA: Sage.

Swartz, O. (1997b). Disciplining the "other": Engaging Blair, Brown, and Baxter. *Southern Communication Journal, 62,* 253–256.

Swartz, O. (2004a). Codifying the law of slavery in North Carolina: Positive law and the slave persona. *Thurgood Marshall Law Review, 29,* 1–26.

Swartz, O. (2004b, Fall). On struggle and edification: Confessions of an academic junkie. *Inventio: Creative Thinking About Learning and Teaching, 6.* Retrieved January 16, 2006 from http://www.doit.gmu.edu/inventio/issue.asp?pID=fall04&sID=issue

Swartz, O. (2004c). Partisan, empathic and invitational criticism: The challenge of materiality. *Ethical Space: The International Journal of Communication Ethics, 1,* 28–33.

Swartz, O. (2004d). Toward a critique of normative justice: Human rights and the rule of law. *Socialism & Democracy, 18,* 185–209.

Swartz, O. (2005a). *In defense of partisan criticism.* New York: Peter Lang.

Swartz, O. (2005b). *The rule of law, property, and the violation of human rights: A plea for social justice.* London: Foxwell & Davies Scientific Publishers.

Wander, P. (1983). The ideological turn in modern criticism. *Central States Speech Journal, 34,* 1–18.

Wander, P. (1984a). The rhetoric of American foreign policy. *Quarterly Journal of Speech, 70,* 339–361.

Wander, P. (1984b). The third persona: The ideological turn in rhetorical theory. *Central States Speech Journal, 35,* 197–216.

Wander, P. (1990). The politics of despair. *Communication, 11,* 277–290.

Weaver, R. (1964). *Visions of order: The cultural crisis of our time.* Baton Rouge: Louisiana State University Press.

Weaver, R. (1970). *Language is sermonic: Richard M. Weaver on the nature of rhetoric.* R. L. Johannesen, R. Strickland, & R. T. Eubanks, Eds. Baton Rouge: Louisiana State University Press.

White, H. (1987). *The content of the form: Narrative discourse and historical representation.* Baltimore: Johns Hopkins University Press.

Zinn, H. (2003). *A people's history of the United States.* New York: Perennial Classics.

2

Social Justice and the Challenge for Communication Studies

Amardo Rodriguez
Syracuse University

I teach a graduate course that explores the relationship between communication and community. Ultimately, the goal of the course is to develop emergent understandings of community. We focus on the following questions: What is community? Why community? How do different peoples do community? Course readings span different theoretical, cultural, and political perspectives on community. Our objectives in the course are to (a) identify the worldview assumptions that inform different understandings of community; (b) understand the different social and political implications that flow from different understandings of community; (c) recognize the communicative, performative, and rhetorical practices that attend to different understandings of community; and (d) probe what different understandings of community suggest about being human. The overarching objective of the course is to deepen our appreciation of the potential contribution of communication theory to emergent understandings of community.

The major writing assignment for this course involves students advancing their own emergent understandings of communication and identifying the ethical, political, and social implications that attend to these understandings of communication. In other words, what models of community do our different definitions of communication implicate? The different definitions of communication my students offer always make for interesting reading. For example:

- Communication is a method of conveying ideas, emotions, information, and directing between people and systems using meaningful symbols.
- Communication is words, sounds, actions used by living beings or things to prepare, transmit, and/or receive and interpret messages.
- Communication is a way of understanding people; what, how, and why they think about certain things.
- Communication is the phenomena of transferring messages, both intentional and unintentional, between two or more individuals.
- Communication is the process of conveying a point or idea to an audience, either directly or indirectly, consciously or subconsciously.
- Communication is the ability to express yourself effectively through language and gestures, while remaining true to your ideals.
- Communication is the process of creating, expressing, and receiving meanings through sets of codes.
- Communication is the process in which the ideas, beliefs, viewpoints, and overall thoughts that embody an entity are expressed.
- Communication is an interaction involving the exchange of meaning, although this meaning may be transformed by the process of interaction.
- Communication is a process of building humanity through giving, taking, and sharing ideas.
- Communication is the avenue, channel, or process in which we are able to construct, define, persuade, and project our interests, beliefs, ideas, and actions to our community.

What is always immediately striking is the ideological similarity found among most of the definitions. Communication is overwhelmingly seen as a transmission phenomenon involving the creating, transferring, sharing, giving, expressing, or conveying of messages and meanings. When I point out this striking similarity to my students, most will contend that their definitions are in no way different from those found in many communication textbooks. Indeed, my students' definitions of communication are quite similar to those that continue to circulate in the field's textbooks and journals. For example:

- "Communication involves understanding how people behave in creating, exchanging, and interpreting messages" (Littlejohn & Foss, 2005, p. 8).

- "Communication occurs only when there are two associated informa-tion producing processes and the output from one process is the func-tional inverse of the other process's output" (Losee, 1999, p. 2).
- "Communication is the transactional process of exchanging messages and negotiating meaning to convey information and to establish and maintain relationships" (Wilson, Hantz, & Hanna, 1989, p.7).

Evidently, and in the face of many compelling critiques (see e.g., Carey, 1989; Cronen, 1998; Deetz, 1994; Pearce, 1989; Powers, 1995; Shepherd, 1993; Sigman, 1995), a transmission view of communication remains domi-nant in communication studies (Cronen, 1998; Davis & Jasinski, 1993; Krippendorff, 1993; Shepherd, 1993). As Shepherd (1993) explains, "The study of communication, in this view, is primarily the study of how a vessel can be manipulated and shaped, in particular contexts and under certain circumstances, in order to best transmit the material it contains" (p. 88).

Accordingly, most of the classes found in communication departments focus on the acquisition of an assortment of communication skills, tech-niques, and strategies that can supposedly help us to be better communica-tors. Thus, if social justice concerns are absent in communication theory and pedagogy, as Swartz (1997, 2005) suggests, then a good place to begin understanding the origins of this absence, as Deetz (1994) and others point out, can be found in interrogating the definitions of communication that frame and guide mainstream communication inquiry and pedagogy. On the other hand, if we believe, as I and an increasing number of scholars believe (see e.g., Anderson, 1994; Blair, Brown, & Baxter, 1994; Cronen, 1998; Deetz, 1994; Krippendorff, 1997; Pearce, 1989; Shepherd, 1993; Sigman, 1995; Swartz, 2005), that communication studies can make an important contribution to social justice theory and practice, then such work needs to begin with advancing definitions of communication that lend more natu-rally to social justice.

I argue in this chapter that dominant definitions of communication un-dermine communication theory's ability to make meaningful contributions to the creation of more just and humane worlds by failing "to see communi-cation for what it is—the source of our humanity and everything else" (Thayer, 1973, p. 130). The absence of social justice in the communication studies that Swartz and others describe is related to the fact that the defini-tions of communication that guide mainstream communication scholarship and pedagogy are of an ontological and epistemological stance that erases social justice. As such, the first task in repositioning communication theory and pedagogy to address social justice and thereby develop "the theoretical and practical ways that ... can redescribe U.S. society so as to enable inclusive and equitable communities to emerge" involves forwarding communication definitions that are more organically amenable to social justice by being of a different ontological, epistemological, and axiological orientation. In what follows, I forward one such definition of communication. In doing so, I join with emerging voices on the periphery of communication studies who are articulating emergent definitions of communication that highlight the constitutive, performative, and redemptive capacity of communication (see, e.g., Cissna & Anderson, 1994; Conquergood, 2002; Davis & Jasinski, 1993; Deetz, 1994; Foss & Foss, 2003; Johnson, 2003; McPhail, 1996; Smith, 1993; Turkey, 1990).

I also aim to demonstrate that such new definitions, besides being more organically amenable to social justice, promote more expansive definitions of social justice. For instance, Frey, Pearce, Pollock, Artz, and Murphy (1996) define social justice as "the engagement with and advocacy for those in our society who are economically, socially, politically, and/or culturally under resourced" (p. 110). This definition, however, calls forth no deep interrogation of the status quo in communication studies. Its focus is on inclusion rather than revolution. Social justice is cast in terms of our commitment to alleviating the injustices against persons from various marginalized and disenfranchised groups. In other words, social justice is cast in terms of our generosity and charity to others who are presumably less fortunate than us. This is, in my view, a privileged definition of social justice. It serves to define and even restrict social justice work to serving in soup kitchens, volunteering in homeless shelters, helping the poor build homes, volunteering with local food banks, marching for various causes, and so forth. Such work is no doubt noble, charitable, and valuable. But what of the larger sociocultural, historical, theoretical, political, and cosmological forces that make for marginalization and disfranchisement? Why is social justice cast in terms of us helping others attain justice, equality, and decency? In short, Frey et al.'s (1996) definition of social justice undermines our ability to speak to larger notions of human misery and suffering by failing to implicate mainstream definitions of communication and the knowledge order that sustains these definitions in the absence of social justice in communication studies.

ON THE ORIGINS OF COMMUNICATION

My students and I spend many weeks unpacking and interrogating our different definitions of communication. The work is intellectually, emotionally, and existentially demanding. We aim to identify the ontological, epistemological, axiological, and pedagogical positions in our different definitions of communication, as well as reckon with the implications that come with these positions. We also aim to identify the origins of these positions and understand how these different positions work in tandem to support each other.

Homogeneity appears prominently in most of my students' definitions of communication. After all, to smoothly and reliably exchange and convey our messages and meanings, we presumably must possess a common vocabulary, or share a common set of codes, symbols, and signs. This belief, of course, is quite prominent in larger discourses about communication and language (see, e.g., Chong-Yeong, 2003). My students, therefore, believe that the absence of a common language or a common set of codes impedes communication and thereby ultimately threatens chaos and social devolution. So I ask, do you therefore believe that a common language should be coercively and hierarchically imposed on a group of linguistically diverse people? Do you believe communities have an ethical and political obligation to promote and sustain one common language? For instance, do you support political efforts to make standard English the legal language of the United States? Most reluctantly and embarrassingly admit "Yes."

Where is this fear coming from, this fear that communities will plunge into anarchy without a common language? Does linguistic and communication diversity really threaten unity and progress? What about the linguistic and communication homogeneity found in places where ethnic cleansing is rampant? What about the linguistic and communication homogeneity found in other societies where racism, sexism, and heterosexism are rampant? Where is it empirically true that linguistic and communication homogeneity makes for unity, peace, equal opportunity, and prosperity for all? The assumption that homogeneity promotes or is even a prerequisite for unity and social evolution has no basis in either reality or theory.

I want my students to reckon and hopefully understand the larger implications of believing and assuming that homogeneity is vital for unity and evolution. This involves appreciating the insidious nature of this belief and how it influences and shapes our discourses about diversity and equality, as well as appreciating how this belief—and the fear that sustains it—makes us discursively suspicious and hostile to difference and thereby the evolution of new and different ways of framing, understanding, and experiencing the world. Thus, in a world where our spaces and distances are increasingly contracting and collapsing, any definition of communication that privileges homogeneity threatens us all.

OTHER DEFINITIONS OF COMMUNICATION
AND SOCIAL JUSTICE

My students are anxious to know my definition of communication. I tell them that communication is about being vulnerable to the humanity of others. Implicit in this dialogic definition is the notion that communication is inherently a constitutive phenomenon—through communication we become human, define our worlds, and help shape the humanity of others. In other words, through enlarging our ability to be vulnerable to the humanity of others we become human. Conversely, practices and arrangements that impede communication by undermining the formation of mutual understanding make us less human and diminish our worlds. Thus, this emergent definition of communication speaks to communication possessing a redemptive quality—a potentiality to heal, to redeem, to make whole. I am assuming that human beings have the potential to heal and that such healing occurs through communication. As such, this definition points to an inextricable relationship between the condition of the world and the condition of our humanity.

Being vulnerable means being open to others' interpretations, experiences, understandings, and truths. It also means recognizing that our own meanings, interpretations, and understandings will never be devoid of ambiguity. Being vulnerable also means embracing human fallibility and thereby recognizing that often our actions will conflict with our intentions and motives. Being vulnerable also means recognizing that many times we will be unable to interpret life's vagaries, complexities, and ambiguities. Confusion and frustration are common human experiences that demand empathy and compassion. As such, being vulnerable also means being tolerant of the anxiety and chaos that come with being human. Finally, being vulnerable means being "generous in our judgments of others, for we can never really know all there is to know about another" (Tutu, 1999, p. 169). Compassion, mercy, and forgiveness are thus integral to being and becoming vulnerable.

Because of our extraordinary capacity to be vulnerable, I locate the origins of communication in our vulnerability rather than in our symbolic and linguistic capacity. Vulnerability distinguishes communication from every other kind of human interaction. It is also our capacity to be vulnerable that makes communication a uniquely human phenomenon and a compelling force in our ability to impact and shape the world. It is also through our vulnerability that we gain the unique ability to reckon with those experiences that no system of codes, signs, and symbols will ever allow us to capture or translate.

To define communication in terms of vulnerability foregrounds the human component and, as a result, moves notions of communication competency beyond that of skills, techniques, and strategies. It pushes us to attend to the larger discourses, worldviews, and institutions that situate and permeate our humanity. Do such discourses, worldviews, and institutions promote our reaching and searching for mutual understanding? Do such discourses, worldviews, and institutions promote trust, openness, and compassion? Moreover, in foregrounding the notion of vulnerability, this emergent model of communication places the burden of communication on us. It obligates us to help each other understand our interpretations and orientations, regardless of the differences that seem to hopelessly divide us. We have to own our ways of encountering others. It also pushes us to examine the larger social, political, and cultural contexts that recursively situate communication by looking at how different contexts bear on our ability to be vulnerable to each other. But most important, this emergent model of communication elevates the study of communication by highlighting our own potentiality to create and shape our worlds. Communication is no longer reduced to merely an expression or product of various mental, psychological, biological, social, or even historical forces. Rather, communication constitutes our capacity to help with the completion of the world. It expands our humanity and enlarges our worlds by constantly demanding of us new meanings, new understandings, new experiences, and, ultimately, new modes of being. In this way, this emergent model of communication commits us to identify and support only those contexts that promote communication, beginning of course with those that make for much more expansive and inclusive communication studies where social justice no longer emerges outside the realm of what we do.

SEARCHING FOR POSSIBILITIES

Most of my students believe that human beings are inherently imperfect. They believe that elaborate and reliable hierarchical institutions are vital to promote and sustain basic human decency. So I ask, why are you framing the matter in terms of perfection versus imperfection? Why do you even insist on framing the matter this way? I point out that this framing device is actually absent in all of the world's great spiritual teachings. Again and again these spiritual texts challenge us to be better human beings, beginning with being better to each other. We are to care more, give more, empathize more, understand more, forgive more, and, ultimately, love more. These spiritual texts assume we are inherently incomplete rather than inherently imperfect; the reason, no doubt, being that perfection is a theoretically undesirable notion. It allows for neither creation nor evolution. It is stasis and such a condition constitutes death for any organic system or entity (Rodriguez, 2003).

There is nothing heuristic in framing discourses about human potentiality in terms of perfection versus imperfection. We are better off with identifying those communication and rhetorical practices that make us more rather than less human, and thereby make for a world with less misery and suffering. We are also better off concerning ourselves with those communication and rhetorical practices that can potentially help us realize new and different understandings of the world. In my view, to look at communication in terms of vulnerability best complements these social justice ambitions.

There are many compelling reasons why a transmission view of communication remains dominant in communication theory and pedagogy, the most obvious being that it demands nothing much from us. It puts no onus on us to enlarge our humanity; that is, to love more, to care more, to forgive more, to give more, and so forth. It also divorces the study and teaching of communication from larger social, political, and intellectual discourses and, in so doing, depoliticizes the study and teaching of communication. We are spared, for instance, from interrogating our own complicity in maintaining a pedagogical order that aids and abets a larger political and ideological order, impeding social justice. There is therefore no onus on us to interrogate and contest the larger sociocultural, political, and ideological systems that situate and penetrate us.

To embody communication in terms of vulnerability and the reaching and searching for mutual understanding is difficult and demanding. Mutual understanding constitutes an understanding that only partially belongs to both persons. It is also an understanding that is emergent, always new to both persons. In other words, the search for mutual understanding dislocates us by always taking us to new mental, emotional, sensual, existential, and even spiritual places. On the other hand, mutual understanding is never complete, never void of ambiguity. So no meaning will ever perfectly or completely describe or capture our realities and experiences. Yet ambiguity vitalizes communication by ensuring meaning remains always unstable, permeable, and changeable. On the other hand, in vitalizing communication, ambiguity vitalizes us by keeping us open to new worlds and new ways of experiencing the communities around us. Ambiguity, meaning, and life are therefore blessedly intertwined (Bateson, 1994; Rodriguez, 2003). Thus, to focus on ending ambiguity only serves to destroy meaning. If ambiguity metaphorically constitutes the world's oceans, meaning constitutes the fish found in those oceans.

NEW METAPHORS FOR COMMUNICATION STUDIES

In my students' many definitions of communication, I nearly always find an assumption of separation. We supposedly have no existential, ecological, or even spiritual bond that joins us. Communication emerges as a bridge that connects people, and communication competency constitutes our ability to build bridges—that is, our ability to express, convey, and share our meaning and messages with others on the other side of the divide. This separation comes from the core of our worldview in the Western world. We assume a world divided by separate and opposing forces. Modern quantum theory, however, posits that this separation is illusory. Everything in the world is interconnected (Bohm, 1980); there is no separation of bodies in communication. We are always connected and continually influencing each other. Our dominant definitions of communication are therefore contrary to emergent understandings of the world (Bohm, 1980; Rodriguez, 2003).

In upholding the notion of separate bodies, we help perpetuate political, social, and ideological systems that trade in human separation. We miss how in acting on one another we are ultimately acting on our own humanity. For instance, our orientation toward ethics in communication studies is on the appropriateness of various practices on others, with no concern for how such practices impact our own humanity. In this regard, communication studies helps perpetuate a knowledge order that undermines social justice. Integral to social justice is the recognition that our fates are bound; the challenge of social justice pedagogy has always been to highlight this reality (Freire, 1995). We are our brothers' and sisters' keepers. In fact, besides quantum theory, the notion of us being interconnected and our fates being intertwined is found at the core of all of the world's great spiritual teachings (Tutu, 1999). Redemption is always dependent on how we treat the weak and most vulnerable among us. Unfortunately, the dominant definitions of communication that characterize communication studies do little to help us appreciate this reality. Neither mainstream communication theory nor communication pedagogy highlight the inextricable relationship between communication and our political consciousness. We surrender discourses about democracy and social justice to political science departments, thereby helping to perpetuate the belief that both are fundamentally institutional matters rather than foremost communication matters. In so doing, we separate ourselves from larger discourses about democracy and social justice. I, therefore, ask my students this: Do your definitions of communication promote democracy, diversity, and social justice? If their definitions are incapable of doing so, how would their communities be democratic, diverse, and just?

What emerges is that my students have a mainstream view of democracy and diversity. They define democracy at the institutional and governmental levels, and diversity at the level of race, ethnicity, sexual orientation, and gender. We presumably promote democracy by upholding various institutions, and promote diversity by including members from various marginalized groupings in our communities. But our common conceptions of democracy and diversity demand nothing much from us (Rodriguez, 2003). Neither enlarges us in any way. Thus, while we profess to be the most democratic nation in the world, we have no qualms about using military aggression against other nations for our own self-interests. What kinds of citizens are therefore emerging from our classrooms?

THE PERILOUS CHALLENGES ON THE HORIZON

The horrors of September 11 have affirmed our deepest anxieties and insecurities of the human condition. We now have a class of human beings on which to project everything we believe is inherently evil about the human condition. Rarely does the other come so perfectly made to order. Besides being of the obligatory different race and ethnicity, this other speaks a different language, conforms to a different dress code, and worst of all, worships what many Americans consider a different and, perhaps, "inferior" God. Moreover, this other was visually captured, again and again and again, committing the most unconscionable actions (i.e., challenging our status and power). As best-selling author Ann Coulter demands, we should "invade their countries, kill their leaders and convert them to Christianity" (Coulter, 2001).

In *Why We Fight: Moral Clarity and the War on Terrorism*, Bennett (2002) writes that we are now in "a war to the finish ... a war about good and evil" (p. 45). For Kaplan and Kristol (2003), "It is a simple fact. The alternative to American leadership is a chaotic, Hobbesian world where there is no authority to thwart aggression, ensure peace and security or enforce international norms" (p. 121). Thus, if the United States retreats "from the position that history has bequeathed us, the turmoil that would soon follow would surely reach our shores" (p. 120). Consequently, the United States "must not only be the world's policeman or its sheriff, it must be its beacon and guide" (p. 121). By any measure, these are all sobering claims. Yet, in my view, they serve to demonstrate that what "really" occurred on September 11 was the end of communication and the elevation of aggression in mediating human affairs.

Aggression is now inextricably interwoven into a grand narrative that includes infidels, crusades, weapons of mass destruction, God, holy wars, jihad, clash of civilizations, spiritual mandates, and the slaughtering of tens of thousands of individuals. Yet nothing much is happening in mainstream communication studies that would suggest that communication was in such peril. However, the task of communication studies must be more than to show how aggression is morally, theoretically, and politically backward and dangerous. We must ultimately show how communication is morally, theoretically, and politically superior to aggression, and we can only do so by showcasing more expansive models and definitions of communication and the possibilities that such definitions contain.

Arguments now in support of aggression are not conceptually different than those used throughout history to justify many wars and horrendous conflicts (Tutu, 1999). In many cases, such wars began with one group concluding that a next group was morally and spiritually inferior, and as a result of this moral inferiority, could be only be dealt with through aggression. September 11 gives us no moral exemption from this company. We invest in war and in acquiring our own massive stockpiles of weapons of mass destruction—at the cost of building more schools, hospitals, and so forth—on the belief that aggression is a superior option to communication because other people in the world, as a result of being morally and spiritually inferior, only understand aggression. September 11 has merely emboldened our belief and thereby serves to justify increased military spending and our willingness to make the horrendous sacrifices that come with waging war.

But how, why, and when do other human beings become the other? How do we discursively, communicatively, and rhetorically construct otherness? That is, how does one group of human beings become not only different from us, but less than us? Otherness begins with where we locate the world and ourselves in the world. When we assume ontologically—as we now commonly do—that other human beings are separate from us, then nothing morally, existentially, or even ecologically binds us to each other. The implications and consequences that come with a highly narrow view of what being human means are no longer bearable. In a world where our spaces and distances are increasingly collapsing, what soon becomes obvious is that we are inextricably and irreversibly interconnected to each other. Our destinies are bound. We have to cooperate and negotiate, which means we have to eventually develop communication models that promote both or risk increased threats to our existence as a species.

We can begin with forwarding a different metaphor for communication studies. I propose we look at communication in terms of an ocean rather than a bridge. The ocean allows us to grasp the centrality and universality of communication to life. It also allows us to understand that communication—as with any other ecology—has an enormous capacity to nurture and sustain an infinite variety and diversity of life. Moreover, like oceans, communication ebbs and flows. We harm communication—and ultimately ourselves—when we suppress such movements. As with any other ecology, however, any ocean can die due to lack of nurturing by all those who constitute that ecology. Regardless of our differences, we all have a sacred stake in ensuring this ecology strives and prospers. Oceans also allow us to grasp the intensity, complexity, and instability that are natural and even necessary to communication and being human. It helps us to be less afraid of the disruption that comes with encountering new peoples and experiences by demanding evolution of all its constituents.

CONCLUSION

Through communication we can alter and expand our worlds. Such is the power communication possesses. Unfortunately, most students graduate from communication studies programs without any appreciation of this power. Sadly, communication studies typically offers no such sense; that is, no expectation that in studying communication we are embarking on the study of our potentiality and our ability to create and shape our worlds.

Communication studies should be more than merely the study of what is. It should ultimately be about what can be (see, e.g., Allen, Orbe, & Olivas, 1999; Boyd, 1999; Ono, 1997; Rodden, 1993; Swartz, 1997, 2005). For instance, starting with the premise that our world is communicational and rhetorical in origin, what new models of community can we imagine? What kinds of communication and rhetorical practices can we invoke to realize such communities? How do we promote these practices and what larger forces, systems, and institutions can we invoke to help nurture these practices? In my view, we can only put communication studies in pursuit of such questions by employing more expansive definitions of communication.

By the end of the semester I hope my students appreciate how our definitions of communication implicate definitions of community, recognize the inextricable connection between communication and community, and understand that discourses about communication are always discourses about democracy, diversity, and social justice. I also hope my students have acquired a larger and more urgent sense of what it means to study communication. If I accomplished some or any of these goals, I would have served the cause of social justice. Ultimately, I hope the course in some way has pushed them to act and behave in ways that expand the realm of what is possible and what is just. For in the end it is action that measures and reflects the worth of any education.

REFERENCES

Allen, B. J., Orbe, M. P., & Olivas, M. R. (1999). The complexity of our tears: Dis/enchantment and (in)difference in the academy. *Communication Theory, 9*, 402–429.

Anderson, R. (1994). Anonymity, presence, and the dialogical self in technological culture. In R. Anderson, K. Cissna, and R. Arnett (Eds), The reach of dialogue (pp. 91–111). Cresskill, NJ: Hampton.

Bateson, M. C. (1994). *Peripheral visions*. New York: HarperCollins.

Bennett, W. J. (2002). *Why we fight: Moral clarity and the age of terrorism*. New York: Doubleday.

Blair, C., Brown, J. R., & Baxter, L. A. (1994). Disciplining the feminine. *Quarterly Journal of Speech, 80*, 383–409.

Bohm, D. (1980). *Wholeness and the implicate order*. New York: Routledge.

Boyd, R. (1999). Compromising positions: Or, the unhappy transformations of a "transformative intellectual." *Communication Theory, 9*, 377–401.

Carey, J. W. (1989). *Communication as culture: Essays on media and society*. Boston: Unwin Hyman.

Chong-Yeong, L. (2003). Language and human rights. *Journal of Intergroup Relations, 29*, 57–65.

Cissna, K. N., & Anderson, R. (1994). Communication and the ground of dialogue. In R. Anderson, K. N. Cissna, & R. C. Arnett (Eds.), *The reach of dialogue: Confirmation, voice, and community* (pp. 9–30). Cresskill, NJ: Hampton.

Conquergood, D. (2002). Performance studies: Interventions and radical research. *Drama Review, 46*, 145–156.

Coulter, A. (2001, September 13) This is war. *National Review Online*. Retrieved January 11, 2006 from http://nationalreview.com/coulter/coulter.shtml

Cronen, V. E. (1998). Communication theory for the twenty-first century: Cleaning up the wreckage of the psychology project. In J. S. Trent (Ed.), *Communication: Views from the helm for the twenty-first century* (pp. 18–38). New York: Allyn & Bacon.

Davis, D. K., & Jasinski, J. (1993). Beyond the culture wars: An agenda for research on communication and culture. *Journal of Communication, 43*, 141–149.

Deetz, S. A. (1994). The future of the discipline: The challenges, the research, and the social contribution. In S. A. Deetz (Ed.), *Communication yearbook 17* (pp. 565–600). Newbury, CA: Sage.

Foss, S. K., & Foss, K. A. (2003). *Inviting transformation: Presentational speaking for a changing world*. Prospects Heights, IL: Waveland Press.

Freire, P. (1995). *Pedagogy of the oppressed*. New York: Continuum.

Frey, L. R., Pearce, W. B., Pollock, M. A., Artz, L., & Murphy, B. A. (1996). Looking for justice in all the wrong places: On a communication approach to social justice. *Communication Studies, 47*, 110–127.

Johnson, E. P. (2003). Race, ethnicity, and performance. *Text and Performance Quarterly, 23,* 105–106.

Kaplan, L. F., & Kristol, W. (2003). *The war over Iraq: Saddam's tyranny and America's mission.* San Francisco: Encounter.

Krippendorff, K. (1993). The past of communication's hoped-for-future. *Journal of Communication, 43,* 34–44.

Krippendorff, K. (1997). Seeing oneself through others' eyes in social inquiry. In M. Huspek & P. Radford (Eds.), *Transgressing discourses: Communication and the voice of the other* (pp. 47–72). Albany, NY: SUNY Press.

Littlejohn, S. W., & Foss, K. A. (2005). *Theories of human communication.* Belmont, CA: Wadsworth.

Losee, R. (1999). Communication defined as complementary informative processes. *Journal of Information, Communication and Library Science, 5,* 1–15.

McPhail, M. L. (1996). *Zen in the art of rhetoric.* New York: State University of New York Press.

Ono, K. (1997). A letter/essay I've been longing to write in my personal/academic voice. *Western Journal of Communication, 61,* 114–125.

Pearce, W. B. (1989). *Communication and the human condition.* Carbondale: Southern Illinois University Press.

Powers, J. H. (1995). On the intellectual structure of the human communication discipline. *Communication Education, 44,* 191–222.

Rodden, J. (1993). Field of dreams. *Western Journal of Communication, 57,* 111–138.

Rodriguez, A. (2003). *Diversity as liberation (II): Introducing a new understanding of diversity.* Cresskill, NJ: Hampton.

Shepherd, G. J. (1993). Building a discipline of communication. *Journal of Communication, 43,* 83–91.

Sigman, S. J. (1995). Question: Evidence of what? Answer: Communication. *Western Journal of Communication, 59,* 79–84.

Smith, C. R. (1993). Finding the spiritual dimension of rhetoric. *Western Journal of Communication, 57,* 266–271.

Swartz, O. (1997). *Conducting socially responsible research: Critical theory, neo-pragmatism, and rhetorical inquiry.* Thousand Oaks, CA: Sage.

Swartz, O. (2005). *In defense of partisan criticism.* New York: Peter Lang.

Thayer, L. (1973). Towards an ethics of communication. In L. Thayer (Ed.), *On communication: Essays in understanding* (pp. 129–144). Norwood, NJ: Ablex.

Turkey, D. (1990). Toward a research agenda for spiritual rhetoric. *Journal of Communication and Religion, 13,* 66–76.

Tutu, D. (1999). *No future without forgiveness.* New York: Doubleday.

Wilson, G., Hantz, A. M., & Hanna, M. S. (1989). *Interpersonal growth through communication.* Dubuque, IA: Brown.

3

Across the Great Divides: From Nonpartisan Criticism to Partisan Criticism to Applied Communication Activism for Promoting Social Change and Social Justice

Lawrence R. Frey
University of Colorado at Boulder

An assumption that many contributors to this volume make is that there is nothing more important than the pursuit of social change for the purpose of promoting social justice. As conscientious people are apt to notice, there is much social injustice in the world. Fortunately, as Frey, Pearce, Pollock, Artz, and Murphy (1996) made clear, communication scholars have much to contribute to the pursuit of social justice through their "engagement with and advocacy for those in our society who are economically, socially, politically, and/or culturally underresourced" (p. 110). Specifically, social justice communication scholarship "identifies and foregrounds the grammars that oppress or underwrite relationships of domination and then reconstructs those grammars" (p. 112).

In light of the importance of social justice communication scholarship, Swartz's (2005) recent text in defense of partisan criticism and this collection of essays are welcome additions to the literature. In this chapter, I seek to extend Swartz's position about the need for partisan criticism by examining the reflexive relationship between partisan criticism and applied communication activist practices as counterparts for promoting social change and social justice. This reflexive relationship suggests that the critique of unjust practices is not sufficient in and of itself; such criticism must be accompanied by concrete interventions on the part of communication scholars that are directed at changing unjust practices. I start by examining the great divide that Swartz has crossed from nonpartisan to partisan criticism, as well as an internecine battle between rhetoricians who seek to promote social change and social justice, and then address the great divide that remains to be crossed from partisan criticism to applied communication activism.

ACROSS THE GREAT DIVIDE: FROM NONPARTISAN TO PARTISAN CRITICISM

Par•ti•san: Adherence to a party, faction, cause, or person.

Crit•i•cism: To consider the merits and demerits of and judge accordingly.

—Adapted from Merriam-Webster Online (2006)

I am not a rhetorical critic by any stretch of the imagination, so I am left wondering, in my naïve understanding of rhetorical criticism, how criticism could not be "partisan" in some way. By definition, it seems that criticism involves some particular perspective taken with regard to such matters as social change and social justice, even if that perspective involves saying that one is not taking a perspective.

Even we in the social sciences, who usually lag far behind our rhetorician cousins in understanding ontological, epistemological, and axiological assumptions, now understand that there is no way to stand outside of the world as objective observers who do not (need to) make political and ethical choices (see, e.g., Andersen, 1993). As Conquergood (1995) so eloquently explained in identifying the ideological choice that confronts applied communication researchers:

> The choice is no longer between pure and applied research. Instead, we must choose between research that is "engaged" or "complicit." By engaged I mean a clear-eyed, self-critical awareness that research does not proceed in epistemological purity or moral innocence: There is no immaculate percep-

tion. Engaged individuals take responsibility for how the knowledge they produce is used instead of hiding behind pretenses and protestations of innocence. ... As communication scholars who traffic in symbols, images, representations, rhetorical strategies, signifying practices, the media, and the social work of talk, we should understand better than anyone else that our disciplinary practice is *in* the world. As engaged intellectuals we understand that we are entangled within world systems of oppression and exploitation. ... Our choice is to stand alongside or against domination, but not outside, above, or beyond it. (p. 85)

Conquergood's (1995) statement easily can be adapted to debunk the notion of a nonpartisan rhetorical critic (or a nonpartisan communication scholar, more generally). Swartz's (2005) position regarding the need for rhetorical critics to explicitly take a partisan stance to promote social change and social justice, thus, meets well Conquergood's call for engaged communication scholarship. Swartz's position, of course, is an extension of the work by those who argued for the ideological turn in rhetorical criticism and for critical rhetoric (see, e.g., McKerrow, 1989; Wander, 1983, 1984; Wander & Jenkins, 1972), whose work, of course, was an extension of those who advanced critical social theory. As Fraser (1985) explained, "A critical social theory frames its research program and its conceptual framework with an eye to the aims and activities of those oppositional social movements with which it has a partisan though not uncritical identification" (p. 97; see also, e.g., Conquergood, 1991; Strine, 1991).

Although the partisan perspective of rhetorical criticism articulated by Swartz (2005) emerges from a long and distinguished history of scholarship, there are many critics of this approach. Hill (1972, 1983), for instance, argued that taking *a priori* advocacy positions on important societal issues (e.g., promoting social justice) does not constitute scholarship. Kuypers (2000) essentially argued the same point, stating that critical rhetoric (partisan criticism) "literally murders the longstanding and widely accepted standard of an objective fairness" ("conclusion," ¶ 2) because "critics will be expected to be advocates, not artisans"; ("conclusion," ¶ 5) he argued, instead, that "critics must be free to analyse any rhetorical transaction, from any perspective, free from constraining and imposed viewpoints," ("Freedom," ¶ 1)and that "we should engage in criticism, not political partisanship" ("conclusion," ¶ 16). Wander (1984), however, in responding to Hill, noted that this position rests on the mistaken notion that advocates constitute "fanatics" who cannot bring their scholarly skills to bear to analyze and critique and, therefore, scholars cannot be advocates and critics at the same time. As Wander (1984) explained:

Partisanship, orthodox Marxism, dogmatism—these terms, in the context of American scholarship, point to concerns about narrowed sensibilities or party discipline in contrast to free-thinking and well-rounded academic humanism. The fear is that intense commitment will result not only in a loss of intellectual independence, but will also render one intolerant, unable to give other than perverse readings of those with whom one does not agree. The underlying ideal is disinterested scholarship and balanced views. (pp. 204–205)

Wander (1984) made clear that there is an important difference between "engaged scholarship and uninformed and poorly reasoned harangues" (p. 200). Thus, one can adhere to a party, faction, cause, or person (be "partisan") and still consider the merits and demerits of an object of inquiry and judge accordingly (engage in "criticism").

Rosenfield (1983) argued that although criticism based on the ideological turn may be scholarship, limiting criticism in this manner would create a "miasma" that would "reduce it to a dreary enterprise indeed" (p. 119). No proponents, however, have advocated that rhetorical criticism should be limited to partisan criticism. Condit (1993), in a more substantive critique, pointed out that although partisan criticism propagates a "sharply divided and two-sided combat ... [between] dominant, empowered and privileged groups of persons who act unjustly to oppress other groups" (p. 184) that is "rhetorically compelling" (p. 186), such criticism is ultimately "closed and totalistic" (p. 185). However, I argue, these tendencies certainly are not endemic to partisan criticism, and even Condit admitted that "critics cannot avoid a partisan inflection in their work" (p. 184).

Although these critiques of partisan criticism can be dismissed relatively easily, a more substantive critique has come from those who are aligned with partisan critics in the goal of promoting social change to eliminate domination, oppression, and social injustice, but who differ on the means by which such social change should be accomplished. An exemplar of such criticism is the "invitational" perspective on social change advocated by Foss (e.g., 2004a, 2004b; see also Foss & Foss, 2002; Foss & Griffin, 1995), which argues, in particular, against the use of persuasive, confrontational communication, a central feature of partisan criticism (see Swartz, 2005), in promoting social change aimed at social justice. As Foss (2004b) explained:

I question the role of communication in the social change process through persuasion. Implicit in persuasion is the desire to control, dominate, and have power over others. It devalues the lives and perspectives of those we are trying to change. It violates our commitment to feminism to disrupt the ideology of domination and oppression that pervade our culture and relationships. Feminist rhetorical theory is concerned with change that doesn't involve persuasion.

The alternative rhetorical approach to social change offered by Foss (2004b) is based on five assumptions: (a) to change other people is difficult; (b) the attempt to change others violates their inherent value and integrity; (c) individuals must change themselves; (d) resistance and opposition sometimes are ineffective options for creating change, resulting in "what we resist, persists"; and (e) the means are the ends in that we cannot produce the future by doing something different in the present. Emerging from these assumptions are two general alternative rhetorical options to persuasion: (a) *enactment*—being or living in the world we desire, and (b) *enfoldment/invitational rhetoric*—encountering different others and respecting the interaction that takes place with them without trying to change them but, instead, (a) offering perspectives; (b) creating environments or atmospheres where other people feel free to share their perspective through the three conditions of safety, value, and freedom; and (c) appreciating them by focusing on positive aspects of people. These alternative rhetorical options can be evaluated according to two criteria phrased in the form of questions: Is this the world in which I want to be living? How do I feel?

This model of communication for social change certainly is appealing, but there are a number of problems that plague this perspective. First, this perspective promotes an essentialist position regarding persuasion. According to Griffin (2003), *persuasion* is an "attempt to change or reinforce an audience's thoughts, feelings, or actions" (p. G-6). Using this definition, a woman reinforcing her friend's decision to leave an abusive relationship constitutes persuasion, but surely such persuasion does not, by definition, violate the person's inherent value and integrity. This essentialist position, thus, conflates the term *persuasion* with something like *coercion*, which would better reference the acts that are being objected to, acts that also would be objected to by partisan critics.

Second, this approach to social change clearly is oriented to the personal or interpersonal domains rather than the public or societal sphere, but even there it demonstrates some serious problems. Not too long ago, a good friend called to tell me that she was going to commit suicide that day. I talked with her for a long time and "persuaded" her not to kill herself. Perhaps I did this because of my desire to control, dominate, have power over her, and all the other evil reasons for engaging in this persuasive act, although I would like to believe that I did it because I valued this person and her life. Does it make any difference to this essentialist view of persuasion that this person was thankful the next day for my persuasive communication? This conception of persuasion as inherently evil, thus, violates the invitational perspective of not imposing one's view on others and respecting how other people see the world.

Third, placing the locus for change solely within individuals (and their interpersonal relationships) ignores the obvious reality that we live in systems not of our own making. I did not choose to be born into U.S. culture, just as girls born into countries where they experience genital mutilation before they reach puberty do not have a choice about their system. It may well be true that people who have many resources at their disposal may have agency over their life, but this certainly is not the case for many who are underresourced and suffering from social injustice. Try telling gay men and lesbians who recently were denied the right to marry in 11 U.S. states that the laws of our country do not make any difference in their life, or tell the one in four prisoners in the United States currently serving time in jail for a drug law violation (James, 2004) that their world is personally constructed and that they still can be free in prison (a statement made by Foss, 2004b). Try telling these individuals, and the many more that could be named who are dominated and oppressed by unjust social systems, that the social and political is not personal. In such cases, the individualistic perspective being advocated does not privilege people's personhood; it essentially blames people for not having "their act together" enough to recognize their absolute agency rather than focusing on changing the system that dominates and oppresses them.

We all know by now, thanks in large part to feminism, that the personal is, in principal, political. However, when we retreat solely within ourselves (or our interpersonal relationships), we run the risk of displacing the political with the personal. Doing so may fit well with the individualistic perspective associated with the United States and the Western world, especially for those who have many resources at their disposal, but it does not provide the type of fertile ground for feminism's emphasis on promoting social change. Even Foss and Griffin (1995) pointed out that (social) "change may be the result of invitational rhetoric, but change is not its purpose" (p. 6). Although this new-age focus on the self-actualization of the individual can and should be an important component of a rhetorical approach to social change, for the personal to also be actively political, it must be firmly tied to the values of connection, cooperation, interdependence, empowerment, and all of the other important values that feminists have articulated, including collective persuasive action in the form of partisan criticism to promote social change and social justice.

Partisan criticism, thus, constitutes an important counterstatement to those who view rhetoric as being nonpartisan and to those who view the persuasive rhetoric that is a central feature of partisan criticism as being inappropriate. By crossing the great divide from nonpartisan to partisan criticism, partisan criticism offers rhetorical scholars an important communicative means by which to advocate for social change and social justice.

ACROSS THE GREAT DIVIDE: FROM PARTISAN CRITICISM TO APPLIED COMMUNICATION ACTIVISM

Ap•plied: Put to practical use, especially by applying general principles to solve definite problems.

Ac•tiv•ism: A doctrine or practice that emphasizes direct vigorous action especially in support of or opposition to one side of a controversial issue.

—Adapted from *Merriam-Webster Online* (2006)

Although I have deep respect for the perspective of partisan criticism that Swartz (2005) offered, I also believe that there is a great divide that needs to be crossed from partisan criticism to applied communication activism. Swartz's position on partisan criticism is based, in part, on the social justice communication perspective articulated by my colleagues and me (Frey et al., 1996; see also Frey, 1998b; Pearce, chap. 11, this volume; Pollock, Artz, Frey, Pearce, & Murphy, 1996). I do not rehash that perspective here, except to say that we argued that a social justice sensibility necessitates, as one of four criteria we articulated (the others being the foregrounding of ethical concerns, performing structural analyses of ethical problems, and identification with others), social actors adopting an activist orientation. As we claimed:

It is not enough merely to define, demonstrate, or bemoan the fact that some of us lack the minimal necessities of life, that others of us are used regularly against our will and against our interests by others for their pleasure or profit, and that some of us are defined as "outside" the economic, political, or social system because of our race, creed, lifestyle, or medical condition, or simply because we are in the way of someone else's project. A social justice sensibility entails a moral imperative to *act* as effectively as we can to do something about structurally sustained inequalities. To continue to pursue justice, it is perhaps necessary that we who act are personally ethical, but that is not sufficient. Our actions must engage and transform social structures. (Frey et al., 1996, p. 111)

My colleagues and I were roundly criticized in a recent essay by Olson and Olson (2003) for claiming that social justice communication scholarship needed to be action oriented, and they certainly have a point. Perhaps we did not make it clear enough at that time, although I certainly did later in editing a special issue of the *Journal of Applied Communication Research* on "Communication and Social Justice Research" (Frey, 1998a), that we explicitly were talking about social justice as a particular form of applied communication scholarship. According to Cissna (1982):

> Applied research sets out to contribute to knowledge by answering a real, pragmatic, social question or by solving a real pragmatic, social problem. Applied *communication* research involves such a question or problem of human communication or examines human communication in order to provide an answer or solution to the question or problem. (Editor's note)

Unfortunately, as my colleagues and I (Frey et al., 1996) pointed out, applied communication researchers, like their nonapplied communication counterparts, have tended to privilege contributions to theory over directly confronting and managing or solving real-world problems (and when such research has featured application, it has tended to be for those who have many resources at their disposal, such as owners of wealthy for-profit organizations). The editorial policy of the *Journal of Applied Communication Research* (2006) makes this focus on theory clear, stating that:

> The *Journal of Applied Communication Research* publishes original scholarship that addresses or challenges the relationship between *theory* and practice in understanding communication in applied contexts. ... Original research studies should apply existing *theory* and research to practical situations, problems, and practices; should illuminate how embodied activities inform and reform existing *theory*; or should contribute to *theory* development. Research articles should offer critical summaries of *theory* and/or research and demonstrate ways in which the critiques can be used to explain, improve, or understand communication practices or processes in a specific context. (italics added)

To counteract this "theory envy," applied communication scholarship needs to focus on confronting and solving real-world problems. However, in a relatively recent forum on defining applied communication scholarship, I

(Frey, 2000) argued that the term *applied communication* had become meaningless, because all research in the practical discipline of communication (see Craig, 1989, 1995) is applied in the sense of it ultimately being devoted to *praxis* that yields wisdom in the form of practical theories (see Cronen, 1995). As Wood (1995) contended, "Applied communication research is practicing theory and theorizing practice" (p. 157). Consequently, I argued that we needed to reclaim this domain of scholarship by starting from the premise that, with regard to applied communication research, "to put into practice" applies to researchers, as opposed to simply anyone who puts communication into practice (e.g., the research participants studied); thus, *applied communication scholarship* should be defined as "the study of researchers putting their communication knowledge and skills into practice. Hence, applied communication scholarship involves scholars bringing their resources to bear to make a difference in people's lives" (Frey, 2000, p. 179).

I certainly am not arguing that every communication scholar needs to be an applied communication scholar or that applied communication scholarship is the only way to promote social change and social justice, for I sincerely believe in a "big-tent" approach, as there is plenty of work for all of us to do. Holding up that big tent, partisan criticism is an important pole for promoting social change and social justice.

However, although criticism can help to promote social change and social justice and, in fact, is a necessary condition for promoting those goals (for something cannot be changed without first identifying the need for it to be changed), criticism often is not sufficient in and of itself for accomplishing those goals; it must be accompanied by concrete application and intervention on the part of someone else that is directed toward actually enacting the social change being advocated. Although McKerrow (1989) claimed that the goal of critical rhetoric "is to understand the integration of power/knowledge in society—what possibility for change the integration invites or inhibits and what intervention strategies might be considered appropriate to effect social change" (p. 91), it does not necessarily produce social change, per se.

The reason such rhetorical criticism does not necessarily produce social change is because of the great divide between the symbolic and material worlds. As Cloud (1994) persuasively argued, although the study of rhetoric is "vital to the projects of critique and social change ... discourse is not the only thing that 'matters' in these projects" (p. 141). She cautioned against falling victim to the "materiality of discourse hypothesis": the belief that "discourse itself is influential or even constitutive of social and material reality" (p. 141). The materiality of discourse hypothesis draws no distinction between symbolic and material acts, because reality is viewed as being a discursive formation. However, as McGee (1986) pointed out:

> Action is doing to the world, the chopping of trees. ... There is a tremendous gulf between action and discourse, the distance between murder, for example, and the "symbolic killing" of name-calling. In truth, *the only actions that consist in discourse are performed on discourse itself.* Speech will not fell a tree, and one cannot write a house to dwell in. One can act through discourse on discourse to guide or control the meaning people see in selected representations of the world. Discursive action, however, always stands in anticipation of its consequences, an act that requires additional acts before one is clear that it ever was more than "mere talk." (p. 122)

Hence, as Cloud (1994) maintained,

> When discourse counts as material, emancipation is seemingly possible in "mere talk" (p. 154), but it is not only discourses and codes from which many people need liberation. A politics of discourse ... assumes that those who are oppressed or exploited need discursive redefinition of their identities, rather than transformation of their material conditions as a primary task (p. 157).

Cloud pointed out that "to say that hunger and war are rhetorical is to state the obvious; to suggest that rhetoric is *all* they are is to leave critique behind" (p. 159). Thus, criticism alone, the textualizing of politics, as Farrell (1993) called it, does not produce social change unless it leads "to some kind of concrete oppositional action—a successful strike, a demonstration that builds a mass movement, or other collective and effective refusal of the prevailing social order" (Cloud, 1994, p. 151); that is, action that results in changes in the material world. As Wander (1984) exclaimed, "Cries of help call for much more than appreciation" (p. 199).

Recognizing the important distinction drawn between symbolic acts and material consequences, communication and rhetorical scholars interested in promoting social change and social justice need to engage in *communication activism*, intervening directly to assist groups and communities to secure social reform. Such interventions, of course, must be based on critiques of the present system, but such critiques, per se, do not necessarily change the material conditions. It also is hard to understand how critique would be viewed as an end goal in and of itself. Wander (1983) argued that "more than 'informed talk about matters of importance,' criticism carries us to the point of recognizing good reasons and engaging in right action" (p. 18), and Andersen (1993) asserted that "the commitment to a set of ideas, once expressed, leads to other kinds of actions. It would be hard to write an ideological critique of Operation Desert Storm, the Federal budget deficit, or the politics of logging, and not feel a need to do more than produce a scholarly article" (p. 248). Critique, thus, should lead naturally to the need to intervene.

Although there clearly is a need for communication activism informed by partisan criticism, the question arises as to where the training is in our graduate programs for how to intervene. The answer is few and far between, unfortunately. In fact, I believe that most doctoral communication programs are somewhat hostile to promoting intervention—seeing theory, criticism, and research as their primary and sole goals. I have some friends, for instance, who have been denied tenure at Research I institutions because their applied communication research was not valued, despite them having a list of publications that would be the envy of most scholars in our discipline. As a member of those committees now, I have yet to be successful in even starting a discussion of the importance of application, let alone activism, in judging colleagues' research when it comes to tenure and promotion, even for those who are hired to engage in applied communication scholarship! In large measure, I believe this is due to academics being some of the most timid people I know when it comes to getting their hands dirty in the mud of social action.

There are, however, some colleagues in our field who are not just, as T. M. Coopman recently exclaimed, "talking about thinking about theorizing about doing something, but actually *praxis*ing what we're preaching" (personal communication, February 11, 2004). I am coediting a two-volume text that features original research studies demonstrating communication activism (Frey & Carragee, in press). Each chapter explains the nature of the communication activism, including the groups and communities involved, the specific projects or interventions designed to secure needed change or reform, the theories and methods that informed the projects, and what lessons scholar-activists might learn from this research about engaging in communication activism. An example from that text helps to demonstrate the point that I am making about the importance of crossing the great divide from partisan criticism to applied communication activism for the purpose of promoting social change and social justice.

McHale (Illinois State University) and his colleagues produced a documentary about Joe Amrine, who was sentenced to death for a crime that he did not commit (McHale, Wylie, & Huck, 2002). McHale, a recent graduate of the University of Missouri at Columbia, was trained in rhetorical theory and criticism. He found out about Amrine and was faced with choices about how to proceed. He could, for instance, have written a scholarly article about the death penalty, in general, or even the fight to save Amrine's life, in particular, and published it in the *Quarterly Journal of Speech* (aiming high) or some other journal that features rhetorical (partisan) criticism. Although he has written a chapter in this forthcoming text (McHale, in press), what he first did was to produce a video documentary about the case, putting his rhetorical skills to use in that way. He then traveled relentlessly all across Missouri to promote the documentary, showing it everywhere he could and getting it into the hands of anyone and everyone who could help, including the governor of that state. The result was that the Supreme Court of Missouri reviewed the case (an unprecedented move, as the Court had never before reviewed a death sentence with a last-minute habeas corpus petition), decided that Amrine was innocent, and set him free.

Amrine repeatedly has stated that he believes the documentary had an impact on his release; as he claimed, "Prior to the documentary, I didn't have a lot of support. I had a little, but not as much as the film. It saved my life" (cited in Youngs, 2003, p. 1). According to Amrine's attorney, as reported in a newspaper article about the case, the documentary "helped to draw enough attention to get the court to take another look at the case" (Blose, 2004, p. 10). The attorney said that he believed the documentary influenced the Missouri Supreme Court's decision to review the case by "turning on the spotlight" to Amrine's plight and that "the influence was to make the courts look at the case, because courts are concerned about how their judgments will appear in the public. For them to sit back silently and let Joe be executed would have created a public backlash" (cited in Heitzman, 2003, p. A10). In the end, the video documentary and the media attention it generated because of McHale's activism were an important catalytic factor in the battle to save Amrine's life and in the larger battle to abolish the death penalty.

It seems hard to argue that McHale's effort, including his scholarly documentation of it, somehow was inappropriate or misguided, but there are those who take exception to the type of activism in which McHale engaged, or even with creating space for communication activist scholarship. Fish (2004), for example, on exiting as dean of the College of Liberal Arts and Sciences at the University of Illinois at Chicago, in an op-ed piece published in *The New York Times*, offered the following advice to academics:

> Don't confuse your academic obligations with the obligation to save the world; that's not your job as an academic .... In short, don't cross the boundary between academic work and partisan advocacy, whether the advocacy is yours or someone else's.

Marx famously said that our job is not to interpret the world, but to change it. In the academy, however, it is exactly the reverse: our job is not to change the world, but to interpret it. While academic labors might in some instances play a role in real-world politics—if, say, the Supreme Court cites your book on the way to a decision—it should not be the design or aim of academics to play that role. (p. A23)

Fish went on to lambaste those who advocate that the university should be concerned with the tasks of "forming character" and "fashioning citizens" to "realize the values and skills of our democratic society"; that is, those who "consider civic responsibility as an explicit and important aim of college education" (p. A23). He claimed that professors should stick to issues "like curriculum, department leadership, the direction of research, the content and manner of teaching, establishing standards—everything that is relevant to the responsibilities we take on when we accept a paycheck" (p. A23).

Although Fish (2004) was talking primarily about teaching (and we all can agree, I am sure, that there is a huge difference between teaching and proselytizing, although we also should keep in mind Conquergood's [1995] point that "the important site for intellectuals working for social change is in their teaching ... practices as much as on the ramparts," p. 92), he probably would say the same thing about scholarship as well, arguing for scholarship that stays away from partisan criticism and applied communication activism. This nonpartisan perspective that Fish advocates is a dangerous view of the role of the academic for those who wish to conduct applied communication scholarship, in general, and for those who wish to engage in communication activist scholarship, in particular.

In the communication discipline, Kuypers (2000) has forcefully questioned the need for partisan criticism and communication activism, arguing that "the leaders of our discipline have gone too far in their attempt to foster social change, both within the discipline and society" ("conclusion," ¶ 1) Vatz (2000) claimed that the National Communication Association "serves its members best as a professional organization devoted to promoting communication scholarship and education, not advocating political ends" (¶ 4) Kuypers suggested that "if critics in our discipline wish to engage in such [political partisanship] they should leave the academy ... We should be professors, not social activists" ("conclusion," ¶ 16).

Fish, Kuypers, and Vatz certainly are entitled to their opinions, but their opinions demonstrate a lack of understanding regarding the impossibility of not being situated in the political struggles of everyday life. They fail to recognize that research is *never* [italics added] a politically neutral act. The decision to study *this group* rather than some other, to frame the research questions *this way* rather than another, and to report the findings to *this group* or in *that journal* rather than in some other forum privilege certain values, institutions, and practices. (Frey et al., 1996, p. 114; see also Becker, 1995; Lee, 1993)

Within such a context, *praxis*, Conquergood (1995) argued, is "fundamentally about placement, about taking a stand, marking (not masking) the self, positioning one's research ethically, politically, as well as conceptually" (p. 86).

CONCLUSION

Kuypers (2000) posed the question, "Must we all be political activists?" The answer, of course, is no, but some of us would like our scholarship to make a difference in the world by promoting social change and social justice. Making that difference begins with the type of partisan criticism that Swartz (2005) has advocated; communication activist intervention subsequently works to change the material conditions that oppress individuals and groups. Communication activist research is grounded in scholars involving themselves in the life of their communities and the broader society as researcher-participants who make important political (cultural, economic, and ethical) choices, take responsibility for those choices, and act on those choices to intervene with—rather than merely descriptively study—others. There are more and more communication scholars who are not content to just stand outside and describe, interpret, and critique the stream of events but, instead, wish to do something about those events. Palmeri (2004) humorously responded to Fish's (2004) op-ed essay that encouraged professors to stay in their ivory tower and avoid immersing themselves in the political struggles of our day by saying:

> I think if I was an artist I would draw a cartoon featuring Rome burning while Stanley Fish lectures Seneca not to douse the flames. 'Your job, Seneca, is to interpret the flames, not put them out,' would be the caption.

Fortunately, there are scholars who are showing how applied communication activist research can put out some of the flames or fan them when needed. McHale's (in press) example, and many more that I could offer from the forthcoming communication activism texts, demonstrates the importance of first crossing the great divide from nonpartisan to partisan criticism, and then crossing the great divide from partisan criticism to applied communication activism to promote social change and social justice. As Andersen (1993) noted, "It is quite a different task to write about ideology and activism than to live it" (p. 251). Had McHale not crossed those divides, had he remained solely a rhetorical critic (even a partisan one), Joe Amrine undoubtedly would be dead today or still waiting to be executed. That is how important it is to cross the great divide from partisan criticism to applied communication activism. The only question is what are we waiting for?

REFERENCES

Andersen, P. A. (1993). Beyond criticism: The activist turn in the ideological debate. *Western Journal of Communication, 57*, 247–256.

Becker, S. L. (1995). Response to Conquergood: Don Quixotes in the academy—Are we tilting at windmills? In K. N. Cissna (Ed.), *Applied communication in the 21st century* (pp. 57–66). Mahwah, NJ: Lawrence Erlbaum Associates, Inc.

Blose, C. (2004). Lights, camera, activism. *Mizzou, 92*, 10–11.

Cissna, K. N. (1982). Editor's note: What is applied communication research? *Journal of Applied Communication Research, 10*.

Cloud, D. L. (1994). The materiality of discourse as oxymoron: A challenge to critical rhetoric. *Western Journal of Communication, 58*, 141–163.

Condit, C. M. (1993). The critic as empath: Moving away from totalizing theory. *Western Journal of Communication, 57*, 178–190.

Conquergood, D. (1991). Rethinking ethnography: Towards a critical cultural politics. *Communication Monographs, 58*, 179–194.

Conquergood, D. (1995). Between rigor and relevance: Rethinking applied communication. In K. N. Cissna (Ed.), *Applied communication in the 21st century* (pp. 79–96). Mahwah, NJ: Lawrence Erlbaum Associates, Inc.

Craig, R. T. (1989). Communication as a practical discipline. In B. Dervin, L. Grossberg, B. J. O'Keefe, & E. Wartella (Eds.), *Rethinking communication: Vol. 1. Paradigm issues* (pp. 97–122). Newbury Park, CA: Sage.

Craig, R. T. (1995). Applied communication research in a practical discipline. In K. N. Cissna (Ed.), *Applied communication in the 21st century* (pp. 147–155). Mahwah, NJ: Lawrence Erlbaum Associates, Inc.

Cronen, V. (1995). Practical theory and the tasks ahead for social approaches to communication. In W. Leeds-Hurwitz (Ed.), *Social approaches to communication* (pp. 217–242). New York: Guilford Press.

Farrell, T. B. (1993). On the disappearance of the rhetorical aura. *Western Journal of Communication, 57*, 147–158.

Fish, S. (2004, May 21). Why we built the ivory tower. *The New York Times*, p. A23.

Foss, S. K. (2004a, February). *An invitational perspective on social change*. Paper presented at the meeting of the Western States Communication Association, Albuquerque, NM.

Foss, S. K. (2004b, March). *Feminist perspectives on social change*. Speech presented to the Department of Communication Colloquium, University of Colorado at Boulder.

Foss, S. K., & Foss, K. A. (2002). *Inviting transformation: Presentational speaking for a changing world* (2nd ed.). Prospect Heights, IL: Waveland.

Foss, S. K., & Griffin, C. L. (1995). Beyond persuasion: A proposal for invitational rhetoric. *Communication Monographs, 62*, 2–18.

Fraser, N. (1985). What's critical about critical theory? The case of Habermas and gender. *New German Critique, 35,* 97–131.

Frey, L. R. (Ed.). (1998a). Communication and social justice research [Special issue]. *Journal of Applied Communication Research, 26*(2).

Frey, L. R. (1998b). Communication and social justice research: Truth, justice, and the applied communication way. *Journal of Applied Communication Research, 26,* 155–164.

Frey, L. R. (2000). To be applied or not to be applied, that isn't even the question; but wherefore art thou, applied communication researcher? Reclaiming applied communication research and redefining the role of the researcher. *Journal of Applied Communication Research, 28,* 178–182.

Frey, L. R., & Carragee, K. M. (in press). *Communication activism* (2 vols.). Cresskill, NJ: Hampton Press.

Frey, L. R., Pearce, W. B., Pollock, M. A., Artz, L., & Murphy, B. A. O. (1996). Looking for justice in all the wrong places: On a communication approach to social justice. *Communication Studies, 47,* 110–127.

Griffin, C. L. (2003). *Invitation to public speaking.* Belmont, CA: Thomson/Wadsworth.

Heitzman, L. (2003, September 23). Amrine, filmmaker revisit case. *Columbia Daily Tribune,* p. A10.

Hill, F. I. (1972). Convention wisdom—traditional form: The president's message of November 3, 1969. *Quarterly Journal of Speech, 58,* 373–387.

Hill, F. (1983). A turn against ideology: Reply to Professor Wander. *Central States Speech Journal, 34,* 121–126.

James, D. J. (2004, October 12). *Profile of jail inmates, 2002.* Washington, DC: U.S. Department of Justice, Bureau of Justice Statistics. Retrieved June 17, 2005, from http://www.ojp.usdoj. gov/bjs/pub/pdf/pji02.pdf

Journal of Applied Communication Research. (2006). *Guidelines for contributors.* Retrieved January 4, 2006, from http://www.tandf.co.uk/journals/authors/rjacauth.asp

Kuypers, J. A. (2000). Must we all be political activists? *American Communication Journal, 4.* Retrieved June 14, 2005, from http://acjournal.org/holdings/vol4/ iss1/special/kuypers.htm

Lee, W. S. (1993). Social scientists as ideological critics. *Western Journal of Communication, 57,* 221–232.

McGee, M. C. (1986). Against transcendentalism: Prologue to a functional theory of communicative practice. In H. W. Simons & A. A. Aghazarian (Eds.), *Form, genre, and the study of political discourse* (pp. 108–158). Columbia: University of South Carolina Press.

McHale, J. P. (in press). Unreasonable doubt: Using video documentary to promote justice. In L. R. Frey & K. M. Carragee (Eds.), *Communication activism: Vol. 2. Media and performance activism.* Cresskill, NJ: Hampton Press.

McHale, J. P. (Producer/Director), Wylie, R. (Producer/Editor), & Huck, D. (Producer/Assistant Editor). (2002). *Unreasonable doubt: The Joe Amrine case* [Videotape]. (Available from John McHale, School of Communication, Illinois State University, Normal, IL 61790–4480)

McKerrow, R. E. (1989). Critical rhetoric: Theory and praxis. *Communication Monographs, 56,* 91–111.

Merriam-Webster Online. (2006). Retrieved January 4, 2006, fom http://www.m-w.com

Olson, K. M., & Olson, C. D. (2003). Problems of exclusionary research criteria: The case against the "usable knowledge" litmus test for social justice communication research. *Communication Studies, 54,* 438–450.

Palmeri, T. (2004, May 26). *So long and thanks for Stanley Fish.* Message posted to mea@lists.ibiblio.org

Pollock, M. A., Artz, L., Frey, L. R., Pearce, W. B., & Murphy, B. A. O. (1996). Navigating between Scylla and Charybdis: Continuing the dialogue on communication and social justice. *Communication Studies, 47,* 142–151.

Rosenfield, L. W. (1983). Ideological miasma. *Central States Speech Journal, 34,* 119–121.

Strine, M. S. (1991). Critical theory and "organic" intellectuals: Reframing the work of cultural critique. *Communication Monographs, 58,* 195–201.

Swartz, O. (2005). *In defense of partisan criticism.* New York: Peter Lang.

Vatz, R. (2000, May 25). NCA should not be an agent of political advocacy. *CRTNET NEWS* (Of Interest No. 5091). Retrieved June 15, 2005, from http://lists1.cac.psu.edu/cgi-bin/wa?A2=ind0005&L=crtnet&T=0&F=&S=&P=8725

Wander, P. (1983). The ideological turn in modern criticism. *Central States Speech Journal, 34,* 1–18.

Wander, P. (1984). The third persona: An ideological turn in rhetorical theory. *Central States Speech Journal, 35,* 197–216.

Wander, P., & Jenkins, S. (1972). Rhetoric, society, and the critical response. *Quarterly Journal of Speech, 58,* 441–450.

Wood, J. T. (1995). Theorizing practice, practicing theory. In K. N. Cissna (Ed.), *Applied communication in the 21st century* (pp. 181–192). Mahwah, NJ: Lawrence Erlbaum Associates, Inc.

Youngs, J. (2003, September 19). Amrine, activists speak out at rally. *The Maneater,* p. 1.

4

Communication, Charity, Social Justice, and the Abolition of Homelessness

Phillip K. Tompkins
University of Colorado at Boulder, Emeritus

In the contemporary United States we see this [the structuring of societies by elites to serve their self-interest] in the naming of high taxes as a (and perhaps *the*) primary political issue. The anti-tax sentiment of our society is fueled and financed primarily by the wealthy. Can anybody seriously believe that the anti-tax movement serves the interests of the society as a whole, and not simply the narrow self-interest of the wealthy? Unfortunately, many do; elites know how to shape public opinion (and thus the system as a whole). (Borg, 2001, p. 144)

I respected the intellectual vigor of my environment [Harvard Law School], but I was appalled by the overwhelming subservience of legal education to the commercial powers and the principalities of property. I thought that a law school should devote at least as much attention in its curriculum to the rights and causes of people as it does to vested interests of one kind or another. I also thought while I was in law school that *justice* is a suitable topic for consideration in practically every course or specialization. Alas, it was seldom mentioned, and the term itself evoked ridicule, as if justice were a subject beneath the sophistication of lawyers. (Stringfellow, 1994, p. 32)

In the first epigraph, Borg succinctly does social criticism and implies that justice is not being served in the United States. Yet there is more in Borg's short footnote—he also diagnoses the cause of social injustice as inherent to the process of communication; that is, "elites know how to shape public opinion (and thus the system as a whole)," a process many critical scholars call hegemony. The second epigraph makes several points, one of which helps us understand part of the process Borg mentioned in which the elites, what Stringfellow calls the "powers and principalities," do shape public opinion and the system as a whole; that is, the process of education in general, and legal education specifically. We return later to both of these quotations for further explication and inspiration.

Until I read Borg's footnote for the first time I had a clear idea how this chapter would unfold. I would return to the philosopher John Rawls, dutifully reproduce his definitions as well as his "principles" of justice—described as they are by some with the terms "liberal democratic" and "liberal socialism" (Freeman, 2001, p. 775), and apply them to the observations and data I have collected over the past 7 years as a volunteer in a homeless shelter and as a member of advocacy groups for homeless people in Denver, Colorado (Housing Justice!, Capitol Hill United Ministries, and the Missions Committee of Trinity United Methodist Church). As I thought through the project a reservation began to develop, the realization that conservatives, particularly those on the religious right, and some moderates, could reject my conclusions out of hand by averring they were derived from "liberal" and "socialist" premises, no matter how tight my reasoning.

An alternative approach suggested itself—rather, it arrived as if a rainstorm—one that persuaded me to assume this less academic but potentially more robust rhetorical stance. Let me describe the shower of ideas that allowed me to engage a new and different approach. The first raindrops fell on me in a formal discussion at the St. Francis Center, a homeless shelter in Denver where I serve as a volunteer on Fridays. Staff members and volunteers have the option of showing up early for work to participate in a "sharing" discussion stimulated often by a handout from or reading by the day's discussion leader. At a recent discussion we received a printout from a Web site attributed to the Office for Social Justice, Archdiocese of St. Paul/Minneapolis. That this is the total extent of my documentation is unimportant because the handout is not definitive; it is used here, as in the group discussion at the shelter, to stimulate interaction and reflection.

CHARITY VERSUS JUSTICE

The handout is in the form of a series of oppositions under the heading: *Charity vs. Justice*: Charity = Social Service; Justice = Social Change. Other oppositional dimensions relevant to this chapter can be paraphrased as private, individual acts versus public, collective acts; responds to immediate need versus responds to long-term need; provides direct service versus provides social change in institution (i.e., food, clothing, shelter); requires repeated actions versus resolves structural injustice; directed at effects, symptoms versus directed at root causes of social injustice. Examples of charity listed in the handout were keenly relevant to my interests: "Homeless shelters, clothing drives, emergency services" involve activities I engaged in at, or for, the St. Francis Center. Under justice were such activities as "legislative advocacy, changing corporate policies or practices, congregation-based community organizing." These were also activities I had been involved in as a volunteer and advocate for homeless people. The document attributed *justice* to the Hebrew Bible, or Old Testament, as described in the actions of Moses to set his people free rather than ask for handouts from the Egyptians; *charity* was traced to the New Testament, to the parable of the Good Samaritan.

The more I reflected on the handout and discussed the concepts with others, the more it seemed to defy, if not contradict, philosophic approaches to criticism. It is set up according to the traditional oppositions of structuralism—as in Levy-Strauss's famous example of "raw–cooked"—and yet it is subtly ambiguous in regard to Derrida's method of deconstruction in which the position of social preference or "privilege" is on the left, inviting a "violent" reversal of the hierarchy. A feminist, for example, might want to transform he/she into she/he. Another strategy open to a deconstructionist would be to reduce the difference within the hierarchy to a state of equality. In the case of the handout, however, what is presumed to be the position of privilege, the left, turns out in some ways to be less preferred, at least to the thinker seeking to discover causes in addition to symptoms, the reformer who searches for long-term rather than short-term solutions. There is also an "extra-dialectical" hint supplied by the imputation of authorship of the document to a Committee for Social Justice, an implication that the terms on the right are preferred if not privileged.

While still in a state of puzzlement about this way of presenting charity and justice, another raindrop fell on me in the form of a brochure produced by Capitol Hill United Ministries (CHUM), the advocacy group in which I participated for several years. In a campaign to discourage the Colorado state legislature from further cutting back social services for poor and homeless people CHUM, an association of 15 to 20 churches and service organizations on Denver's Capitol Hill, chose the slogan "Justice Beyond Charity, Lent 2005, 'Let Justice Roll Down Like Waters,'" a second recognition of a troubled relationship between the two terms. CHUM's brochure announces training in the skills of lobbying and legislative action for its members; their plan includes pledging the food savings from fasting 1 day a week to social service agencies. The brochure calls for weekly fasting, charity, and just action to attend to the "welfare of the most vulnerable in society. [The brochure warns that] We cannot depend on private charity to do so—in fact, our charities are already at maximum capacity even when fully partnered with government." This sets an absolute limit on the effectiveness of charity, beyond which reform can only be accomplished by legislation seeking social justice. Although both charity and justice have positive connotations, CHUM's slogan, "Justice Beyond Charity," implies that charity may be a lower form of justice, and that true justice lies beyond charity.

Still another raindrop fell late in 2004 in the form of a newsletter from Housing Justice! A column in it, "Affordable Housing Is a Matter of Practicing Our Faith," by Rabbi Joel R. Schwartzman, also addressed the relationship between charity and justice. He had recently led his congregation—B'nai Chaim—through the High Holy Day season, 10 days culminating in Yom Kippur. "During services, I explained that the word 'charity,' was actually a mistranslation of the Hebrew word, *Tzedakah*, which actually means 'righteousness' or 'justice.' When we perform *Tzedakah* and give what is ours to others, we are actually sharing, in some way, what God merely has loaned to us." In Hebrew there is semantic confusion due to mistranslation; with the corrected or preferred translation, however, there does seem to be the implication that justice is in some way preferred to charity.

I turned to English dictionaries for help. My *Shorter Oxford English Dictionary* (OED; 1965) defines *charity* in the following way:

Charity: 1. Christian love; *esp.* the Christian love of our fellow men. Often personified. ME. 2. Love, natural affection; spontaneous affection ME. *pl*, Affections 1667. 3. A disposition to judge hopefully of men and their actions, and to make allowances for their shortcomings 1483; fairness, equity—1647. 4. Benevolence, *esp.* to the poor; charitableness; alms-giving OE. *pl.* Acts of charity done to the poor 1607. 5. Alms ME. 6. A bequest, foundation, institution, etc., for the benefit of others, *esp.* of the poor or helpless.

The definition of *justice* in the same dictionary is too long to be reproduced here, but the key terms used are "the quality of being just or righteous" and "legal proceedings." It does acknowledge a theological meaning of "divine law" and the "state of being 'just before God'—1622."

A more recent source, *The New International Webster's Dictionary & Thesaurus of the English Language* (*NIWD*; 2002), gives a definition of charity quite similar to the older *OED* entry just considered. Both definitions, for example, indicate the word can apply to an institution as well as an individual. Its definition of justice differs a bit from the earlier source, evidence that there have been changes in meaning over the past 40 or 50 years. For example, the *NIWD* gives as its third definition "adherence to truth of fact; impartiality" and its first two synonyms are "equity, fairness." Equity and fairness, interestingly, are terms used either as definitions or as synonyms for both of our key terms, acknowledgment that there is a family resemblance between the two. We still do not have, however, an explanation as to why one religious organization would give preference to social justice over charity and why another one wants "Justice Beyond Charity" and a rabbi wants to translate charity into justice.

Fortunately, raindrops kept falling on my head, providing some insight into this semantic puzzle. The book in which the first epigraph of this chapter appeared is Borg's (2001) *Reading the Bible Again for the First Time*. Borg is the Hundre Distinguished Professor of Religion and Culture at Oregon State University. In a lifetime of reading, studying, and teaching the Bible, Borg has come to an understanding of justice that fits my need in this chapter. He reports that as a young man during the 1960s he found the Prophets of the Hebrew Bible to be relevant to the world around him. He was energized by their passion for social justice. Passages in Amos particularly moved him, verses such as "You oppress the poor and crush the needy. You trample on the poor and take from them taxes of grain" (Borg, 2001, p. 118). He was also moved by Amos's prophetic criticism of the elites who "live lives of luxury and are indifferent to the misery in their midst" and wanted exactly what Amos wanted: "Let justice roll down like waters, and righteousness like an ever-flowing stream" (Borg, 2001, p. 119). Borg admits he went to seminary in part because of Amos. There he learned that the rhetorical structure of the "prophetic speech" was the IndictmentThreat Oracle," defined in this way:

- *The indictment:* An accusation or a list of offenses.
- *The threat* (or sentence): What will happen because of the offenses.
- *The summons to the accused:* The naming of the offenders. (Borg, 2001, p. 120)

Why is it, one might ask, that the religious right and other church members are not energized by the teaching and criticism of the prophets? If so, they could be expected to focus less on "values" prohibiting abortion and gay marriage, and more on the need for social justice. Borg believes there are several reasons. Some members of the religious right have been blinded by the teachings that the prophets are important merely because they are said to predict or foresee the coming of Christianity; others resist hearing the prophets because they make those of us who enjoy the affluent life feel uneasy and uncomfortable; finally, there is the ambiguity or semantic confusion surrounding the word justice.

Borg explains this third reason with examples from his students. He could not understand why his students were not responding to his teachings about the prophets the way he had responded as a student. They dutifully took notes, but did not act as if they were moved by his passionate exposition of the prophets' passion for justice. He paused to ask them what they thought of when he used the word justice. After some silence, a student said he thought of the criminal justice system. Of course he would. In the United States, the Department of Justice is concerned with criminal justice. His students had simply not heard the prophets, for "if you hear the prophets' passion for justice as being about convicting and punishing criminals, one has not heard them at all" (Borg, 2001, p. 139).

A second meaning of justice he discerned was procedural justice, the concern for procedures and rules that ensure fair play. This meaning is widespread because it assumes the procedures will be the same for all people, for every individual. This meaning aligns perfectly with individualism—a core cultural value in the United States. Procedural justice does matter greatly in our system, particularly in regard to the adjudication of criminal defendants, but it is not what Amos and the other prophets were speaking of.

The third meaning, according to Borg (2001), is social justice:

> More comprehensive than criminal justice and procedural justice, social justice is concerned with the structures of society and their results. Because it is results-oriented, it discerns whether the structures of society—in other words, the social system as a whole—are just in their effects. Do they produce a large impoverished class or result in a more equitable distribution of resources? Do they benefit some at the expense of many or serve all equally? Do they produce conflict or peace? Do they destroy or nourish a future? (Borg, 2001, p. 139)

Borg thus distinguishes among criminal justice, procedural justice, and social justice; his emphasis on the results of a society gives us an additional dimension not present in the earlier oppositions. He goes on to write that social justice is what the prophets proclaim. It also refers to a conflict between the kind of social justice imagined or idealized and the domination system of our society, the key terms in a prior body of theological criticism of 20th-century United States.[1] The final sentence of the preceding paragraph runs thus: "The structuring of societies by elites to serve their interest continues" (Borg, 2001, p. 140). That sentence is marked by footnote number 55, the content of which is the first epigraph of the chapter, thus completing the circle in which Borg talks about hegemony, the ability of the elite to shape public opinion and produce systemic injustice.

In the epilogue of his book, Borg (2001) makes a distinction between charity and justice. After doing so he uses the word compassion as a synonym for charity. He sees the relationship as similar to those sources considered earlier. Both justice and compassion are required. Justice without charity or compassion sounds like politics as usual. Yet the word justice is "utterly essential":

> Charity and kind deeds are always good; there will always be need for help. But the individualization of compassion means that one does not ask how many of the suffering are in fact victims. Compassion without justice can mean caring for victims while quietly acquiescing to a system that creates ever more victims. Justice means asking why there are so many victims and then doing something about it. (p. 301)

In other words, both charity and justice are needed for a humane society; justice, however, moves beyond the individualism assumed in charity and compassion, it moves beyond to public, collective acts produced by rational deliberations; justice looks beyond the symptoms to the root causes of injustice; it seeks to go beyond helping individual victims to producing the kind of social change in the domination system that will prevent new victims.

THE POWERS AND PRINCIPALITIES

To understand better the domination system Borg invoked to explain injustice, it is necessary to introduce a modern prophet, a prophet of the 20th century and author of the second epigraph of this chapter, William

---

[1]The critique of the domination system was begun by an extraordinary thinker, William Stringfellow, and carried further in four volumes by Walter Wink. We take a look at their work after completing our discussion of Borg.

Stringfellow (1928–1985). The essential biographical facts are provided in Ellsberg's (1997) book *All Saints: Daily Reflections on Saints, Prophets and Witnesses for Our Time*, which describes Stringfellow as a lay or nonacademic theologian, social critic, and prophet. We know from self-reference in the second epigraph of this chapter that Stringfellow went to Harvard Law School and was appalled by the subservience of the law to power and property he found there. "Emerging as 'someone virtually opposite' of what a Harvard Law School graduate was expected to be, [Stringfellow] settled into a vermin-ridden apartment in Harlem to practice poverty law. From this vantage point he acquired a particular perspective on the world that later informed his writing on the 'powers and principalities'" (Ellsberg, 1997, p. 184). Raised as an Episcopalian, Stringfellow came into conflict with his own church by becoming an early advocate of ordaining women as priests, and for advocating the rights of homosexuals. He became a fierce critic of the Vietnam War and, while acting out his social criticism, he was arrested by the FBI for harboring a fugitive, Daniel Berrigan, the Jesuit priest who was convicted of destroying draft files as a form of antiwar protest. Stringfellow's theme as a Christian theologian was the "Constantinian Compromise," the "accommodation of Christianity to the [Roman] empire and the preservation of the status quo" (Ellsberg, 1997, p. 185), thus allowing the powers and principalities to have their way. After law school Stringfellow encountered other powers and principalities.

The powers and principalities include "all corporations, all ideologies, all images … all conglomerates … all nations, all idols" and specific examples considered by Stringfellow in his social criticism include but are not limited to "the Pentagon or the Ford Motor Company or Harvard University … or the Methodist Church or the Teamsters Union" (Stringfellow, 1994, p. 205). He held that these institutions were creatures that are autonomous, free of human control. Their existence reverses the biblical assumption of human dominion over the creatures: "In reality they dominate human beings" (Stringfellow, 1994, p. 208). Writing in 1973, Stringfellow said that "dehumanization" was one term of then-current jargon for the reversal of the dominion between persons and principalities. In a passage prophetic of the crisis of homelessness today in the United States, Stringfellow illustrates the powers and principalities with the example of "the separation of citizens in apartheid, enforced as the case may be, by urban housing and development schemes" (Stringfellow, 1994, p. 209). Stringfellow realized that developers make more money on expensive homes than housing affordable to the people who do what are considered lower forms of work. By using the word apartheid, he anticipated an argument I take up toward the end of this chapter; namely, that homelessness is today's counterpart to racial segregation in the 20th-century United States and slavery in the 19th century.

To round out this terse summary of Stringfellow's social criticism as theology, I add that there is the force of rivalry among the powers and principalities. There are instances of cooperation among them such as the "Pentagon, some self-styled think tanks, and the weapons industry" (Stringfellow, 1994, p. 211); these are expedient and transient; the real motive of the powers and principalities is simple survival. Thus, he argued that an important subtext of the Vietnam War was the survival of the beasts behind it. The powers and principalities demand and acquire commitment, loyalty, identification, and idolatry. They possess those who are dependent on them for survival. Political leaders, including presidents, are not stupid or wicked, they are instead "captivated, dominated, obsessed by the demonic" (Stringfellow, 1994, p. 211). The relationships among the powers and principalities and their victims are so complex, he concluded, they defy description other than as a "milieu of chaos."

Borg and others, as mentioned earlier, trace the concept of justice to the prophets of the Old Testament or Hebrew Bible. Stringfellow, by contrast, emerges as a modern prophet of justice on the basis of his reading of the New Testament, the Book of Revelation in particular. Wink aligns himself with Stringfellow. Wink's (1998) fourth book on the powers and principalities, *The Powers That Be*, cites the Book of Daniel, although he, like Stringfellow, relies most heavily on the New Testament. The powers that be are networks of organizations and institutions that are idolatrous; idolatry is when a power pursues a vocation "other than the one for which God created it and makes its own interests the highest good—then that Power becomes demonic"(Wink, 1998, p. 29). This demonic spirit is a concept Wink compares to what business writers call corporate culture, the personality of an organization that no individual can control.[2] Taken together these networks constitute the domination system, which is "characterized by unjust economic relations, oppressive political relations, biased race relations, patriarchal gender relations, hierarchical power relations, and the use of violence to maintain them all" (Wink, 1998, p. 39).[3]

---

[2]My own way of expressing this phenomenon is the notion of culture within a corporate body practicing what Weber called instrumental rationality; see Tompkins (2005).

[3]The domination system produces good results and bad, the bad results including systematic social injustice. The domination system and even its individual corporate members cannot be confronted by individuals with a charitable orientation, only by movements and coalitions who gain strength by numbers and the power stemming from a desire to see justice. My own view, following Burke, is that hierarchy is a defining characteristic of human beings, and although I accept the "demonic" as metaphor, I would stress that corporate bodies produce positive social effects as well as negative ones.

Returning to the relationship issue, verbal oppositions or dialectics can, of course, be transformed for analytic purposes into continua. Thus, charity versus justice or charity/justice can be converted into charity ... justice. An advantage to this conversion is that it allows an individual to find her or his space or place along the continuum at any given time, with the possibility of movement from time to time. It also avoids putting one concept in an inferior position, implying a bad connotation. Think of the horrifying results if charitable institutions all shut down to pursue the goal of long-term justice. Both ends of the continuum, therefore, are necessary to a humane, civilized society. Neither term has meaning except in relation to the other, as in cool ... warm. In the sharing discussion described earlier in this chapter, the executive director of the shelter said movement from charity to justice represented a developmental pattern; that is, that many people who wind up on the right end started on the left (it is in doing charity that many people come to realize there are victims of the system and that to prevent this victimization from continuing and expanding, one must join others in trying to get to the root causes of the injustice). This describes my personal experience, starting as a volunteer at a homeless shelter almost 7 years ago and gradually coming to the understanding that I needed to join and support groups advocating social justice for homeless people, groups such as Housing Justice!

As an addendum to this section, I must report that after the preceding text had been composed I stumbled across a book, *Credo* (Coffin, 2004) that supports my analysis—even if the notion of a continuum between the two concepts is implicit. Coffin's life has been an acting-out of the need for justice; when he was Chaplain at Yale, Coffin was jailed as a Freedom Rider for marching alongside Martin Luther King, Jr., in the civil rights movement. He was also jailed for his role in the march on the Pentagon, a protest against the Vietnam War. *Credo* is a treasury of passages from his later sermons at the Riverside Church in New York City, organized under nine headings, two of which are "Social Justice and Civil Liberties" and "Social Justice and Economic Rights." One rhetorical passage is representative of his views on the charity ... justice continuum. It is, ironically, addressed to the churches, an important member of the powers and principalities:

> Had I but one wish for the churches of America I think it would be that they come to see the difference between charity and justice. Charity is a matter of personal attributes; justice, a matter of public policy. Charity seeks to alleviate the effects of injustice; justice seeks to eliminate the causes of it. Charity in no way affects the status quo, while justice leads inevitably to political

confrontation. Especially I would hope that Christians would see that the compassion that moved the Good Samaritan to act charitably—that same compassion prompted biblical prophets to confront injustice, to speak truth to power, as did Jesus, who, though more than a prophet, was certainly nothing less. (Coffin, 2004, pp. 62–63)

Consistent with the earlier analysis, Coffin indicates that charity is a personal attribute, justice a matter of public policy; charity alleviates the effects of injustice, justice seeks to eliminate its causes; charity has no effect on the status quo, justice requires confrontation; neither charity nor justice is limited to either the Hebrew Bible or the New Testament. Coffin (2004) also sees a political alliance of powers and principalities in this passage: "Handouts to needy individuals are genuine, necessary responses to injustice, but they do not necessarily face the reason for the injustice. And that is why President Reagan and so many business leaders today are promoting charity; it is desperately needed in an economy whose prosperity is based on growing inequality" (pp. 64–65).

IS HOMELESSNESS THE MORAL EQUIVALENCE OF SLAVERY AND RACIAL SEGREGATION?

Before considering homelessness as a form of injustice, it will be necessary to define it. Burt (2003) defines homelessness by using language from the McKinney-Vento Homeless Assistance Act: "The Act defines a person as homeless if the 'individual lacks a fixed, regular, and adequate nighttime residence.' People sleeping in 'a public or private place not designed for, or ordinarily used as, a regular sleeping accommodation for human beings,' as well as those staying in shelters for homeless people, are part of the definition" (p. 2). This is a general, catch-all definition stressing that a homeless person lacks a regular residence in which to spend the night. Others have come up with definitions that emphasize degrees or stages of homelessness.

Australian writers, for example, have come up with three categories of homelessness:

Primary Homelessness: People without conventional accommodation, such as people living on the streets, sleeping in parks, squatting in derelict buildings, or using cars or railway carriages for temporary shelter. Secondary Homelessness: People who move frequently from one form of temporary shelter to another. It covers: people using emergency accommodation (such as hostels for the homeless or night shelters); teenagers staying in youth refuges; women and children escaping domestic violence (staying in women's refuges); people residing temporarily with other families (because they have no accommodation of their own); and those using boarding houses on intermittent basis. Tertiary Homelessness: People who live in boarding houses on a medium to long-term basis. Residents of private kitchen and bathroom facilities; their accommodation is not self-contained; they do not have security of tenure provided by a lease. (quoted in Lynch & Cole, 2003, p. 141)

Lynch and Cole (2003), members of the University of Melbourne Law Faculty, argue that homelessness is a violation of fundamental human rights, including but not limited to the "right to freedom of expression, the right to freedom of association ... and the right to health" (p. 1). They ground their argument in national and international declarations of human rights. They urge people to invoke human rights law in litigation and public policy advocacy.[4]

Our previous discussion of the continuum between charity and justice prepares us now to take a fresh look at homelessness and poverty. It is a counterintuitive truth that in the richest of societies, the United States, poor and homeless people are increasing in numbers and percentages. Is this an issue at the charity end of the continuum or at the justice pole?

Few would deny that the abolition of slavery in the United States during the 19th century was a triumph of justice and a triumph for our society as a whole. Few would deny that the abolition of de jure segregation in the 20th century was a triumph for justice and our society as a whole. Neither could have been achieved by charity alone. Both of those achievements were ardently opposed by many of the powers that be, by owners and their attorneys.

A professor of law at the University of Indiana, F. Roisman (2000) advanced in an article in the *Saint Louis University Public Law Review* the thesis that homelessness is the moral equivalent of slavery and racial segregation practiced in preceding centuries. The title of her article is "The Lawyer as Abolitionist: Ending Homelessness and Poverty in Our Time." Beyond the observation that it is not obvious why the role should be restricted to lawyers, I find her argument appealing only up to a point. After exploring her arguments, I state my reservations.

---

[4]Incidentally, Coffin (2004) would agree that homelessness is a violation of human rights: "This isn't a matter of charity, but of justice. Just as to the slaves freedom was not a gift but the restoration of a right no one had any business taking from them, so a home is a right; the homeless are being robbed" (p. 34).

Her argument by analogy—that the battle to abolish homelessness is like the ones to end slavery and segregation—is supported by three reasons:

1. Homelessness and poverty disproportionately claim the same kind of victims as did slavery and segregation: people of color, African Americans, and Latinos. Although there are variations in the studies documenting this fact, Roisman relies on numbers from a 1999 publication of the Interagency Council on the Homeless; that is, 40% of homeless clients are African American, 11% Hispanic, and 8% Native American. In Denver the local population of homeless people is somewhat different than the national averages by having lower percentages of African Americans, higher percentages of Hispanics or Latinos and Native Americans. The abolition of slavery addressed political freedom, but the abolitionists knew there was an issue of economic freedom involved as well. They insisted that slaves be given "40 acres and a mule," but this, of course, was not done. Dr. Martin Luther King, Jr., similarly came to see the economic issues in segregation, hence his organization of the Poor People's March to achieve *economic* justice.

2. The concept of property owners' rights was invoked in opposition to the abolition of slavery and segregation. Slave owners' property rights had to be respected; the owners of apartments, hotels, and restaurants had the right to decide who could and could not be accommodated and fed. Roisman does not use the acronym NIMBY (not in my backyard) in her analysis of how property rights are used against homeless people today, but she does note the "arguments ... that services for homeless people should not locate near homes and businesses for fear of reduced property values and, more generally, that money should not be redistributed from wealthier people to enable every human being to live decently. To challenge *homelessness* and poverty means to challenge a system of private property" (p. 3). My experience is that NIMBYism is one of the most powerful forces against ameliorating the plight of the poor and particularly homeless people. I have seen neighborhood associations of decent people fight to prevent the development of affordable housing for working people, fight to prevent the construction and existence of shelters. Here I would couple Roisman's first argument to her second in an explicit manner; that is, we must see that homeless people are being systematically excluded from a place of propinquity or closeness in relation to the domiciled, and that a disproportionate

number of them are people of color. The powers that be want them at a distance and invisible; this is similar, of course, to the injustice of segregation.

3. Each of the three campaigns is a "moral crusade" (p. 3). The word crusade is perhaps an unfortunate lexical choice, given the tension between the United States and others who think of the European Crusades as neither moral nor righteous. It is good to recall that the abolitionists fighting against slavery and those fighting segregation were inspired, in part, by theology. It is not clear as I write how many of the third wave of abolitionists will be inspired by scripture and theology.

Roisman goes further than I am willing to venture. Although I see similarities among the three movements, it is difficult for me to accept homelessness as identical to slavery. My first reason is illustrated by a conversation with an African American man of my acquaintance; when I mentioned the comparison he fired a rhetorical question without pause: "Are they being hung from a tree?" Second, there is the danger that slavery can be seen as something less depraved and immoral than it is if equated with homelessness and poverty. Third, and this may be a variation of the second reason, I find again that there is a temptation by some self-righteous reformists to equate their cause with abolitionism. I refer to Frank's (2004) political study of my home state: *What's the Matter With Kansas? How Conservatives Won the Heart of America*. His answer to the question raised in the book's title is that conservative Republicans came to power by adamantly advocating an antiabortion, and at times an antievolution, antigay stance. As Frank puts it, "Anti-abortion leaders everywhere are fond of comparing themselves to abolitionist and to civil rights leaders of the past—much to the irritation of civil rights leaders of the present" (p. 84). My fourth reason is that despite the power of NIMBYism, I do not accept Roisman's claim that to challenge homelessness one must challenge the system of private property. Many homeless people dream of having private property of their own; many of them cherish memories of even a most humble homestead of their parents. Finally, a subtheme of Burke's (1984) *Permanence and Change* is that abolition is sometimes just another term for *transformation*. These five reasons lead me to say that I reject the literal analogy between and among the movements and reject the notion that Abolitionism, with an uppercase A, is identical to the movement against homelessness. I do accept the similarities among the movements and can call what is underway in Denver at this moment an abolitionist movement—with a lowercase "a."

TOWARD ENDING HOMELESSNESS IN DENVER

I am a member of an urban church that feeds and helps homeless people 3 days a week. Knowing of my role as an advocate for homeless people, a member of the clergy asked me to organize a Forum Series at the church on the "Faces of Homelessness" to be held in the church on the evenings of the last two Thursdays of January and the first two Thursdays of February 2005. Although I frequently briefed the clergyman, I was given a fairly free hand. My first impulse, as an academic, was to find academic experts on the subject—let's get some economists and sociologists, I thought—and indeed my first invitation was to an adjunct professor in New York City who has done important research on intervention with homeless children. The professor accepted my invitation, until he realized he was expected to accept an award from a foundation on the same day. That allowed me to see that I should cast down my buckets into my own environs, the metropolitan Denver area. There was something happening in Denver that needed attention, scrutiny, and analysis—and support.

I confess to being excited about the emerging movement. During the 7 years I had served as a volunteer at a homeless shelter (charity), the problem grew fairly steadily. I realized the need to participate in advocacy groups in an attempt to get at the causes of homelessness (justice), slow its growth, and perhaps eliminate it. There continue to be sources of resistance to our advocacy attempts other than NIMBYism. There was also what I call the political and ontological problems. The political problem can be characterized as an increasing degree of polarity between the right and the left in the United States in general and Colorado in specific, making it nearly impossible to reach agreement about social problems. The ontological problem can be characterized by the disagreement about the essence of the homeless being, illustrated by reactions of people to my activities as a volunteer and advocate. Some people appreciated what I was doing for the poor and the oppressed; others, however, denied it was useful because, after all, homeless people chose to be on the streets and that made me a mere enabler, or as one person put it, a "pimp." It seemed to me the political problem was less important than the ontological one. Solutions to homelessness are hard to work out and accept if discussants do not agree on the degree of volition possessed by homeless people.

Nonetheless, in talking to members of the community of people who serve homeless persons in Denver, I sensed a feeling of enthusiasm for the project. I sensed there was a growing political will to do something about homelessness. After all, our highly popular mayor—John Hickenlooper—had appointed a Commission to End Homelessness in Denver Within a Decade. Attempting to end homelessness can be fairly described as an abolitionist exercise, even if one must use a lowercase a. There was a resolve, expressed frequently, by our mayor. At a news conference the mayor said about homelessness, "This is a problem we can do something about." He appointed the Commission. He named as chair a member of his cabinet, the manager of the Denver Department of Human Services, Roxane White, who had founded Urban Peaks, a shelter for homeless teenagers in Denver known by knowledgeable people as a particularly effective support service. Shortly after taking the job she realized there was a shortage of shelter beds in the city so she put cots in the lobby of her own department's office building.

White promptly accepted my invitation to speak at our forum series. So did two other members of the Commission who are representatives of the downtown business community. So also did another member of the Commission, Randle Loeb, a homeless writer for the *Denver Voice*, the newspaper that speaks for Denver's homeless citizens. Loeb gained the rapt attention of the audience of 120 people as he identified himself as a "chronically homeless person" and explained the cause of his status: "I am bipolar." After saying that he was unable to sleep in shelters because of their overcrowded conditions, he coped by working nights cleaning up offices and sleeping in a church where he was a caretaker. He recommended a book for the audience to read: Kusmer's (2002) *Down and Out, on the Road*. Loeb also plaintively asked the audience why he and they could not accept each other as brothers and sisters.

Tom Luehrs, Executive Director of the St. Francis Center, the shelter where I work as a volunteer, is also the head of Metro Denver Homeless Initiative, the coalition that conducts the annual census of homeless people. He agreed to speak about numbers, the growing numbers and changing makeup—more and more children—of the population, as well as the causes of their plight. He was followed up by an outreach worker, Bernie O'Connell, who reported the results of his interviews with panhandlers and loiterers on the 16th Street Mall, the central artery of the downtown area limited to pedestrian traffic and free shuttle buses. Significantly, his work was funded by a grant from the Downtown Denver Partnership, a combination of some 500 urban business owners who were coming to realize the reciprocal impact of homelessness and business, how each affected the other. O'Connell's findings encouraged the business community and members of the Commission, reinforced them in the belief that homelessness was a problem that could be solved. In fact,

O'Connell's grant had just been renewed for a second year. He elicited a discernable response from the audience when he admitted to having been homeless himself after an automobile accident and operations during which he got severe staph (*staphylococcus*) infections. He also created considerable sympathy for the homeless people he interviewed on the mall, particularly those with serious mental illnesses. In some cases he was able to get them to a free clinic for diagnosis and prescribed medications that helped get them off the street.

To humanize the numbers and abstractions, a musical conductor named Tom Jensen spoke about discovering a precocious homeless boy in the Denver public schools. Jensen was performing a concert in a grade school when he paused to ask, as he always does, how many symphonies Beethoven composed. This time he got the correct answer—nine—from an 11-year-old boy. After the concert the boy's teacher told Jensen that she was happy that Loren got the right answer because, although he and his mother were homeless, he went to the library regularly to listen to and read about music. When Jensen told me about this story we both made a pledge. He pledged to refurbish the mother's old wooden clarinet and get lessons for Loren. I pledged to find transitional housing for Loren and his mother.

As I explained to the audience, Jensen was able to accomplish his goals quickly. Not so for me. Before I could get started I learned they were about to be evicted from their shelter because they had stayed the allotted 90 days. Suddenly my project to get them housing was transformed into preventing them from winding up on the street. Learning on the job, I was going up against what Stringfellow called the dehumanization practiced by the powers and principalities, even when they were trying to help. To start, when I got a check from my church to extend their stay in a motel on Colfax Avenue we learned that the clerks accepted only vouchers from the city, not checks from churches or from me. Second example: One bureaucrat said the mother had to bring her son for an interview (during a school day), another said it was not necessary. Third example: One can only appeal for an extension in a motel at the last minute of the last day of the stay. Fourth example: While Loren's mother was taking time off from her job to apply for help, the human services office had a fire drill, ending all possibilities of interaction for the day. Fifth example: Phone calls from a motel where they stayed were so expensive she could not call me from there. Sixth example: The social workers who were trying to help me got off work 2 hours before the social worker at Loren's shelter came to work. The stress began to get to me: Two social workers I consulted diagnosed my problem as compassion fatigue.

Jensen did get the clarinet repaired and got an outstanding teacher who doubled Loren's lessons from two a month to four at her own expense. I was finally able to scrape up enough money from a friend, the St. Francis Center, my church, and the Junior Symphony Guild to make up the "balloon" payment of deposit plus rent for transitional housing subsidized by Catholic Charities. I then introduced Loren and his mother to the audience; Loren responded by playing, after only four lessons, a Native American song of a spiritual nature on his clarinet and singing the lyrics. The audience of 120 people gave him a standing ovation.

The faith community was given its own evening for a forum on the prophetic mission and tradition: Included was a minister who had worked at the Denver Rescue Mission; a Methodist Bishop; the Executive Director of Housing Justice!, a faith-based initiative; and the head of the Colorado Council of Churches. One speaker said in conversation after the forum that he was disappointed that the mayor had not appointed anyone from the faith community to the Commission. It was clear that the religious leaders were in support of the project to end homelessness.

One highlight of the series came in the second forum when Roxane White, Chair of the Mayor's Commission to End Homelessness in Denver, presented the first draft of the Commission's Action Plan. The audience was impressed not only by getting an insider's briefing about their plan but also by the comprehensiveness of it. She presented the eight strategies to end homelessness they were proposing:

1. Invest in housing.
2. Increase shelter beds.
3. Prevent people from becoming homeless.
4. Twenty-four-hour outreach and enhanced public safety.
5. Adequate support services to help people leave the streets and maintain housing.
6. Provide education, training, and employment to provide stability.
7. Improve community awareness and a coordinated response to the issue of homelessness.
8. Address zoning, urban design, and land use to support housing.

There were too many specific, tactical proposals in the plan for White to discuss, but it was remarkable that the many diverse interests represented on the Commission had agreed to these strategies and specific proposals. For example, the original composition of the Commission included 3 staff members (including White), 7 nonprofit and funding representatives, 7 elected members of the city council, 7 people representing city and government agencies, 3 representatives of neighborhood associations, 10 members of the homeless community (including Randle Loeb), and 8 members of the business community. Neighborhood associations are often opposed to shelters and affordable or low-income housing in their backyard; business people generally advocate lower taxes, not the higher taxes that would be necessary to invest in affordable housing and more shelters (those who provide services to homeless persons never have enough revenue). It is hard to generalize about homeless persons but their grassroots advocacy group wanted first of all a tent city—a goal rejected by the city and the Commission.

I knew from interacting with people who attended the forums that they feared that if we improved conditions for homeless people in Denver, the word would get out and poor people all over the country would descend on the city. This is the so-called magnet theory of housing. This kind of logic could prevent any city from improving their services for homeless people. As moderator of the forum series, I made sure that this question was asked of White after she explained the action plan. She replied that the Commission had been in communication with the political leaders of Denver suburbs surrounding Denver and stretching up and down the front range of the Rockies, that these entities were cooperating. She also could have mentioned that some 150 cities in the United States were also coming up with action plans at the same time.

I had invited two members of the business community on the Commission to End Homelessness to participate in the Faces Forum. The first was Richard Scharf, the President and CEO of the Denver Metro Convention & Visitors Bureau. He represented those business interests who wanted to attract tourists to Denver. I pressed him to address the question of group process. He admitted that during the first two meetings of the Commission he doubted they would ever be able to agree on much of anything. The other speaker at the forum series representing business interests was John Desmond, Director of the Downtown Environment for the Downtown Denver Partnership, an association of city businesses that taxed themselves to help keep the city clean. At first he shared Scharf's fear that the Commission would get nowhere, but he continued to listen to others in the group. He repeated that the business community was concerned about surveys that revealed that pedestrians feared aggressive panhandlers on the mall. He stressed that these were perceptions, not reality, conceding that the downtown area was no doubt one of the safest areas in the metropolitan area.

Many if not most people are uncomfortable when beggars make appeals for money. The Downtown Denver Partnership encourages people not to give to individuals, but urges them instead to give to those charitable organizations that provide services for homeless persons. One court—the U.S. Court of Appeals for the Second Circuit—ruled in 1993 that "a member of a charitable, religious or other organization who seeks alms for the organization and is also, as a member, a beneficiary of those alms should be treated no differently from one who begs for his or own account" (Loper v. NYPD, 1993, p. 7). Moreover, the court in that case ruled that begging is protected by the Constitution, and is in fact a form of political speech (i.e., an implicit criticism of the system). It is for this reason that communities pass laws prohibiting not panhandling, but aggressive panhandling—begging for money in a way intended to intimidate the audience, whether by blocking a person's way, touching, or behaving in a threatening way.

For the final forum, "Bringing the Sectors Together for the Last Word on Homelessness," I invited the state's Episcopal Bishop, Robert O'Neill; John Desmond, the officer of the Downtown Denver Partnership; and the newly elected Speaker of the Colorado House of Representatives, Andrew Romanoff, an outspoken advocate for poor and homeless people. Here I was, enlisting the powers that be, flawed and fallen as they are, to cooperate with each other in bringing about reform and justice. I am pleased to report that all segments pledged to cooperate in promoting justice for homeless people. As the moderator of the series, I thought it was fair to say that we had all become abolitionists, committed to ending homelessness in Denver.

How did this remarkable consensus develop? This was not the paradigm case of a speaker persuading like-minded citizens to adopt a course of action. It is clear that the various members of the Commission had not been inculcated with the same set of value premises, and lacked the homogeneity assumed by the classical theories of persuasion; that is, find those common value premises and deductively link one's proposal to them. Some of the people representing the city and the charities and service providers were operating with humanitarian and religious value premises, plus a desire to move beyond charity to justice. Political leaders function with the desire to achieve what is possible. The business leaders operated on the value premise of doing what is good for business; they clearly wanted the homeless persons on the mall to become invisible to tourists and other shoppers. And as indicated previously, different groups had different attitudes about taxation as a means to abolition.

Twenty-five years ago Cushman and Tompkins (1980) offered a theory of rhetoric for contemporary society. Noting that the conditions of homogeneity experienced by the Greeks and Romans no longer existed in the 20th-century United States, they set about in a deductive development to explain how agreement and consensus can be produced in today's conditions of heterogeneity. That heterogeneity was itself a result of three trends they saw in 1980 (one of which may be reversing itself to some degree 25 years later): "(1) an increased tolerance for a plurality of cultural positions; (2) an increased interdependence between nations, groups, and individuals; and (3) an increased need to manifest respect for diversity as an antecedent for coordinated action" (p. 47). Note the phrase "coordinated action" as the descriptor for the new rhetoric. Instead of doing audience analysis to find a common value set and appealing in a one-way direction to the group to accept a proposal, today's conditions call for coordinated action, precisely the process employed by the Commission to End Homelessness.

Cushman and Tompkins (1980) also argued that the modern test of achieving coordinated action—as opposed to speaker–audience persuasion—"is whether those who are interdependent in regard to some problem form a *rational consensus* that they have understood and manifested respect for each point of view" (p. 58). This seems to be what the divergent interests on the Commission did: They listened, understood, and respected each other's point of view. They learned that all recognized a problem they desired to eliminate—too many homeless people on the streets of Denver—but instead of having a common set of value premises they had different reasons for solving it. This can create in the individual a sense of obligation:

> When one must act in cooperation with others who hold divergent ideologies and must as a condition for cooperation understand and respect those differences in selecting an appropriate principle for guiding collective action, then in order to do what is wanted, *one has to do things that he or she does not want to do for their own sake* (Cushman & Tompkins, 1980, p. 47, italics added).

Although homeless persons and service providers desire more shelters and affordable housing for their own sake, business people might not. However, more shelters—open during the day for education and training—would take homeless people off the 16th Street Mall, an outcome that would be desirable for its own sake. The director of a shelter might not want to be open day and night because it puts an additional strain on the staff and makes it difficult to do cleaning and maintenance, but additional support

from the city for the shelter, education, and affordable housing could ultimately reduce the population of homeless persons, a goal desirable for its
own sake. Politicians would not want to raise taxes for their own sake, but
creating an improved business climate and helping destitute people get jobs
are desirable outcomes in their own right. Members of the Commission had
an obligation to listen to others and accept what they did not want to accept
to get what they did want for its own sake. Obligation seems to have been a
key factor in achieving consensus and a coordinated action plan inside the
Commission.

One must also give credit to the excellent leadership and resources the
Commission enjoyed. Mayor Hickenlooper made it clear he wanted to solve
the problem. He and the Chair, Roxane White, appointed people to the
Commission who had a direct interest in the problem of homelessness and
an interest in solving it. The leadership created an ambiance or culture of
respect for others, a willingness to listen to differing ideas and ideologies,
and the obligation to accept what one did not want to get what one did
want. This became a rational process to all when data were presented indi-
cating that doing little or nothing for homeless people is as expensive as providing shelters, education, affordable housing, and rehabilitation programs.
Incarcerating people is a very expensive way of making undesirable people
invisible.

During the process of moving toward a coordinated action plan, the
Commission also moved beyond charity to justice despite the absence of
common value premises. Justice can, therefore, be achieved within a heterogeneous culture if there is an interdependence in regard to problems to be
solved, a willingness to listen and respect other points of view, and a rational
sense of obligation to accept some things one does not want to get that
which is desirable in its own right. Such coordinated action need not require ontological agreement about the essence of the homeless being. That
is, one can agree to accept 24-hour outreach plans to monitor homeless
people whether one believes them to be autonomous authors of their own
fate or helpless, dependent beings who are what they are because of
economic factors, physical handicaps, and mental illness.

As of the writing of this chapter, the Commission has not released its final
action plan. When it is released the city council and the mayor and subur-
ban neighbors will also have to give their approval. The fact that seven
members of the city council participated in the Commission is a positive political indication that much of it will be approved. Neighborhood associations will, however, manifest NIMBYism and stiff resistance against the
construction of hygiene centers (public restrooms), affordable housing, and

new shelters. Nonetheless, there is reason to hope that the city of Denver is attempting to move beyond charity to justice for the poor and homeless.

REFERENCES

Borg, M. (2002). *Reading the bible again for the first time.* San Francisco: Harper.
Burke, K. (1984). *Permanence and change* (3rd ed.). Berkeley: University of California Press.
Burt, M. (2003). Chronic homelessness: Emergence of a public policy. *Fordham Urban Law Journal, 30,* 1267–1280.
Coffin, W. S. (2004). *Credo.* Louisville, KY: Westminster John Knox.
Cushman, D., & Tompkins, P. (1980). A theory of rhetoric for contemporary society. *Philosophy & Rhetoric, 13,* 43–67.
Ellsberg, R. (1997). *All saints: Daily reflections on saints, prophets, and witnesses for our time.* New York: Crossroad.
Frank, T. (2004). *What's the matter with Kansas? How conservatives won the heart of America.* New York: Metropolitan Books.
Freeman, S. (2001). Rawls. In R. Audi (Ed.), *The Cambridge dictionary of philosophy* (pp. 774–775). Cambridge, UK: Cambridge University Press.
Kusmer, K. (2002). *Down and out, on the road: The homeless in American history.* Oxford, UK: Oxford University Press.
Loper v. New York City Police Department, 999 F.2d 699 (1993).
Lynch, P., & Cole, J. (2003). Homelessness and human rights: Regarding homelessness as a human rights violation. *Melbourne Journal of International Law, 4,* 139–177.
Roisman, F. (2000). The lawyer as abolitionist: Ending homelessness and poverty in our time. *Saint Louis University Public Law Review, 19,* 237–258.
Stringfellow, W. (1994). *A keeper of the word: Selected writings of William Stringfellow.* Grand Rapids, MI: Eerdmans.
The new interactive Webster's Dictionary and Thesaurus (2002). Naples, FL: Trident Press International.
The shorter Oxford English Dictionary (3rd ed.). (1965). Oxford, UK: Clarendon Press.
Tompkins, P. (2005). *Apollo, Challenger, and Columbia: The decline of the space program.* Los Angeles: Roxbury.
Wink, W. (1998). *The powers that be: Theology for a new millennium.* New York: Doubleday.

5

Voice and the "Other": Interactive Theatre as a Model for Education and Liberation on University Campuses

Jennifer Lyn Simpson
Rebecca Brown Adelman
University of Colorado at Boulder

Many scholars and educational institutions have recognized the importance of increased voice to scholarship, to decision making, and to learning. Wrapped up in this notion of voice are implications of increased access, diversity of perspective, and institutional or systemic mechanisms that value, rather than suppress, difference. In practice, institutional efforts to address this concern have variously focused on increasing forums for participation (literally spaces in which people can come together to "have their say"), diversity (as demographic representation of different groups, primarily by race or ethnicity, calculated in numeric percentages), or dissemination of information (this has taken many forms ranging from offering specific courses, seminars, or training sessions that provide information about diversity, producing institutional literature that touts demographic breakdowns and diversity offerings, and making more information accessible to more people using new technologies). Although all of these strategies have been somewhat successful in increasing numbers, broadening the range of information

available, and increasing access to certain vehicles for expression, they have
had less success achieving the ideal of increased voice.

In keeping with Katz's (2002) concern that social justice "has seldom
been the principal term of reference for campus debate, and I think that universities are the poorer for that" (p. B7), this chapter begins with an overview of the principal terms of reference that do infuse campus debate, and
reviews scholarship about the transformation of higher education. We then
suggest that through a richer understanding of the interrelationship of
voice to otherness (concepts we develop in greater detail later) we are able
to identify organizational practices that lend themselves both to transforming knowledge and to reshaping understanding of ways of meaning that create a context more conducive to social justice. The bulk of this chapter
explores this premise in practice through close examination of the Interactive Theatre Project, a model rooted in Boal's methods of Theatre of the
Oppressed (1979, see http://theatreoftheoppressed.org), used regularly as
an educational and training tool at the University of Colorado at Boulder.

THE LANGUAGE OF PARTICIPATION AND DIVERSITY
ON UNIVERSITY CAMPUSES

Recent reports on the state of U.S. universities have emphasized the importance of increased participation and campus diversity to promoting a strong
climate for learning. Since the beginning of the 1990s, national institutions
of higher education such as the American Association of University Professors (AAUP), American Council on Education (ACE), the Carnegie Foundation, the National Association of Student Personnel Administrators, and
the American College Personnel Association have produced reports that
foreground the importance of attending to issues of participation, voice,
and diversity on college campuses. As universities and educational foundations across the United States call for increased "engagement" (American
Association of Higher Education) and a re-envisioning of scholarship
(Woodrow Wilson Foundation), the discipline of communication can play
an important role in rethinking how meaning is constructed in interaction.

Scholarship produced both by communication researchers and scholars
of higher education has often linked notions of participation, diversity of
perspective, and deeper learning. Boyer's (1990) landmark study of campuses, "In Search of Community," proclaims, "the free expression of ideas in
a community of learning is essential" (p. 17). What this free expression of
ideas looks like in practice, however, tends to be more elusive. Peters (1999)
suggests that "felicitous communication—in the sense of creating just com-

munity between two or more creatures—depends more basically on imagination, liberty, and solidarity among the participants than on equal time in
conversation" (p. 34). Yet, in the absence of unfettered imagination, unrestricted liberty, or unwavering solidarity, the call for equal access to forums
for participation, especially across differences, continues to increase on university campuses.

A recent joint report produced by ACE/AAUP (2000) further articulates
the ambiguous notion of voice with that of difference:

> Today's selective liberal arts colleges have tried to build communities crafted
> to offer the benefits of encounters across differences to faculty and students
> who enter as strangers and become collaborators in exploring a universe of
> ideas and perspectives shaped in part by the history each brings. In the last 30
> years, these colleges have broadened their vision beyond traditional forms of
> difference (of interest, talent, geographic region, social class, national cul-
> ture, and the like). Race has emerged as a valued source of different insights.
> (Gudeman, 2000, p. 38)

As matters of difference have become increasingly salient in all types of organizations, scholarly calls for "voice" have touted the value of increasing
the diversity of perspectives brought to bear on organizational issues. In
practice, however, the ways in which differences have mattered to organizational decisions have often not fundamentally challenged institutional
structures that support and reproduce the status quo. As such, these approaches have not often met the test of creating more socially just organizational forms (Frey, Pollock, Artz, & Pearce, 1996).

A significant amount of scholarship in the discipline of communication
has focused on the academy as a site of struggle around matters of difference
(Allen, 1995, 1996, 2000; Allen, Orbe, & Olivas, 1999; Ambrozas, 1998;
Barnett, 1994; Bergquist, 1995; Buttny, 1997; Collier, 1995; Nicotera,
1999; Porter & Catt, 1993; Simpson, 2001) where participation and voice
are at issue (Ambrozas, 1998; Bérubé & Nelson, 1995; Eisenberg, Murphy,
& Andrews, 1998), and where the campus climate affects both of these
(Ambrozas, 1998; Boyer, 1990; Cheatham, 1991; Goodall, 1999; Simpson,
2001). There is already a clear sense that these are important and interrelated issues, yet the complex interconnections between increased "voice"
and genuine encounters with otherness can be difficult to conceptualize
(Deetz & Simpson, 2004, Simpson, 2005). Our own campuses, however,
may provide delightful and powerful examples of how learning may happen
differently, both in and out of the classroom, when genuine encounters with
the other become possible (Simpson & Allen, 2005). Next we unpack the

contributions that understandings of voice and otherness can make both to transforming knowledge and to reshaping the social justice landscape.

VOICE AND THE "OTHER": RETHINKING WHAT AND HOW WE KNOW

The concept of voice goes beyond a general understanding of participation or involvement in recognizing the way that our voices position ourselves and others in relationship to one another in interaction. This notion of voice goes beyond the simple act of expression. As Strine (1997) suggests, "voices locate individual persons as speaking subjects socially and culturally by enabling communicative interactions and, through interaction, the formation of self-identity" (p. 448). In other words, voice positions us in relationship to one another and to a sociocultural context. In this way voice becomes a theory of agency. How my voice, my position, becomes articulated with those of other social actors in the scene defines, and may alternately challenge or reproduce, existing social relationships. Furthermore, voice is implicated with matters of both difference and culture. As voices that more closely approximate the ideological status quo often have increased access to vehicles of dissemination, their positions are given increased likelihood of falling on hearing ears (Peters, 1999), and thus becoming culturally perpetuated.

Many recent writings on voice are adamant that everyone has multiple voices, multiple positions, from which they might speak, although some of those voices are more socially sanctioned than others. Ono (1997) cautions "listeners who expect to hear unified voices, whether 'academic' or 'real,' deny our multiple voices and perhaps forget that we are not born speaking; all voices are learned ones" (p. 119). This learning happens because the people around us, and the culture in which we are embedded, constantly send messages that affirm or deny potential identities, potential ways of expressing, potential voices. Nakayama (1997) warns that "we are constrained in the ways that our voices construct, and contradict our identities .... We are taught and we learn to obey the rules of language and society" (p. 236). Voice, then, becomes intimately tied to otherness because how our voice is positioned in relationship to others is largely a function of whether and how our voices support or challenge dominant social positions. Here, we use otherness to describe the radical difference that we may be confronted within an encounter that necessitates the calling into question of taken-for-granted assumptions and ways of knowing. When Other is capitalized, we are generally referring to an interlocutor who embodies this difference, whereas other, uncapitalized, is used in its more colloquial sense of somebody else.

The voices that are most often heard in organizational contexts (including university campuses) are those that support, affirm, and reproduce dominant ways of knowing and understanding. These voices typically have greater access to forums for input, and the perspectives they represent are often disseminated more broadly to demonstrate support for existing policies and procedures. These voices do not typically "[engage with or advocate for] those in our society who are economically, socially, politically, and/or culturally under-resourced" (Frey et al., 1996, p. 110). Voices that challenge commonly held values, beliefs, and assumptions on the other hand may be systematically excluded or suppressed. Sometimes this happens in overt ways by controlling access to forums, but more often it happens more subtly as the norms, ideals, and ways of knowing of the dominant group form the common ground upon which participants must stand in negotiating meaning (Deetz & Simpson, 2004; Simpson, 2001). When this happens, our capacity to learn from and grow with one another diminishes. Performance, however, has the potential to break open the spaces in which identities become calcified, and renews the possibility of deeper, more genuine encounters with otherness, creating space for a social-justice orientation to develop and be explored. As Warren (2001) suggests, "Performativity denies, in some fundamental way, the stability of identity, moving toward a notion of repetition as a way of understanding that those markers used to describe one's identity (i.e., gender, class, race, sexuality) get constructed through the continual performance of those markers" (p. 95). Interactive Theatre, as we discuss later, provides a space in which the unreflective, continual, day-to-day performance of identity can be challenged, and otherness more genuinely encountered.

Levinas (1969, 1985, 1987) elaborated a notion of otherness in which our capacity to know ourselves is expanded through our encounter with the Other. In encountering the Other in a genuine fashion, our own commonly held assumptions and beliefs can be called into question. Insofar as we place limits on the Other's identity, we not only close off opportunities for deeper understanding of ourselves; we do violence to the other with whom we interact. When, for example, we see our interlocutor through constructed lenses of race, gender, sexual orientation, or religion, we place parameters around who that Other may be in interaction with us. Because we do not create space for the radical difference of the Other to enter the encounter, our potential growth in the relationship is limited. This does violence to the other by denying them the right to autonomous definition of self.

This connection we all have to different others places individuals in responsible relationship to the subjects with whom they interact. In fact, as Levinas)(1985) argues, "the tie with the Other is knotted only as responsibility" (p. 97). In this sense, our own subjective existence is inextricably intertwined with our relationships to Others and in our responsibility toward those relationships. Responsibility, in this sense, does not mean protecting the other from conflict, however, for, as discussed earlier, it is only when the possibility of conflict exists that participants may engage authentically.

Both the *Pedagogy of the Oppressed* (Freire, 1970) and the *Theatre of the Oppressed* (Boal, 1979) provide rich models for how educators, trainers, and facilitators can work to create spaces in which the radical difference of otherness can be experienced. The premise behind these models is precisely that in exposing ourselves to difference, we open up space for alternative action, create ways of seeing and knowing that challenge the status quo, and create the possibility of liberation for those marginalized Others typically at the periphery of organizational or social life. Green (2000) reflects:

> There is extraordinary power in [Boal's] foundational idea of transforming spectators into "spect-actors" who become active subjects in the theatre rather than passive observers, thereby giving power, authority, and responsibility to the audience. Spect-actors are given the opportunity to rehearse active resistance to oppression in the theatre, to "try-out" different possibilities within the relative safety of the theatre and evaluate the success of each ....The theatre, Boal famously says, is a rehearsal for revolution. (p. 47)

Revolutions come in many shapes and sizes, however, and can serve a broad spectrum of functions. At the University of Colorado at Boulder, a large Western public campus, the Interactive Theatre Project (ITP) provides a striking example of how these methods can be used to surface conflict in meaningful and productive ways, explore difference through uncomfortable yet empowering means, and create the conditions under which both routine knowledge and ways of knowing can be revolutionized.

As we turn to reflect on our experiences crafting, writing, acting, facilitating, and growing through our connection to Interactive Theatre, it should be noted that the narrative(s) that follow serve a function not entirely dissimilar from that of the theatre we describe. All repetitive action has the power and potential to calcify knowledge and ways of knowing; to make over the contestable under the guise of the normal and natural. As Taylor (2002) suggests, "texts configure the relationships between significant symbols.... . Over time, and through repeated articulations, such relationships become sedimented" (p. 33). Later, we draw on various narrative modalities to challenge, break open, and problematize traditional readings of academic discourse as we explore the development of the ITP and the significance it has for our thinking about voice, "otherness," and meaning-making in interaction.

THE INTERACTIVE THEATRE PROJECT

As with many university campuses, the University of Colorado at Boulder, a predominantly White campus, struggles with matters of difference and diversity. Since 1998, we have both been actively involved in a set of initiatives grouped under the rubric Building Community Campaign (BCC). This project's core objective is a commitment "to developing a campus environment that welcomes and respects all people of diverse perspectives, races, ethnic backgrounds, ages, genders, religions, sexual orientations, abilities, economic status, family situations, national origins, and other individual differences." To fulfill this commitment, the campaign has spearheaded and supported a wide range of events, programs, and forums for educating and empowering the campus community around matters of difference. In this chapter, we focus specifically on the development and implementation of the ITP as a model for opening spaces for genuine encounters with difference. Throughout our narrative, we move back and forth between a scholarly review and analysis of this project and our own voices and narratives of our experience as members, creators, actors, participants, and facilitators of this project.

A Brief History of the Project

The ITP was modeled after Brazilian visionary Augusto Boal's Theatre of the Oppressed (1979). Theatre of the Oppressed is a popular community-based education model that uses theatre as a tool for transformation and is used the world over for social and political activism, conflict resolution, community building, therapy, and government legislation. Interactive theatre also has roots in Freire's (1970) *Pedagogy of the Oppressed*. The second author of this chapter founded the ITP at University of Colorado at Boulder in 1999 to provide an alternative vehicle for exploring difficult issues on campus. Next, Rebecca Brown Adelman remembers the early stages of this process.

Rebecca Remembers. When I founded the Interactive Theatre Project at CU Boulder in the spring of 1999, I had worked at the university for over 5 years doing rape and gender education work, as well as serving as a victim's advocate. My training is as an actor and drama therapist, and early on in my career I developed a deep commitment to the transformative and healing potential of theatre, especially when working with individuals and small groups in a therapeutic context.

While I was in graduate school at NYU, I studied the works of Augusto Boal and was intrigued and fascinated by his use of theatre in a community context, not for therapeutic or educational purposes, but to foster social change within communities, and I began to expand my vision of what theatre could do for learning and growing in this way. While I was thinking through the potential of this work, Boal came to New York and performed a piece of Forum Theatre with his theater troupe and I could not resist the opportunity to attend.

As I quickly learned, Forum Theatre is a powerful tool for engaging groups in difficult discussion, because it allows actors and audience members to interact with one another in transforming a problematic social situation. First, the actors enact a scenario depicting a problematic social situation with no clear resolution. The scene is then performed again and audience members become participants in the construction and resolution of the scene as they have an opportunity to take on the role of the character they most identify with and experiment with alternative actions and reactions to change the outcome of the scene.

When I saw Boal and his troupe perform, I experienced, firsthand, theatre's power and ability to create community among strangers in a short amount of time and participate in action and dialogue around challenging issues. My vision of theatre began to shift as I came to see theatre not only as a tool for personal transformation, but also as a vehicle for social and cultural change. I saw that theatre could enable participants to explore roles that are played out in their communities and investigate the consequences of both action and inaction. I also began to envision how theatre could become a tool for reaching larger groups of people in a broader social context. This growing belief in theatre as an engaging tool for education and change motivated me to incorporate theatre in much of the prevention and education work on sexual assault that I did in my early years at CU-Boulder. Doing this early work led to collaborations that gained me an invitation to a conference hosted by Cornell University on their Interactive Theatre Ensemble. I was impressed by Cornell's program within a university setting and was encouraged when the Building Community Campaign was developed at the University of Colorado at Boulder.

Given CU-Boulder's newly declared commitment to community (Deetz & Simpson, 2004; Simpson, 2001), I started to think about how an Interactive Theatre model could be adapted to meet the needs of the campus. The more I thought about it, the more I liked the idea, and I approached the Vice Chancellor for Student Affairs with a request for funding a program that would address difficult issues impacting the university community using theatre. I was awarded the money, and what started out as a small program with one scene and a few actors has grown and become institutionalized through support from the Wardenburg Student Health Center.

Grand Opening: Interactive Theatre.   The first interactive theatre performance entitled "Interactive Theatre Comes Out!" debuted on campus in October 1999. This performance addressed issues of sexual assault among men, and was chosen as the debut topic for several reasons. First, the issue was important to Rebecca because, as a victim's advocate, she had several male clients who were survivors of sexual assault perpetrated by other men. Furthermore, as difficult as sexual assault is as a topic of discussion, for men, the issue is even more taboo. Finally, this topic demonstrated to the university community a commitment to not only broach challenging topics in new ways, but also to create a space in which topics that are often outside the scope of acceptable discussion can enter the dialogic realm.

The performance was well attended by members of the University of Colorado at Boulder community, and many university officials, several of whom had already made a financial commitment to the project, were also present. A short scene was performed by two male actors who then engaged in a facilitated discussion with the audience as they remained in role. During this performance the university community was able to share in Rebecca's vision of the ITP. Soon, conversations began to develop that would eventually incorporate Interactive Theatre into orientation for new students and in many other ways throughout the university community. Five years after the debut performance of Interactive Theatre on the University of Colorado at Boulder campus, with the help of a grant from the federal Violence Against Women Act and further financial commitment from the university, the ITP has grown into a resource for students, faculty, and staff on campus. Rebecca is now the full-time director of the project and, in the fall of 2002, created a troupe of 12 student actors who now meet and rehearse on a weekly basis.

As this brief history suggests, the ITP has consciously and conscientiously worked to create alternative spaces for exploring matters of difference in ways that challenge routine and traditional ways of knowing. Next we explore the explicit philosophy of the ITP and draw some connections to theoretical assumptions and recommendations about voice, difference, and otherness. Then, Jennifer reflects on her involvement with the ITP. We conclude with several illustrative examples of how Interactive Theatre has allowed, encouraged, and challenged audiences to engage otherness differently at the University of Colorado at Boulder.

PHILOSOPHY OF THE INTERACTIVE THEATRE PROJECT AT THE UNIVERSITY OF COLORADO AT BOULDER

The stated goal of the ITP at the University of Colorado at Boulder is to raise awareness about diversity on campus and break down barriers that impede the development of community. Forums that do not provide an opportunity for genuine encounters with difference limit our ability to grow individually as well as collectively. The ITP strives to open doors for collaboration, discussion, and problem solving among students, faculty, and staff from across backgrounds on campus. Guinier and Smith (2000) argue that this kind of theatre is "about exciting the mind and exciting the soul and exciting the people to become citizens in their own democracy" (p. 45) and that is precisely the vision that the ITP brings to the Boulder campus. The project works toward providing voice and visibility to marginalized groups on campus and forming bridges among campus community members. The project, in turn, works to empower students, faculty, and staff to contribute to building a stronger sense of community at the University of Colorado at Boulder.

In Interactive Theatre there are no experts, only one's own experience. The presented issue or conflict is brought forth through a theatrical context that touches people intellectually as well as emotionally. Different issues surface and participants find themselves freed from organizational constraints that might close down discursive opportunities to explore more richly the conflict before them. In discussions, a broader range of issues becomes contestable.

One of the main strategies that the ITP at the University of Colorado at Boulder uses to accomplish this is scripted theatrical scenes where actors stay in role during a facilitated discussion. These creative forums are designed to engage community, faculty, staff, and students around questions of social justice. In this way, the performance becomes a springboard for dialogue among the characters, facilitators, and with one another. Participants can experience empathy for and identification with those involved in the performed scenario, they are freed to fully think through what happened in the scene, they are enabled to think about possible consequences of the performed situation, and they are freed to discuss possible solutions and potential strategies for transforming what they have witnessed. Having this interaction often allows groups to explore difficult, complex issues and contributes to greater community strength, creativity, and competence.

As the ITP continues to grow at the University of Colorado at Boulder, the mission and intended impact of the project is twofold. In developing a troupe of student actors and a coalition of staff and faculty members, the ITP participates in a deeper experience of Boal's Theatre of the Oppressed techniques. Boal (1995) states that the "Theatre of The Oppressed is a system of physical exercises, aesthetic games, image techniques and special improvisations whose goal is to safeguard, develop and reshape this human vocation, by turning the practice of theatre into an effective tool for the comprehension of social and personal problems and the search for their solutions" (p. 15). Thus, the transformative process may occur on two levels: Troupe and community members may experience an ever-deepening understanding of social justice issues; as their own learning develops the nature of the impact on audience groups may also be altered.

This multilayered transformation can also occur across time and space as actors grapple internally with conflicts, as audience members are transported to other moments in their own lives, and as the work that happens in the performance transforms those who have participated in a way that shapes and influences future perceptions of their world. As Landy (1993) argues:

> Paradox is at the heart of the dramatic experience. The individual as actor or group as chorus lives simultaneously in two realities. These realities are diverse: present and past, rehearsal and performance, the studied moment and the spontaneous moment, everyday life and the life of the imagination, internal and external, fiction and nonfiction, the ordinary and the wonderful, the expected moment and the enhanced moment, actor and role, "me" and "not me." (p. 11)

Although this potential is present in many theatrical performances, in Interactive Theatre it is amplified as the line between actor and audience, script and life blurs. Next we turn our gaze back on ourselves to explore how this process unfolds in practice.

A SELF-REFLEXIVE PAUSE

The ITP at the University of Colorado at Boulder provides a unique opportunity to explore how embodied knowledge can transform ways of knowing and break open spaces for encountering otherness in powerful ways. One of the greatest advantages of such a model is its capacity to include the audience, to ground difficult topics in scenarios that ring true and feel real, all the while protecting the participants from being individually targeted or challenged too directly in a public context. Participants in ITP performances (whether actors or audience members; as we have seen, the line between the two often blurs) often find their deeply held values, beliefs, and expectations challenged, called into question, and opened to new understanding and construction. It is in moments such as this when the radical difference of the Other calls our own understanding of ourselves and the world in which we live into question in such a way that those things that seemed normal, natural, and given become, all of a sudden, open to contestation. In such moments we are able to catch glimpses of Gadamer's (1975, 1980) genuine conversation, Habermas's (1980, 1984, 1987, 1995) ideal speech situation, and Deetz's (1992, 1995a, 1995b) process of dialogic open formation. Suddenly (although also carefully and strategically), new ways of knowing the world become possible. One senior faculty member at the University of Colorado at Boulder, who saw the first set of Interactive Theatre performances used in new student orientation, remarked:

> I just went and watched some of the Interactive Theatre Program during orientation, I watched it because it was wonderful and uplifting to watch. I watched young people in the audience, our new freshmen, become involved and interested in issues that they need to be involved and interested in and I kept thinking to myself, "My God, this is really good. This is good stuff." We're still doing good stuff on this campus. (D. VanGerven, personal communication, September 22, 2000)

Remarks such as this highlight the impact that the ITP can have on audience members and underscore the sense that this program is a departure from the norm in significant ways. Jennifer reflects next on her experience encountering and growing through her engagement with Interactive Theatre.

Jennifer Reflects.   I first heard about the new Interactive Theatre Project at CU Boulder through my work with the Building Community Campaign. As the program has evolved, I have brought many lenses to thinking about and understanding the impact that this program can have on the CU Boulder campus. The first lens I brought to my interpretation was that of a researcher, studying questions of building community on university campuses. I was intrigued by what I saw as a multifaceted approach to building community coming out of the BCC, and saw the ITP filling an underserved niche. From early descriptions, I had the sense that this program could really help the campus get at difficult and challenging issues in powerful ways. As a scholar with interests in the intersection between voice and otherness, I was curious to see if, and how, the scenarios developed might create a space in which controversy might become the stuff of dialogue and transformation instead of debate and polarization.

I was not sure what to expect when I went to see Interactive Theatre Comes Out! but was immediately impressed by the power of the scenario to evoke emotion, elicit reaction, and raise questions that a lecture or presentation would almost certainly have glossed. Having now witnessed, facilitated, and/or acted in several scenarios, the power of the performance seems genuinely to come from the space (physical, intellectual, and emotional) that the scene creates for the actors, facilitators, and audience members to engage, almost visibly, always palpably, in the conscious construction of new meaning and new understanding in the moment. No two performances are ever alike because what shows up in the room each time is always different, and the scenarios and characters must always interact with the values, beliefs, and ideals that audience members bring with them.

In fact, it is really amazing to watch the same scenario performed to different audiences, and even by different actors. The scene, for instance, that I have seen performed most often, is the one that all first-year students experience during orientation. The scene, titled "Just Another Party," explores many of the complexities surrounding heterosexual date-rape situations and allegations. The scene is complicated and messy. Both the male and female characters are drinking heavily. He's older. He encourages her to keep drinking. She breaks her "buddy pact" with her friends and goes to his room, very drunk. At the end of the scene, she feels violated, convinced that he raped her. He feels like he met a fun girl and had a great time. There are no easy answers provided in the scene, and much space for challenging and reflection in the question and answer session. In the many times I have seen it, I am amazed at how differently I react to the characters depending on who is playing them, and how this influences the kinds of questions that come from the audience. So, while the scenes are often explicitly about something, they also always provide spaces to explore how the otherness that confronts us shapes our own understandings, perceptions, and reactions.

Rebecca Interjects.   You know, that reminds me of something. I was doing a public performance of "Just Another Party" one night, and something happened that really drove home just how powerfully time and space collapse in these scenes. You never quite know whether transformation is going to happen because of prior experiences the audience brings to the room, or if they will take something away from the performance that would not grab them until later on. As I was warming up the audience this particular spring night, I asked the crowd, as I often do, why they were at the performance and what they hoped to get out of the evening.

One young male student answered that he had seen "Just Another Party" at orientation the previous fall. He said that when he first saw the performance he did not believe that what it depicted could be the reality of the CU Boulder campus. He was here tonight, he said, because now, two semesters later, he realized that every party he went to was just like this performance in many ways and, he said, he wanted to see the scenario again so that he could test out who he was when he first saw it with who he was now.

Jennifer Resumes.   That is a nice example. I think that dynamic plays out in so many ways with Interactive Theatre. Having acted in several scenarios, I have also really come to appreciate the challenge that this work presents. In rehearsal, actors not only memorize lines, block movement, and practice timing as one would for any performance, we also do a lot of character work to prepare for questions and answers. Where all actors must have a sense of their motivation, in Interactive Theatre, there is an entire internal life that must be developed and accessible to allow the "performance after the performance" to be believable and effective.

When scenes have run into challenges, this is often where it happens. Personally, the character work has forced me to examine many deeply held and often underexamined assumptions. Digging deeper into the characters I have played has often reinforced, and made more real, the complex interconnections between different forms of oppression as I have discovered that a scene I thought was about class, also taught me a lot about race, or vice versa. The categories and labels that we so easily assign, and that limit our potential for growing in our encounters become more difficult to maintain as actors are forced to examine interconnections more closely. In doing this prework, the stage is set for a richer experience during the performance and space is created for the audience to engage the script and the characters through their own lenses. I have found that in the process, the nature of those lenses often becomes more visible.

INTERACTIVE THEATRE IN ACTION

So far we have described our theoretical grounding, explored the potential of Interactive Theatre to transform inquiry into questions of voice and otherness, walked through a history of the project, and each reflected on some of our experiences working with Interactive Theatre at the University of Colorado at Boulder. Next, we invite you, the reader, to engage an actual scenario with us. This piece, written in the days following the attacks of September 11, 2001, explores several sets of feelings, reactions, and struggles being felt and expressed across campus. The scenario was performed in two sessions, one at noon, and one in the evening, both shortly after September 11. Each drew very different crowds and a wide range of response. In many ways, this scenario epitomizes the potential of Interactive Theatre to respond to timely issues, yet evoke them in ways that still allow space for the otherness in the room to shape the transformative experience of participants. The following script moves in and out of the words initially written by Rebecca and our subsequent reflections on both the script and the performance(s).

What Happens Next

Rebecca: I wrote this scene almost a month after the September 11 attacks. Our University community was still reeling from the aftermath, as was I. Being a native New Yorker, September 11 hit very close to home. This was one of the first times we used Interactive Theatre as a method of response. The actual incident portrayed in this scene occurred on our campus. The feelings and struggles around the incident were shared by many. It was clear that we needed a venue for these opposing views to be vented and explored.

Jennifer: As the co-chair of the Building Community Campaign, I knew that we needed to have a campus response to September 11, and we quickly organized a discussion forum. As tension escalated, though, incidents were happening on campus that bespoke the fear, confusion, and uncertainty that so many were feeling. When Rebecca offered to write an Interactive Theatre piece that would deal with some of what was happening, I hoped it would allow us to get at issues that other forums were ill equipped to deal with.

Rebecca: In the question-and-answer period of Interactive Theatre performances, I always tell the actors to allow the audience's participation to affect them, especially if it has an emotional quality to it. Ideally, we strive for the characters to transform in a way that is realistic for the character.

The Script

(It's a beautiful day on the CU Boulder campus. The date is September 14, 2001. A bunch of students are socializing on the campus green.) Life is going on "as usual." (Two students, Julia and Mark, are walking out of class.)

Julia: Can you believe we had a quiz?
Mark: I know! What's up with that …

Some conversation … light … laughter … etc.

Mark: Man, I can't believe how nice it is out.
Julia: I know. I'm digging this weather. It hasn't been so great for classes though. All I want to do is hang out outside.
Mark: Yeah, totally.
Julia: It's not like I can concentrate right now anyway.
Mark: God I can't imagine what it is like in New York right now. It's so sad.
Julia: Well I can, it sucks.
Mark: Yeah. I'm sure. I'm scared of what's going to happen next. I might get drafted.

(Beat)

Julia: Let's talk about something else, this is too depressing. So, what's up for the weekend?
Mark: I'm not sure. Ellie is coming up Saturday night. I might go over to Mike's house later. I think they're having a few people over.
Julia: Sweet.

Mark: (Getting up) Hey, let's go to the hill and get something to eat. You want to? I'm starving.

Julia: Sounds good to me. Where do you want to go?

Mark: I don't know … maybe … the deli?

(They start to walk)

Julia: Yeah, or how about Chinese?

Mark: We could do Chinese. I'd be into some sweet and sour beef.

(As they walk and bullshit they come across some writing in spray paint on the ground)

Mark: Wow. Oh my god.

Julia: Somebody's pissed off.

Mark: Yeah, I can't believe somebody spray-painted that.

(A student walks by on the way to class and stops where Mark and Julia are. S/he looks at the writing, looks at Mark and Julia, looks back at the writing and keeps walking.)

Aside

Rebecca: Julia's sentiments were ones that I had come in contact with in my own personal life. Many people that I knew who were impacted by the September 11 attacks had much anger and wanted or needed something to happen. This may not have been the most popular view or politically correct perspective, but it seemed important in creating the character of Julia that the fact that she had an emotional connection to September 11 be voiced. This allowed for people to probe deeper into who she was rather than writing her off because they do not agree with her perspective.

The Script Continues

Mark: This is going to be hard for them to get rid of.

Julia: Well maybe they shouldn't get rid of it. You can't pretend
            things didn't happen. The World Trade Centers are a
            freaking pile of rubble, and we have to look at that. This is
            nothing.
Mark: I don't think leaving it is really the answer.
Julia: Well, I do. (Under her breath) I think we should bomb the
            shit out of them.

Aside

Jennifer: Most Interactive Theatre pieces have strong statements or
            remarks designed to provoke a response from the audi-
            ence, coupled with a competing perspective or response.
            In this way "otherness" that may be filtered, hidden, or
            suppressed in public spaces becomes an available topic of
            discourse. Situations that may be threatening, frightening,
            or angering if encountered in one's daily experience are
            presented as topics for discussion.

The Script Continues

Mark: What? That's not going to solve anything … .
Julia: What? You think we should sit down and have a conversa-
            tion with them? Give me a break. They've asked for it. It
            serves them right.
Mark: Serves who right?
Julia: Anyone who's an Arab.

(Mark looks at her)

Julia: Well … I mean what are we supposed to do? After what
            has happened these people deserve what they get.
Mark: Oh! So, you think all the Middle Eastern students deserve
            to be subjected to this graffiti? You think anyone who is
            Arab deserves to be the target of our anger? Julia, I know
            you're upset, but you can't blame everyone who looks Mid-
            dle Eastern … that's ridiculous, don't you think?

Julia: They've been screwed for centuries, what makes us think
            it is ever going to get better? I think we should just blow
            up that whole part of the world.

Mark: Well, you should call the President and let him know that
            ... .

Julia: Listen to the news. There are terrorists living "normal"
            lives here until they get the OK to strike. On TV they
            were showing those people celebrating in the streets after
            the bombing. I'm not going to suck up to them. I want to
            stay clear of them ... . I've heard that people on airplanes
            are freaking out when someone who looks Arab gets on
            the plane. They should just not let them fly.

Mark: Julia ... who are you right now? I can't believe how racist
            you're being.

Julia: What? I think there is something in the law that says that
            if passengers on a plane feel uncomfortable because of
            someone the airline can ask them to leave.

Mark: It's one thing to be uncomfortable by the way someone is
            behaving, it's another thing to judge people by the color of
            their skin.

Julia: Give me a break, Mark. I mean, come on, be honest. If
            you got on a plane right now and some dark-skinned guy
            with a turban sat next to you tell me you wouldn't feel un-
            comfortable.

Mark: Are you listening to yourself? No, I wouldn't feel uncom-
            fortable.

Julia: Oh come on ... .

Mark: No.

Julia: Not even a little bit?

Mark: No!

Julia: Right ... .

(Mark gives in, but with visible frustration)

Mark: Whatever, all right, I might be uncomfortable, but I don't
            necessarily think it's right.

Julia: But you'd feel it right? Sorry, people get what they ask for.
            Arab people are going to have to buck up and deal with

what has happened to our country. And, if they don't like
it they can just go back where they came from ... if we
haven't blown it up already.

Mark: Wow, bitter table for one.

Julia: Yeah, of course I'm bitter. You, of anyone, should know
             that! And, I bet everyone in New York and Washington,
             DC, are feeling the same way.

Mark: I can understand that you're angry ... but everything
             you've said ... it doesn't help what's happened. You know
             what ... I don't think I have time for lunch after all. I need
             to run some errands and head to class.

Julia: OK ... I thought you were starving.

Mark: I was, but I think I've lost my appetite.

Julia: Suit yourself.

Mark: I'll see you later.

Julia: Later.

Curtain

In the question-and-answer period that follows a performance like this, audience members first interrogate the characters (while the actors stay in
role), then the actors derole and participate in a discussion about the construction of the scenario. Here, we begin in the same way. In dialogue with
one another, we interrogate first the content of the scene, then its construction, and finally the reflexive process we have engaged in while writing this
piece.

Debriefing

Jennifer: Wow. That was a pretty powerful scene. Wasn't it a bit
             harsh in places though?

Rebecca: Well, the whole point here is really to provide a space
             where we can say things we might be thinking, but not be
             willing to say, so that the audience can talk about them.

Jennifer: I know, I know, but this feels pretty targeted. What do you
             do if people get offended?

Rebecca: People do get offended. In real life, people get offended,
             but then they usually storm off, get in a fight, or stop talk-

	ing. Here when people get offended, that's the beginning of the conversation, not the end.
Jennifer:	I only got to see one of the performances of this piece, what were some of the things people seemed to get offended about?
Rebecca:	Well, in the first session, the character of Mark was asked if he would ever join the military. His answer was no, and that led to a deeper exploration of who actually fights the wars for our nation. Although Mark's character was looking for a peaceful resolution to what had happened to our country, he was also challenged to look at what it means for many people when our country goes to war. The fact that the actor was a White, male college student also brought in the issue of privilege. Although participants agreed with his desire for peace and a concern for racial profiling in our country, he was also questioned around his patriotism, and there was a visible reaction to his reluctance to serve.
Jennifer:	So what did that discussion seem to do for the group?
Rebecca:	Well, part of what we work to do is really get across the idea that neither of these opposing perspectives is right or wrong. People walk away seeing that the issue is more complex and complicated and much can be learned about ourselves and others when we delve into the conflict rather than avoiding it.
Jennifer:	I remember in the performance I saw that Julia's character really got a lot of flack for being so angry.
Rebecca:	Yes, some people in the audience felt so uncomfortable with how angry she was that they did not even want to deal with her character.
Jennifer:	What do you mean did not "want to deal with her character"?
Rebecca:	I mean that some of them moved really quickly to that essentializing kind of place where all the complexities of the person get wrapped up in the labels we assign them. Like, some people commented on how she might just be mad because she was a woman.

Jennifer: So what were people missing in seeing her as "just a
              woman"?
Rebecca: Well, I think one of the really interesting things in this
              scene was that this character had these negative feelings
              and she needed a place to have them expressed. Many
              people were feeling like that after September 11, and it
              was really hard to talk about.
Jennifer: I seem to recall a pretty lively discussion after that first in-
              terchange. What was your take on it?
Rebecca: I think that once participants were able to sit with Julia's
              anger they were able to uncover that beyond the anger
              was fear and sadness. As participants engaged with the
              character around those feelings, they were able to see her
              as more of a human being than as just someone who had
              expressed anti-Arab sentiment.
Jennifer: Didn't Julia's character also undergo some transformation
              through that dialogue?
Rebecca: Yes, once Julia hit that place of sadness she was also able
              to be more open to people's feelings of concern for people
              of Arab descent in the U.S. This was a tough scene for the
              actors too because it was so soon after September 11, and
              the issue really hit close to home. I think the resolution in
              Julia's character might have happened more easily in the
              discussion than it would have in real life; the actor who
              played Julia was almost her antithesis in real life and the
              transformation came easily for her, but it still let people
              work with ways of challenging or confronting the perspec-
              tive that she voiced.
Jennifer: That's usually what you're working for in writing these
              scenes, isn't it?
Rebecca: Yeah, but this one was especially hard because it was so
              close, and there were so many ways we could have gone
              with it. The thing that always amazes me is that when you
              have a rich topic, the audience brings the complexity. In
              some ways, the scene doesn't need to be, shouldn't be, too
              complicated. Its job is to create a space in which the norm
              is to challenge, confront, and see the things we take for
              granted in another light.

Jennifer: That's really what's struck me about the scenarios, both in watching and in performing. You know, I work with this notion of otherness all the time, and Interactive Theatre amazes and delights me in the way it facilitates its emergence.

Rebecca: Right. I never really used the word otherness to describe it before, but I have always talked about how the humanness of the characters in the scene defies the labels we want to ascribe to them. When we are forced to encounter the other, as you put it, our preconceptions about them and about ourselves are called into question.

Jennifer: Do you think we could do the same thing with writing?

Rebecca: How do you mean?

Jennifer: Well, what if we were to write about our experience working with Interactive Theatre in a way that grabbed people's attention, felt real, and made them stop and think about their assumptions about how they come to "know" things?

Rebecca: What would that look like?

Jennifer: I do not know, when you're trying to decide on how to write a script for Interactive Theatre how do you decide what it will look like?

Rebecca: I guess I put it in a context people are familiar with, talk about issues and ideas that have relevance and meaning, then try to make it feel personal.

Jennifer: So what if we wrote an academic book chapter that started out looking very much like a typical book chapter, felt familiar, comfortable, developed this connection between voice, and otherness, and how Interactive Theatre can tap those ideas, and then helped people feel what it was like to be there?

Rebecca: You mean like include a script?

Jennifer: Sure. And maybe include personal reflections, too. Write about the process from multiple angles, give the readers a sense for how the creative process is all wrapped up in this transformation we're talking about. You could talk about the writing, the visioning, how the program developed ...

Rebecca: And you've got experience facilitating, participating ....

Jennifer: ... and acting.

Rebecca: Right, and acting. So we could really cover the full spectrum of experience. Although ... what about the interactive part, the question-and-answer period? How would we
get at that?

Jennifer: Just like we do in Interactive Theatre. Create the space,
set the stage, and see what happens.

Rebecca: It could be kind of cool. Do you think we can pull it off?

CONCLUSION

This chapter has been a journey through, an exercise with, and a reflection
on the myriad ways that performance can open up spaces for discussion,
challenge commonly held assumptions, and create space for the production
of alternative meanings. In thinking, writing, theorizing, and performing
this chapter into being we have become ever more sensitized to the power of
theatre to make visible the constructive and constitutive process of organizing social experience that is so routinely taken for granted in everyday life.
As Corey (1996) suggested:

> To view the social construction of identity as an activity, a performance, is to
> imbue the process with play and discovery. The production of identity, nego-
> tiation of meaning, arbitration of power, and definition of self are constructs,
> to be sure, but these constructs are produced, refined, and re-produced
> through performance. Thus, the study of performance provides a heuristic
> device for social constructionism. (p. 148)

Our experience working with Interactive Theatre, and engaging in
the more careful analysis and reflection of the process that writing this
piece has called for, reinforces this point on several levels. First, as
should be evident from the playful quality of several of our reflections,
thinking about performing affords a certain latitude in exploring the
constructive, productive process of meaning formation. One need not
stray far from the habits of daily life to access the behaviors, words, attitudes, and choices that one makes in performing, but knowing that one is
engaged in performance makes always evident and ever-present the fact
that conscious choices are being made. Second, both the study and act of
performance problematize the taken for granted necessity of reproduc-
ing the world as we know it or as things are. Because there is an expectation in performance that motivations will be explored and alternatives

investigated, the production–reproduction cycle is arrested. Further, in Interactive Theatre, interrogation and questioning are the norm, and the otherness resides not only in the elements of the script, but also in everything that the audience brings with it into the room. In writing this chapter, we have reaffirmed our belief that this potential resides in writing as well as in embodied performance. What makes possible alternative ways of knowing are spaces that jar, give pause, and challenge our sense of the way things are. When writing is made interactive it, too, becomes performative.

In engaging this process of performative writing several key themes have emerged as important to our inquiry. First, our conviction that the opportunity for voice is intimately linked to the presence and possibility of otherness to emerge in an exchange has been reinforced. Our work with Interactive Theatre has driven home how being confronted with difference, and challenged and encouraged to interrogate one's own beliefs and perspectives, can create the possibility for transformation.

Second, we find that this possibility is often more readily accessible in this format because of the safe distance that the scenario provides from personal experience. This highlights an interesting tension between proximity and distance evident in some of the preceding examples. On the one hand, the interactive performance is more real than reality in that it makes visible that which might be left invisible and says openly that which might be withheld. On the other hand, the forum in which the scene is presented is clearly artificial, and the scene is not real in any concrete sense of the word. It simultaneously portrays experiences and feelings that may be common to many, and is not about anyone in particular. As one student remarked after experiencing a performance, "I am all of these characters." And yet, because the audience is never any of the characters really, they are liberated to ask questions and engage the scene in ways that the constraints of other social forums might preclude.

Third, to blend our voices in expressing the concept, Interactive Theatre allows the humanness of the characters to challenge, confront, and problematize the labeling and calcifying of the Other. The process of doing character work both supports this potential and enables our final insight as well: Interactive Theatre enables multiple layers of transformation as it works on and through authors, actors, audience members, and facilitators; and, it transcends time and space as the scenarios evolve and transform over time, as audience members engage them on multiple occasions, as the past enters the room through the actors and the audience, and as the life of the performance lives on after the curtain falls.

REFERENCES

ACE/AAUP. (2000). [Online]. *Does diversity make a difference? Three research studies on diversity in college classrooms.* A joint report of the American Council on Education and American Association of University Professors. Retrieved January 9, 2006, from http://www.acenet.edu/programs/omhe/div-rpt-sec2.pdf

Allen, B. J. (1995). "Diversity" in organizational communication. *Journal of Applied Communication Research, 23,* 143–155.

Allen, B. J. (1996). Feminist standpoint theory: A Black woman's (re)view of organization socialization. *Communication Studies, 47,* 257–271.

Allen, B. J. (2000). "Learning the ropes": A Black feminist critique. In P. Buzzanell (Ed.), *Rethinking organizational and managerial communication from feminist perspectives* (pp. 177–208). Thousand Oaks, CA: Sage.

Allen, B. J., Orbe, M. P., & Olivas, M. R. (1999). The complexity of our tears: Dis/enchantment and (in)difference in the academy. *Communication Theory, 9,* 402–429.

Ambrozas, D. (1998). The university as public sphere. *Canadian Journal of Communication, 23,* 73–89.

Barnett, R. (1994). *Academic community: Discourse or discord.* London: Jessica Kingsley.

Bergquist, W. H. (1995). *Quality through access, access with quality: The new imperative for higher education.* San Francisco: Jossey-Bass.

Bérubé, M., & Nelson, C. (Eds.). (1995). *Higher education under fire: Politics, economics, and the crisis of the humanities.* New York: Routledge.

Boal, A. (1979). *Theatre of the oppressed* (C. A. & M.-O. L. McBride, Trans.). New York: Urizen.

Boal, A. (1995). *The rainbow of desire: The Boal method of theatre and therapy* (A. Boal, Trans.). New York: Routledge.

Boyer, E. L. (1990). *Campus life: In search of community.* Princeton, NJ: Carnegie Foundation.

Buttny, R. (1997). Reported speech in talking race on campus. *Human Communication Research, 23,* 477–506.

Cheatham, H. E. (Ed.). (1991). *Cultural pluralism on campus.* Washington, DC: American College Personnel Association.

Collier, L. M. (1995). College campus hate speech codes: A personal view from an absolute perspective. *Howard Journal of Communication, 5,* 263–278.

Corey, F. C. (1996). Performing sexualities in an Irish pub. *Text and Performance Quarterly, 16,* 146–160.

Deetz, S. A. (1992). *Democracy in the age of corporate colonization: Developments in communication and the politics of everyday life.* Albany: State University of New York Press.

Deetz, S. A. (1995a). Character, corporate responsibility and the dialogic in the postmodern context. *Organization: The Interdisciplinary Journal of Organization, Theory and Society, 3,* 217–225.

Deetz, S. A. (1995b). *Transforming communication, transforming business: Building responsive and responsible workplaces.* Cresskill, NJ: Hampton.

Deetz, S. A., & Simpson, J. L. (2004). Critical organizational dialogue: Open formation and the demand of "otherness." In R. Anderson, L. Baxter, & K. Cissna (Eds.), *Dialogue: Theorizing difference in communication studies* (pp. 141–158). Thousand Oaks, CA: Sage.

Eisenberg, E., Murphy, A., & Andrews, L. (1998). Openness and decision making in the search for a university provost. *Communication Monographs, 65,* 1–23.

Freire, P. (1970). *Pedagogy of the oppressed.* New York: Continuum.

Frey, L. R., Pollock, M. A., Artz, L., & Pearce, W. B. (1996). From medium to context to praxis and process: Transforming the undergraduate communication curriculum. *World Communication, 25,* 79–89.

Gadamer, H. G. (1975). *Truth and method* (G. Barden & J. Cummings, Eds. & Trans.). New York: Seabury.

Gadamer, H. G. (1980). *Dialogue and dialectic: Eight hermeneutical studies on Plato.* New Haven, CT: Yale University Press.

Goodall, H. L. (1999). Casing the academy for community. *Communication Theory, 9,* 465–494.

Green, S. (2000). Boal and beyond: Strategies for creating community dialogue. *Theatre, 31,* 47–54.

Gudeman, R. H. (2000). College missions, faculty teaching and student outcomes in a context of low diversity. In *Does diversity make a difference? Three research studies on diversity in college classrooms* (pp. 37–60). Washington, DC: American Council on Education and American Association of University Professors.

Guinier, L., & Smith, A. D. (2000). Rethinking power, rethinking theatre: A conversation between Lani Guinier and Anna Deavere Smith. *Theatre, 31,* 31–45.

Habermas, J. (1980). *Discourse ethics: Notes on philosophical justification, moral consciousness and communicative action* (C. Lenhart & S. Weber Nicholson, Trans.). Cambridge, MA: MIT Press.

Habermas, J. (1984). *The theory of communicative action: Vol. 1. Reason and the rationalization of society* (T. McCarthy, Trans.). Boston: Beacon Press.

Habermas, J. (1987). *The theory of communicative action: Vol. 2: Lifeworld and system* (T. McCarthy, Trans.). Boston: Beacon Press.

Habermas, J. (1995). *Legitimation crisis* (T. McCarthy, Trans.). Boston: Beacon Press.

Katz, S. (2002, May 17). Choosing justice over excellence. *Chronicle of Higher Education,* p. B7.

Landy, R. J. (1993). *Persona and performance: The meaning of role in drama, therapy, and everyday life.* New York: Guilford.

Levinas, E. (1969). *Totality and infinity: An essay on exteriority* (A. Lingis, Trans.). Pittsburgh, PA: Duquesne University Press.

Levinas, E. (1985). *Ethics and infinity: Conversations with Phillipe Nemo* (R. Cohen, Trans.). Pittsburgh, PA: Duquesne University Press.

Levinas, E. (1987). *Time and the other* (R. Cohen, Trans.). Pittsburgh, PA: Duquesne University Press.

Nakayama, T. K. (1997). Les voix de l'autre. *Western Journal of Communication, 61,* 235–242.

Nicotera, A. M. (1999). The woman academic as subject/object/self: Dismantling the illusion of duality. *Communication Theory, 9,* 430–464.

Ono, K. A. (1997). A letter/essay I've been longing to write in my personal/academic voice. *Western Journal of Communication, 61,* 114–125.

Peters, J. D. (1999). *Speaking into the air: A history of the idea of communication.* Chicago: University of Chicago Press.

Porter, W. M., & Catt, I. E. (1993). The narcissistic reflection of communicative power: Delusions of progress against organizational discrimination. In D. K. Mumby (Ed.), *Narrative and social control: Critical perspectives* (pp. 164–185). Newbury Park, CA: Sage.

Simpson, J. L. (2001). *The making of multivocal culture: Building community on a university campus.* Unpublished doctoral dissertation, University of Colorado, Boulder, CO.

Simpson, J. L. (2005). Engaging communication: Politically responsive theory in action. In J. L. Simpson & P. Shockley-Zalabak (Eds.), *Engaging communication, transforming organizations: Scholarship of engagement in action* (pp. 245–262). Cresskill, NJ: Hampton.

Simpson, J. L. & Allen, B. J. (2005). Engaging difference matters in the classroom. In J. L. Simpson & P. Shockley-Zalabak (Eds.), *Engaging communication, transforming organizations: Scholarship of engagement in action* (pp. 149–171). Cresskill, NJ: Hampton.

Strine, M. S. (1997). Deconstructing identity in/and difference: Voices "under erasure." *Western Journal of Communication, 61,* 448–459.

Taylor, B. C. (2002). Organizing the "unknown subject": Los Alamos, espionage, and the politics of biography. *Quarterly Journal of Speech, 88,* 33–49.

Warren, J. T. (2001). Doing Whiteness: On the performative dimensions of race in the classroom. *Communication Education, 50,* 91–108.

6

Challenges of International Women of Color in the United States: The Complicated "Rights" of Belonging in Globalization

Raka Shome
Arizona State University

This chapter focuses on the issue of social justice and community—in particular issues of race and multiculturalism—by arguing for the importance of centralizing globalization in this discussion. It arises from a growing concern that much of critical communication scholarship within the National Communication Association (NCA),[1] which purports to be sensitive to issues of democracy, justice, and equality, is too squarely situated within the boundaries of the United States when those boundaries themselves are implicated in larger global flows of violence, (in)justice, and power.[2] Addition-

---

[1] Although this is less so in the International Communication Association (ICA), American-ness also, for the most part, tends to dominate the frameworks of the ICA.

[2] Some exceptions to this, especially within NCA circles, include scholars such as Lawrence Grossberg, Toby Miller, Michael Curtin, Cameron McGarth, Angharad Valdivia Dilip Gaonkar, John Erni, and others. In addition, scholars such as Radhika Parameswaran, Meenakshi Gigi Durham, Soyini Madison, Hemant Shah, Rona Halualani, Marwan Kraidy, my own work, Stephen Wiley, Paula Chakravari, Radha Hegde, and some others also incorporate global issues in their engagement with the phenomena of communication. Although these and other scholars have provided some important interventions, a critical engagement with internationalism for the most part continues to remain absent in mainstream intellectual discourses of the NCA.

ally, at a time when increasing numbers of immigrant international scholars of color are beginning to occupy our discipline, due to global flows of capital and culture, discussions of advocacy, democracy, equality, rights, and all such terms that we associate with social justice remain limited, and even perhaps anachronistic, unless they are placed against the various complexities and incommensurabilities of globality that are interrupting America today.

To say this another way, given that one of the goals of this volume is to rethink issues of community and justice, I want to argue that central to this rethinking should be a consideration of the way in which U.S.-centric issues of community and justice are interrupted by the colliding and colluding flows of various global modernities that are informing and remaking the U.S. public sphere—including that of the academy. Thus, I seek to contribute to the discussion of partisan criticism in this volume by arguing for the centrality of a transnational and postcolonial critical perspective in disciplinary considerations of justice and community.

In the first section of this chapter I address limits of the discourse of multiculturalism and diversity as it is often engaged within the U.S. public and academic imagination. Given that globalization, with its various colliding and colluding modernities, has complicated the meaning of "rights" and "belonging," I posit that discussions of multiculturalism are inadequate without an engagement with globalization and the asymmetrical postcolonial flows of power into and out of the United States. In the second section, I focus on the ways in which race, nationality, and complex global flows of culture impact international women of color in the United States (including the academy) and how the complex positioning of these women invites us to rethink discussions of multiculturalism in the United States and the North American script that often regulates and contains it.

I focus on international women of color not merely because of my own investments in postcolonial feminist knowledge production, but also because international and immigrant women of color in the United States—especially after 9/11—constitute one of the most vulnerable populations in the country. Not citizens, and sometimes not even permanent residents (i.e., green card holders, given that there are many who work on H1B visas or are dependent on their spouses' visas), they often lack the nation-centered protection of diversity. Straddling multiple national borders, they are forced to navigate through multiple and often incommensurable gender and sexual scripts. For them, the body, too often, is literally the site on which geopolitical collisions of diverse modernities and their corresponding masculinities and patriarchies are enacted. Hence, an examination of their complex positioning enables us to address the numerous intersections and collisions of gender, race, sexuality, class, nationality, geographies, and temporalities that continually interrupt (whether recognized or not) narratives of belonging in America.

PROBLEMATIZING THE NATION CENTEREDNESS OF "DIFFERENCE"

Today, the discussion of diversity in the U.S. academy, with its unreflexive celebration of "cultural difference" is beginning to lose its radical potential as a critique of the racialized and nationalized modernities that inform the structures, spaces, and disciplinary techniques of knowledge production (Giroux, 1994; Grossberg, 1993, 1994; Moreiras, 2001, among others). This is especially the case when we re-consider difference in conditions of globalization and the complex postcolonial relations that shape our contemporary realities.[3] For instance, Giroux (1994) notes that while identity politics had been central in challenging the cultural homogeneity of the 1950s, it "failed to move beyond a notion of difference structured *in polarizing binarisms and an uncritical appeal to a discourse of authenticity*" (p. 31, italics added). Indeed, the concern here is that while the excavation of difference in multicultural studies may have had some initial gains in questioning dominant White power structures, its terms of discussion too often recentered the very fixity of identity that it was attempting to move beyond. Given my own investment in postcolonial theory, my particular interest in this issue has to do with the ways in which discussions of multiculturalism in the academy, the larger public sphere, and our discipline frequently function to protect and preserve the boundaries of American-ness. In so doing, they often reify a binary of the national–international, citizen–noncitizen, when, in fact, this binary is being disrupted and complicated every day by numerous unpredictable relations of globalization.

If one is a recognizable minority (i.e., when one carries that globally privileged imperial appendage "American" to one's recognizable ethnic marking) that can be slotted into a recognizable state-sanctioned category of difference, one too easily finds a place in discussions of multiculturalism in the U.S. academy. For instance, in NCA there are divisions and caucuses such as the African American Studies, the Asian American studies, Latino

---

[3]In communication studies, Grossberg's (1993) seminal essay is especially relevant for recognizing the limits of difference. Putting forward his concerns about identity politics, Grossberg argues for the necessity of spatializing our understanding of culture in ways that can address the complexities of a global spatial economy.

Studies—the three most clearly recognized categories of cultural difference in the U.S. imagination. However, we do not have divisions where immigrant or third-world scholars of color with completely different postcolonial histories and complexities can find a place. This is not an identity politics argument that I am making; rather it is an argument geared toward calling attention to the contradictions between the domestic (and domesticated) categories of difference that rule our racial imaginations, and difference whose existence may escape such maps of imagination.

Lee's (1995) call for a "critical internationalism" in area and cultural studies research, and Desmond and Dominguez's (1996) discussion (in the context of American Studies) of how engagements with diversity too often reflect an inward orientation that reifies a logic of American exceptionalism, are particularly relevant for my argument.[4] Although these scholars rightly lamented the logic of American-ness that informs celebrations of difference, we continue to find that, for the most part, discussions of multiculturalism in the academy too often deploy difference as a national being instead of a global interruptive becoming. In so doing, they function ironically to regulate various forms of global otherness or alterity that haunts the boundaries of America, given that those boundaries are built on America's geopolitical relations with "other worlds." That is, difference that may have been produced outside of the U.S. public sphere, outside of North Atlantic modernities, and outside of our available cultural (U.S.-centric) tools for recognizing difference, is too often erased from the register and discussions of multiculturalism in the United States.

Such issues could be seen clearly after 9/11. On many campuses after the terrorist attacks, there was, on the one hand, a clear liberal drive to celebrate our differences (where the "our" too often was an American "our"). In the commercial media too, public awareness advertisements displayed faces of various American scripted ethnicities touting "We are all Americans." Yet, on the other hand, the harassment (implicit or explicit) of individuals who were South Asian, Middle Eastern, or non-English-speaking immi-

---

[4]The field of cultural studies, for instance, has recently witnessed some debates about the Euro-American centered-ness of the cultural studies project and the problematics it tends to work with. See here the recent anthology by Abbas and Erni (2005). Other works, still limited for the most part, that also reflect such moves include Radway (1999), Wiegman (2002), Kaplan and Grewal (2002), among others. See also the discussions that ran on the crossroads listserv, devoted to American studies, on the topic of "Towards critical internationalism" from October 1996 to 1997, located at http://cross-roads.georgetown.edu /interroads/toc.html. Although many of these discussions are beginning to occur in fields such as American studies and cultural studies, in the field of communication studies, however, the American-centered logic of multiculturalism and race, for the most part, continues to remain unmarked.

grants of color grew in alarming proportions. In the city of Phoenix, from where I write, one of the bloodiest and well-known acts that received significant global attention took place when a Sikh convenience store owner, Balbir Singh Sodhi, was ruthlessly shot to death in Mesa, a suburb of Phoenix. Even more recently, in May 2003, Avatar Singh, an Indian immigrant who had parked his 18-wheeler in North Phoenix while making a phone call to his son, was shot by two young White men who yelled, "Go back to where you belong" (see http://www.sikhnet.com/s/phoenixshooting).

Indeed, after 9/11, America's color line has been drastically contained and regulated by national lines. In saying this, I want to emphasize that 9/11 is not the cause of this. Rather, 9/11 brought to the surface more visibly the nation-centered logic of multiculturalism that has always underwritten American discourses of cultural belonging and civil rights. This is a logic that is, as I suggested earlier, anachronistic. It denies naively the constant (yet unacknowledged) interruptive global and postcolonial alterities through which contemporary lines of U.S. society are constituted. It is anachronistic also because it does not recognize the pitfalls in making the boundaries of race coincide with the legal and spatial boundaries of the nation when those boundaries themselves are so complexly intertwined and imbricated in numerous unseen elsewheres to which the nation (especially one such as the United States that is constantly built and rebuilt on various forms of global violence, genocide, and economic pillage) has an ethico-political responsibility.

As South Asians (and I do not just mean South Asian Americans) were targeted in violent ways after 9/11, what shamefully slipped from the American imagination is how the technology industry in this country is built on the backs of brilliant South Asian minds on HIB visas, how Bangalore and Hyderabad—technology hubs in India—make possible the running of many software companies in the United States and contribute to much of the operation of our technocentric lives in contemporary America. As Arabs (including many Middle Eastern students) were regularly detained by the FBI, what once again fell out of the mainstream discourse were instances of how U.S. arms and constructions companies have made billions of dollars in Saudi Arabia in the past two decades (Marable, 2003), how close to 30,000 U.S. citizens are employed by Saudi companies or Saudi–U.S. corporate ventures, and how Exxon made an agreement with the Saudi government to produce gas projects worth $20 billion to $26 billion (Marable, 2003).

In the context of our discipline, in which discussions and recognition of race, for the most part, are embarrassingly American-centric, these arguments are especially urgent if our discipline is to reconsider its modes of intellectual belonging, imagination, and practices in globalization. Gupta and Ferguson (1998), for instance, have argued cogently about the dangers of mapping and regulating cultures, or in the context of my argument, multiculturalism, through fixed-place-based notions of belonging. Given the constant movement and flows of peoples and cultures in globalization and postcoloniality, the notion of a place as being static, fixed, and bound to a homogenous national culture is being problematized. Places are continually being remade by new relations of global hybridity. As Gupta and Ferguson note, today "India and Pakistan reappear in postcolonial simulation in London and Teheran rises from the ashes in Los Angeles" (p. 38). Given this, discussions of multiculturalism that do not see the global in the local and the local in the global remain out of touch with the complex ways in which places and spaces are being remade through unpredictable flows of internationalism and diasporas. Indeed, the goal today for radical scholarship should be less to center difference (oversaturated as we are with too many state-sanctioned categories of difference that are often also theoretically internalized in our academic worlds and parlance). Rather, the goal should be to focus on the alterity, the ambivalence, the *differance*, that exceeds and disrupts nation-sanctioned regimes of difference, such that we may not have a term for marking, naming, or slotting it (and what is unnamed is always subject to greater violence).

Today in the United States, most tend to have a recognition and awareness of difference, given that difference is precisely what is so often used by contemporary global capitalist formations including the academy to market identities and products. The cultural logic of neoliberalism (as the latest manifestation of neocolonialism), it could possibly be argued, is cultural difference (and not monoculturalism), whereas the cultural logic of (pre-World War II) territorial colonialism was the suppression and denial of difference. For economic globalization to be successful and tap global markets effectively, it must be able to strategically utilize and articulate difference to produce a larger homogeneity—of consumption habits, material desires, worldviews, and notions such as democracy and freedom. If modernity, as Dube (2002b) suggested, stages itself through seductive enchantments that cover over power inequities, then one of the enchantments of contemporary American modernity, with its overriding logic of consumption and consumerism, is an enchantment with difference—but a difference that is recognizable, usable, translatable, and, most important, can be regulated and recuperated into the logics (cultural, political, and economic) of American-ness.

Further, when difference is seen as an outcome only of the designs of North Atlantic and Euro-American modernity—as it usually is in American discourses of multiculturalism, the deployment of difference denies the criss-crossing and collisions of multiple modernities that push and pull, route and reroute the politics of difference in different ways in different conjunctural moments and spaces.[5] For example, in the United States, African Americans are often positioned as the ultimate or even the primal signifier or sign of multiculturalism in the public imagination (given that Whiteness is constituted through Blackness). Underlying this positioning, of course, is the guilt and shame of chattel slavery. But however horrendous and abhorrent slavery might have been, however inexcusable might have been its practice and its continued effects, its story is still the product of, and rooted in, a North Atlantic temporality and history. That is, there is still a privileging of the abuses only of Western modernities that occurred in a particular time frame. What remains occluded then are the numerous ways in which Western modernities, in their imbrication in other modernities, have also produced gross abuses outside of North Atlantic times and geographies.[6]

I want to emphasize here that in arguing the preceding, I do not in any way mean to minimize the continued oppression and victimization of African Americans in the United States. I am simply inviting us to recognize how the abuses of North Atlantic modernities, including the current structures of neoliberalism, that impact and articulate modernities, spaces, and populations beyond North Atlantic geographies need as much attention. There are other forms of slavery today—for example, "illegal" undocumented immigrants from third-world countries working in sweatshops, garment factories, and electronics factories in the United States, producing products for multinational companies, or, after 9/11, "suspicious" immigrants of color being detained. There is also slavery (of labor) being produced by the United States (but not only) in "other worlds" as American businesses are outsourcing their labor—such as call centers—to cheaper

---

[5]The concept of multiple modernities has recently constituted a new theoretical move in cultural studies that is geared toward pointing out the importance of examining modernities beyond the Anglo/Euro framework. Some especially influential works are Gaonkar (1999, 2002), a special issue of *Public Culture* (1999) on alternative modernities, among others. Although the concept of multiple modernities has centralized the importance of addressing modernities beyond the Anglo framework, my focus in this chapter is more on recognizing the intertwining and colliding realities of diverse global modernities that inform and impact the U.S. public sphere.

[6]Spivak's (1988) "Can the Subaltern Speak?" in which she critiqued Foucault's theorization of marginality in Europe for its lack of attention to how the histories of Europe also produced marginalities on the other side of the international division of labor remains, to date, one of the most sophisticated and complex theorizations of this problematic.

offshore markets at low wages. Distinguished critic Harish Trivedi of Delhi University recently lamented such outsourcing of work as producing the new "cybercoolies of our global age [who work] not on plantations but on flickering screens" (in Das, 2003). These are examples of an unrecognized slavery that are rooted not just in North Atlantic modernity, but more complex postcolonial collisions (as well as coming together) of contemporary American modernities with other modernities. Thus, a serious reconsideration of race in globalization throws into crisis and ruptures the map of multiculturalism in the United States. It shows how this map itself may be a product of a parochial attention only to North Atlantic modernity that denies the loud, jangled, and yet often deliberately unheard, collision and collusion of numerous and complex global histories and geographies, and their unseen flows into and out of the United States under cultural and economic globalization. As Dube (2002a) notes:

> It is a matter of being self conscious about the particular ways in which we put forward notions of difference and premises of power …. In other words … what conceptions of present history/progress do we bring to bear upon our renderings of power and difference? What anterior idea animates our appropriation of history? (p. 200)

It is precisely the importance of complicating difference against international histories and geopolitics that Dube and others emphasize that, in my view, makes postcolonial theory a more complex theoretical enterprise than just theories of multiculturalism for interrogating the productions of race and rethinking issues of community and belonging in globalization. In saying this, I do not mean to minimize the rich and influential work that exists on multicultural identity politics but, rather, want to point attention to some of their limits for theorizing the complexities of race in globalization especially when such work remains bound to an American geography and culture.

In the discipline of communication, there is now a growing interest in postcolonial scholarship[7]—although in comparison to numerous other disciplines such as anthropology, English, women's studies, geography, history, theater, and cinema studies that have been vastly transformed by postcolonial scholarship, the discipline of communication, overall, has been relatively slow to embrace the potential and significance of postcolonial scholarship. This is because postcolonial theory throws into

---

[7]See, for example, Durham, 2004; Grossberg, 1993, 2002; Drzweicka & Halualani, 2002; Hasian, 2002; Kraidy, 2002; Lee, 1998; Parameswaran, 2002, 2004; Rajagopal, 2000; Shome, 1996, 1998; Shome & Hegde, 2002b; Supriya, 2002, 2004; Zacharias, 2003, among others.

crisis the positivist and modernist foundations of our field by linking those foundations to continuing and past colonial effects in "other worlds" and showing how those foundations themselves are imbricated in the dominant (U.S.) ideologies and assumptions that drive contemporary geopolitics.[8] Given the relative newness of our field in the academy, this would certainly engender significant intellectual and political anxiety.

Indeed, few other left-oriented theoretical discourses confront and unsettle—with such intellectual sophistication—the imperial and geopolitically dominant impulses of U.S. and Western knowledge formations as postcolonial theory, for postcolonial theory does not rest merely with excavating race; rather, it forces our intellectual imaginations to connect constantly to global violence in numerous elsewheres in which the West (but not only) is implicated. Thus, there is an increasing recognition among a growing number of scholars in our field that the object of our scholarship, communication—and some familiar topics through which we engage it, such as technology, media, information systems, discourse, identity, culture, space, community, the public, and more—is continuously informed by larger unfolding relations of globality and postcoloniality.[9]

Postcolonial theory, as a theoretical framework that is situated within (while also interrupting the British-American version of) the larger project of cultural studies, is concerned with interrogating modernities and colonialism as one central effect of modernity (Barlow, 1997; Chakraborty, 2000; Dube, 2002a; Spivak, 1988). Where postcolonial theory remains useful is that it tries to interrogate race not just by exclusively focusing on race; that is, it does not begin with race, but, rather, understands race as one central product effect of larger global relations. Given that its larger impetus is to theorize the relations between modernities and colonialisms—and race is one effect (but not the only one, although certainly a central one) of colonialism—postcolonial theory is concerned with larger structural issues of nation, geographies, histories, geopolitics, (incommensurable) modernities, temporalities, subalternity (which is not the same as marginality), and global relations (past and present) of economy and culture that mediate such categories in the productions of various colonialisms.

---

[8]For some other discussions of the relevance of postcolonial theory for communication studies see the August 2002 special issue on postcolonialism in *Communication Theory* and Shome (1996, 1998). Outside the discipline see Afzal-Khan and Seshadri Crooks (2000), Moore-Gilbert (1997), and Gandhi (1998).

[9]See, for example, Curtin (2003), Durham (2004), Grossberg (1993, 1997), Halualani and Drzweicka (2002), Parks and Kumar (2002), Kraidy (1999, 2002), Madison (2005), Malek and Kavoori (2000), Mongia (1999), Miller, Govil, and McMurria (2001), Shome and Hegde (2002a, 2002b), Parameswaran (2001, 2002, 2004), Valdivia (1995), and Wiley (2004), among others.

Postcolonial theory brings a geopolitical and historical situatedness to any discussion of race. It is always concerned with mapping and remapping global connections and disconnections, unsettling the binaries of the here and the there, the then and the now (Hall, 1996), and showing how these binaries themselves are constantly being reconfigured with different outcomes in different nodal points in globality. In its attention to such larger global structures, postcolonial theory enables us to move beyond the (frequent) frozen fixity and acontextualism of mere identity politics. This is not to say that postcolonial studies jettisons identity or says that identity politics is irrelevant; rather, what it says is that identity is best understood by moving to larger international structural levels in which geopolitics is always central. In postcolonial theory, the personal is not merely political; the personal is always *geopolitical*.

Thus, when we use postcolonial theory to interrupt multiculturalism, we move multiculturalism itself to a larger international and geopolitical level that, in invoking complex issues of intertwining and incommensurable modernities, might make visible the often regulative presence of the (U.S.) nation and subject positions in our theoretical maps of multiculturalism. As Kaplan, in her introduction to *Cultures of U.S. Imperialism,* notes about the models and theories of multiculturalism that rule our academic imaginations:

> American nationality [in them] can still be taken for granted as a monolithic and self-contained whole … if it remains implicitly defined by its internal social relations, and not in political struggles for power with other cultures and nations, struggles which make America's conceptual and geographic borders, fluid, contested, and historically changing. (Romero, 1997, p. 244)

Additionally, what must also be understood is that while multiculturalism in the United States is concerned with identities that have been excluded from the limits of (Anglo) modernity, postcolonial theory, while embracing this concern, operates within a larger focus. Its concern is not just with the margins (in fact, it problematizes the binarist logic of center and margins) but with that which cannot be recuperated into institutionalized cultural frameworks (including geographies, spaces, and time), that which escapes the imagination of knowledge, that which is outside of recognizable systems of desire and knowledge—the supplement that exceeds the conceptual frameworks of Western, and other geopolitically dominant modernities, while always silently (and sometimes, as with the attacks of 9/11, not so silently) haunting them. This perspective is powerfully articulated in the project of subaltern studies, which is a subarea in postcolonial studies. Postcolonial critic Seshadri-Crooks (2000) explains the critical impulse of postcolonial theory in this way:

> [i]n other words [in postcolonial theory] modernity is no longer a question of knowing the limits of knowledge, as with classical philosophy, but one of discerning the constitutive negativity, the otherness, the non-recuperable, the 'unthought' that makes positive knowing possible (p. 13).

INTERNATIONAL WOMEN OF COLOR AND THE POLITICS OF BELONGING IN GLOBALIZATION

Against the preceding theoretical framework, I now want to visit the complex positioning of international women of color in the United States (including the academy). Before I begin, let me offer a caveat. I recognize that the term *international women of color* is broad and that not all international women of color have the same experiences, given that their relation to the United States is forged through different histories and geographies, movements and removements, desires and violences. Nonetheless, there are certain broader theoretical issues related to their positioning as third-world immigrants in which I am interested, in terms of how they interrupt U.S.-centered discourses of gender and race. Because of my own cultural location as South Asian Indian (and not South Asian Indian American), I primarily speak from this subject position; however, I hope that the larger theoretical questions raised here call attention to the collisions of geographies, histories, modernities, nations, memories, and the divergent and often oppositional gender and cultural scripts, through which third-world women of color are displaced in the United States.

My interest in this topic emerges from several issues (or concerns): First, as I posited earlier, international women of color too often tend to fall out of discussions of race and gender in the academy—in the literature on multiculturalism, critical race studies, in the feminist literature, and even in the women of color literature—which for the most part, whether recognized or not, are organized to express the interests and desires of women and minorities who are U.S. citizens. Wiegman (2002), for instance, has recently called attention to how "histories of U.S. nationalism and racialization [have] performed themselves within Women's Studies curricula and research" (p. 4).

One sometimes senses an anxiety from domestic minority scholars working on gender and culture that a focus on the international women (or people) of color may undermine the salience of domestic racial issues. Although the anxiety is understandable—given the continued practices of exclusion through which domestic women (or people) of color are treated in the United States, including in the academy—it is ultimately not a politically reflexive move. It reifies a binary between the national and global, the citizen and noncitizen, and remains reluctant to recognize that the global is here, inside the United States, and that inside is itself produced through, and productive of, various (unseen and unknown) outsides.

One only has to take a look at the way in which some women's studies courses and departments are organized as well as ethnic studies departments. It is often standard in women's studies programs to offer courses on women of color—but if one looks at the content of this, it is frequently, for the most part, designed to speak to U.S. women of color. One also finds additional courses taught separately under labels such as, for example, global feminism, international feminism, or transnational feminism. The curricular organization of women's studies departments often reifies the problematic that I am addressing. But should not the category of gender always be studied through global feminist perspectives? Is the global merely "out there"—outside of the nation—as a free-floating abstraction that seemingly does not touch, shape, and interrupt gendered lives in the United States? Gender was always already global and geopolitical even before we discovered transnational feminism as a theoretical framework. The global has always worked through nations. Kaplan and Grewal (2002) have recently offered a much overdue critique of such nation-centered intellectual imaginations that often govern feminist programs in the United States and, I would add, could also be relevant to many ethnic studies programs.

I have firsthand knowledge of such complexities. As an international woman of color, I am sometimes tired of being coded as a woman of color and generically cast with domestic women of color, rendering invisible my own complex global history. I get tired of not being seen as a valid recognizable and identifiable minority (i.e., I am not a citizen). Or, I am the foreign woman from elsewhere when, in fact, I am subject to the constant and violent racialization of the U.S. nation (and South Asians, being only a recent although still limited presence in the U.S. imagination, remain one of the most misunderstood geopolitical categories). My reality is shaped by complex transnational relations and histories of colonialism and decolonization that cannot just be equated with that of domestic minorities who have, and will continue to have, much more nation-centered protection in the United States than I can ever hope for (which is not to deny that domestic minorities, in relation to the White power structure, continue to face gross abuses of race and gender in the academy).

Nor can my reality be denied as though it has nothing to do with the nationalist logic of the U.S. nation-state whether I am "here" in the United States or "there" in India, given the increasing presence of the U.S. in Indian markets since the 1990s. I am not a citizen—but a resident alien. Yet my political and economic reality is constantly shaped and exploited by the intersecting forces of race, nation, globalization, sexism, and various colliding modernities that have produced me. This is to say, my reality as an international woman of color is not adequately captured, understood, dignified, and legitimated when discussions of diversity merely focus on race and gender without adequately addressing issues of geopolitics and postcoloniality. Addressing such issues would include recognizing how the U.S. nation's complex relations with other nations impact, at an affective and intellectual level, the lives of international faculty of color, international students, and other members of color in the academy who may not be citizens but certainly have as much a stake in narratives of belonging (intellectual and material) in the United States. The larger point I am making is that for international women of color, our entire bodies, how we perform them, how we are performed on them by the U.S. nation-state, are already caught in various untranslatabilities of global modernities that exceed nation-centered assumptions of difference. As Mohanty (2003) notes, questions "of difference and equality in education take on a certain urgency in a world where the fate of First world citizens is inextricably tied to fate of the refugees, exiles, migrants, immigrants in the [f]irst world/north and of similar constituencies in the rest of the world" (p. 189).

Mohanty's (2003) words insist on recognizing that the sphere of education—a sphere that is so centrally tied to the production of democracy and citizenry—is, in our current global context, inextricably linked to various incommensurable flows of internationalism and colliding modernities into and out of the United States. By flows of internationalism, I mean flows of bodies and ideas into our academic cultures that throw into crisis U.S.-centered assumptions about research, pedagogy, professionalism, collegiality, and community and invite us to hear the sounds and silences of multiple modernities (some of which we in the United States may simply not be able to grasp or be aware of) that interrupt the social assumptions that inform such categories.

Feminist and critical race scholarship interrogating gender and racial biases in the academy have long shown how many academic practices and assumptions (of being and belonging) are informed by a White masculinist heterosexual bias. However, there needs to be more attention to, and problematization of, how the culture of the academy (and our discipline in particular, including our modes of relating to each other) are written by U.S.-centered assumptions about what it means to belong—as a scholar, intellectual, colleague, or simply a human being. American-ness (and not just race) must be problematized and critiqued in our assumptions of gender and social relations in the academy and beyond.[10] When the politics of being an intellectual and the politics of being "human" today are caught in various unfolding, messy, interruptive, and colliding relations of globality, we must allow our politics, including the politics of relating to each other, to be continually interrupted by global otherness—of bodies, ideas, imaginations, and desires—that may at times be incommensurable with (or unimaginable to) our American scripts of difference and our American assumptions about community.

A topic on which much more interrogation needs to occur in critical and cultural studies is that of friendship as transnational politics.[11] Friendship, as Derrida (1997) had famously suggested, underpins all basic assumptions of such phenomena as solidarity, alliance, belonging, ethics, community, familiality, hospitality, and so on. It is political. But what do we do when the terms and assumptions about friendship are caught, not just in divergent, but colliding, modernities and their corresponding ideologies and values about caring, communication, giving, relating, desire, and love? When we raise the issue of friendship to the level of geopolitics, whose terms and assumptions of friendship structure and dominate our relations as Americans with transnational or immigrant others in the United States? How do we (and can we) negotiate (across) such incommensurabilities—assuming that we recognize them as such—if we are to envision the possibility of thinking of community beyond the United States (which is not the same as saying one can somehow "escape" the nation), if we are to envision a global coalition of intellectuals and allies working toward common political goals. Most important, are we willing to reexamine the assumptions of our geopolitically, economically, and nationally privileged positions as U.S. citizens, especially when we allow the global to enter our worlds, in the

---

[10]As noted earlier, in the field of American studies, for instance, there has been a recent reflexivity on critiquing an unmarked American-ness in the literature, an American-ness that is often not connected to larger global histories of violence within which the United States is implicated. Radway's (1999) presidential address, "What's in a Name?" and Desmond and Dominguez (1996), among others, are noteworthy here. Although these are clearly important and much needed moves, what also needs to be explicitly emphasized is the imposing American-ness that even informs our professional, collegial, and social relations with each other, and especially with international scholars.

[11]McRobbie's (1996) discussion of interethnic friendship is one of the few works that I am aware of that moves in this direction. Although McRobbie does not focus explicitly on transnational friendship (which has a different complexity than merely interethnic friendship), the move made in this piece is significant for recognizing friendship as an important area of work that needs greater theorization.

thinking through of what such maps of negotiations and friendship might look like.

> Dear ex-friend
> I am saddened by the fact that we simply couldn't agree ...
> ... I was too suave and talkative
> you were plain rude ... for my chilango taste
> I called you "gringo" de carino
> You called me "minority" twice
> We didn't mean it of course
> But we were somehow damned by history (Gomez-Pena, 1996, pp. 161–164)

Additionally, we must be willing to look actively for those interruptions, those untranslatabilities of being and becoming (intellectual and bodily), instead of just slotting them into some fixed U.S.-centric framework of multiculturalism and gender difference or relating to them in a patronizing manner as something that has to be "fixed" and brought into our recognizable (U.S.) maps of civility, communication, and community. Worse still would be comparing one immigrant with another and wondering why X is not more like Y (where X may offer a more recognizable and safer point of identification whether because of X's deliberate assimilation or simply her or his geographical and cultural proximity, or in some cases even the length of time spent in the West). Comparing immigrants with each other (often to rank them in some map of hierarchy or identification) erases the localities that inform the production selves in globality, including historical localities within a particular nation.

My own country, India, for instance, has numerous divergent cultures, each with many histories of struggles—beyond British colonialism—against the numerous conquests that the nation has historically undergone for several thousand years. These cultures each have their own particular traditions, histories of resistance, and differences in language. As a Bengali, from Bengal, I have been produced by a culture that—especially after the British partitioned Bengal into two states (and later two countries around the time of independence in 1947)—never had much economic power (in comparison to the rest of India). However, Bengal has always burst with passionate intellectual energy—that has also significantly included women (given its strong roots in leftist and Marxist politics). One finds this in arts, theater (especially street theater), poetry, fiction, academy (producing Nobel Laureates such as poet Rabindranath Tagore and the economist Amartya Sen, among others), cinema (in the works of Mrinal Sen, Satyajit Ray, and Aparna Sen), and in the long history of intellectual revolutionaries and intellectual insurgency (e.g., the Naxalite movement of the 1970s).

The now cliched, and admittedly inflated, phrase "what Bengal thinks today, India thinks tomorrow"—that became popular during the nationalist revolution against the British, and the corresponding image of the "Bong intellectual"—has been a signature through which Bengal has often been positioned in the Indian imagination. Irrespective of whether this signature is still relevant (especially under the logic of economic liberalization and the invasion of multinationals), my point is that it is a culture that is significantly different from some North Indian cultures—including in gender politics and some of its historical relations with the British (given that Bengali revolutionaries were often excluded from the National Congress party). Thus, when I am sometimes asked in the United States why other Indian women may not always share my views on things, I am tired of constantly having to explain that many third-world nations have often internally been forged through local histories of numerous and often divergent struggles and politics. These histories, although certainly situated within the nation, may also position us divergently on maps of colonial histories. In histories of decolonization, the map is never fixed; it always goes through multiple changes and is forged through multiple conflicts. At a basic level, all this minimally has to do with dignity—human dignity, cultural dignity, the indignities of our divergent histories as third-world people, the dignity of being, of belonging, of not having to constantly explain oneself and the multiple violences through which one's national and local histories have been constituted, especially to people in the United States who too often ignore the geopolitical privileges that inform their everyday interactions with international people of color, in relation to past and present histories of colonialism.

Second, what must also be recognized is that given that international and postcolonial women of color are often historical products of diverse modernities (and thus cannot be reduced to a single history and geography), this production brings multiple interruptions into U.S.-based narratives of multiculturalism and gender. Because of the politics of decolonization that occurred in the third world since World War II, many third-world populations have often geographically routed and rerouted themselves in multiple ways in the process of negotiating decolonization and later globalization. For instance, South Asian populations often have multiple histories—given that the South Asian diaspora, especially under globalization, has been so widely dispersed in different parts of the world. I spent most of my formative years in India, but I also spent parts of my formative time in the Middle East (in Oman, a small powerful, moderate, nation where my parents worked for several years).

These trajectories that have had significant impact on my own sense as a postcolonial individual (at a fairly young age when I did not really have the tools to understand) constantly force me to rethink belonging in globality and make it impossible for me to entertain any homogeneous notions of community. Although we might be shaped by multiple modernities in postcoloniality, they do not shape us in equal ways. In offering this personal example, I am not positing a celebration of hybridity as the answer as has often been the trend in cultural studies work. Rather, I am calling attention to the jostlings and gratings of global incommensurabilities in postcoloniality.

All this is to say that the reality of a postcolonial, international, non-U.S. national, woman of color in the United States or the West may have been produced at the intersection of multiple (and often colliding) transnational gender scripts that may make it impossible for her to relate to maps of patriarchy that are just theorized through an attention to a single modernity or a single national time.[12] As South Asian female fiction writer Vijay Lakshmi (2004) states in an interview in *Little India*—an important online magazine for South Asians in the United States, it is "harder for women if only because they are supposed to be the keepers of their culture on the one hand, and on the other they must keep in step with the new culture. It's the paradoxical nature of adjustments required of them that makes it difficult for women."[13]

Postcolonial women of color in the academy and in the larger intellectual community have cogently begun writing about such issues, including pointing to generational, class, and local differences of gender politics among immigrant women. Works of writers and intellectuals such as Meena Alexander, Chitra Divakaruni, Vijay Lakshmi, Jhumpa Lahiri, Himani Bannjeri, Rajni Srikanth, as well as the rich emerging South Asian popular films in the United States such as *American Chai, Green Card Fever, Desi, ABCD, Flavors, Leela, Wings of Hope, Monsoon Wedding,* and *Friend,* among others, have also begun touching on such issues. Often, the goal of this emerging popular culture is to draw attention to the various postcolonial incommensurabilities that South Asians experience in the United States.

Frequently, the focus of the films is on the tensions, complexities, and emotional challenges that South Asian women face when they have to ne-

---

[12]An important essay that illustrates such gendered collisions and collusions of cultural scripts is Bhattacharjee (1997).

[13]See www.littleindia.com/february2004/InterviewVijay.htm.

gotiate the often widely different scripts of romance, sexuality, and intimacy of the dominant U.S. culture in relation to their own cultural frameworks (e.g., in relationships with American men who are sometimes represented as simply not understanding their cultural scripts, or operating from divergent assumptions about the terms of an intimate relationship). Consequently, such films, by raising issues of geopolitical inequities, sometimes show these transnational relationships as being unsuccessful—a representation that although correct in pointing to the frequent incommensurabilities and tensions of transnational intimacy, remain problematic, at another level, for implicitly slipping back into the logics of cultural absolutism and comfort zones of cultural homogeneity.

This leads me to my final argument regarding the destabilization of scripts of sex and sexuality, longing and desire, and intimacy and love in the context of globalization. In an excellent study on sex and globalization, Altman (2001) asserts that, increasingly, sex and sexuality "become a terrain on which are fought out bitter disputes around the impact of global capital and ideas" (p. 1). Indeed, it could be argued that globalization is increasingly resulting in a situation in which the very battle over modernity is being fought on the terrain of sex and sexuality. What are the bounds and scripts of sex and desire that make up the modern and civil sexual subject when modernity today is visibly multiple and heterogeneous and resides across different times and spaces, while also traversing them? This is an important point of interrogation given that scripts of intimacy in the Western imagination are so tied to assumptions about morality, freedom, the modern (vs. tradition), civility, autonomy, transparency, and the self.[14]

What do we do in situations of global contradictions in which the relations and understandings of gender and sexual identity, sexual scripts, narratives of intimacy, sexual sociality, verbal and nonverbal behaviors (e.g., sexual cues, signs of desire), and their gender codings that script our bodies and behavior get caught in webs of global excess where meaning exceeds and interrupts our available North American scripts of sexual difference? For instance, what could be seen as a sign or cue of heterosexual interest, or an acceptable script of romance and intimacy, according to U.S. standards, might signify something quite different, or even inappropriate and uncivil, in meaning systems of civility in another national culture. Such considerations require us to rethink nation-centered scripts and ideologies of intimacy, and rethink desire and love itself in the context of geopolitics, diverse modernities, and colliding national cultures.

---

[14]See Alexander (1997) and Stoler (1995) for powerful illustrations of this point in other contexts.

One noteworthy essay that addresses some of these problematics is Boym's (2000) "On Diasporic Intimacy." The notion of intimacy, explains Boym, "is connected to home," to feelings of safety; it pertains to the "inner-most," "one's deepest nature" (p. 227). She states that for many immigrants and culturally alienated individuals in the United States who bring with them different traditions of social interaction that are often in opposition to the U.S. culture and its facile pop culture psychology of always speaking your desire in plain language, experiences of intimacy with an individual from the dominant culture can bring considerable dread and anxiety. This is because as an immigrant, in such situations, one's sense of "homely" safety becomes further uprooted, given that "you'd have to feel at home to be intimate, 'to say what you mean'" (p. 227).

Gender and class complicate such situations. Situating the artificial bi-naries of the private and the public against geopolitical realities and diverse global modernities, Boym theorizes the possibility of diasporic intimacy as an alternative and interruptive framework for reimagining transnational inti-macies in the United States, in opposition to the dominant U.S. scripts of in-timacy, which often emphasize overt directness, transparency of the self, and individualism:

> [Diasporic intimacy] is spoken in a foreign language that may often reveal the inadequacies of translation. Diasporic intimacy does not promise an un-mediated emotional fusion but only a precarious affection—no less deep, while aware of its transience. In contrast to utopian images of intimacy as transparency, authenticity, and ultimate belonging, diasporic intimacy is dystopian by definition; it is rooted in the suspicion of a single home .... It is haunted by images of home and homeland, yet it also discloses some of the furtive pleasures of exile. (pp. 227–228)

I want to be clear again that in arguing for the importance of recognizing divergent (and colliding) scripts of intimacy and the ways in which they re-main linked to feelings of transnational safety, memory, home, and home-land, I am not arguing for relativism or global pluralism. Further, I recognize that some sexual scripts—such as the rape of a woman, child marriage, child pornography, or bride burning—universally remain inexcusable, no matter the culture, although their complexities should still be culturally situated. I hope that it is clear, in light of the larger argument of this chapter, that I am suggesting that we recognize the unequal global and international power re-lations through which colliding scripts of desire operate—some of which enter our terms of recognition, whereas others simply fall out of them, or never quite enter them. These are important issues that need to be unpacked. The negotiation of such issues in globality is central to the possibility of imagining, however difficult, not just (nationally contained) interracial relationships but tenuous and precarious transnational relationships across diverse and colliding times and spaces, and the continuously unfolding relations of globality. It is important that we situate desire not merely in the context of a national body politics, but in light of a messy, unequal, and colliding transnational body politics.

CONCLUSION

The modest discussion I have offered in this chapter seeks to clarify how multiculturalism and diversity today may be best engaged not just from the perspective of national translatabilities, but global untranslatabilities; not just from the perspective of borders coming together, but borders (temporal and spatial) colliding and interrupting each other. We need to focus not just on the diversity that we can translate, but on the otherness, the alterity, that defies and exceeds our nation-centered paradigms of translation. For it is in that defiance that we can perhaps begin to peer into the various incommensurabilities of globality that move in and out of our national boundaries and, in the process, mock the boundedness of those boundaries.

REFERENCES

Abbas, A., & Erni, J. (2005). *Internationalizing cultural studies: An anthology*. Malden, MA: Blackwell.
Afzal-Khan, F., & Seshadri Crooks, K. (Eds.) (2000). *The pre-occupation of postcolonial studies*. Durham, NC: Duke University Press.
Alexander, J. (1997). Erotic autonomy as a politics of decolonization. In J. Alexander & C. Mohanty (Eds.), *Feminist genealogies, colonial legacies, and democratic futures* (pp. 63–100). New York: Routledge
Altman, D. (2001). *Global sex*. Chicago: University of Chicago Press.
Barlow, T. (1997). Introduction: On "colonial modernity." In T. Barlow (Ed.), *Formations of colonial modernity* (pp. 1–20). Durham, NC: Duke University Press.
Bhattacharjee, A. (1997). The public/private mirage. In J. Alexander & C. Mohanty (Eds.), *Feminist genealogies, colonial legacies and democratic futures* (pp. 308–329). New York: Routledge.
Boym, S. (2000). On diasporic intimacy. In L. Berlant (Ed.), *Intimacy* (pp. 226–252). Chicago: University of Chicago Press.
Chakraborty, D. (2000). *Provincializing Europe*. Princeton, NJ: Princeton University Press.
Curtin, M. (2003). Media capital: Towards the study of spatial flows. *International Journal of Cultural Studies, 6*, 203–229.
Das, G. (2003, September 7). Cyber-coolies or cyber sahibs. *Times of India*. Retrieved August 1, 2004, from http://timesofindia.indiatimes.com/articleshow/169677.cms
Derrida, J. (1997). *Politics of friendship*. New York: Verso.

Desmond, J., & Dominguez, V. (1996). Resituating American studies in a critical internationalism. *American Quarterly, 48,* 475–490.

Drzewiecka, J., & Halualani, R. (2002). The structural–cultural dialectic of diasporic politics. *Communication Theory, 12,* 340–366.

Dube, S. (2002a). Introduction: Colonialism, modernity, and colonial discourse. *Nepantla, 3,* 197–220.

Dube, S. (2002b). Mapping oppositions: Enchanted spaces and modern places. *Nepantla, 3,* 333–350.

Durham, M. (2004). Constructing the "new ethnicities": Media, sexuality, and diaspora in the lives of South Asian immigrant girls. *Critical Studies in Media Communication, 21,* 140–161.

Gandhi, L. (1998). *Postcolonial theory: A critical introduction.* New York: Columbia University Press.

Gaonkar, D. (1999) Alternative modernities. *Public Culture, 27,* 1–19.

Gaonkar, D. (2002). Towards new imaginaries: An introduction. *Public Culture, 14,* 1–21.

Giroux, H. (1994). Living dangerously: Identity politics and the new cultural racism. In H. Giroux & P.McLaren (Eds.), *Between borders: Pedagogy and the politics of cultural studies* (pp. 29–55). New York: Routledge.

Gomez-Pena, G. (1996). *The new world border.* San Francisco: City Lights.

Grossberg, L. (1993). Cultural studies and/in new worlds. *Critical Studies in Mass Communication, 10,* 1–22.

Grossberg, L. (1994). Bringin' it all back home: Pedagogy and cultural studies. In H. Giroux & P. McLaren (Eds.) *Between borders: Pedagogy and the politics of cultural studies* (pp. 1–25). New York: Routledge.

Grossberg, L. (2002). Postscript. *Communication Theory, 12,* 367–370.

Gupta, A., & Ferguson, J. (1998). Beyond culture: Space, identity and the politics of difference. In A. Gupta & J. Ferguson (Eds.), *Culture, power, place* (pp. 33–51). Durham, NC: Duke University Press.

Hall, S. (1996). When was the post-colonial? Thinking at the limits. In I. Chambers & L. Curti (Eds.), *The postcolonial question: Common skies, divided horizons* (pp. 242–260). New York: Routledge.

Hasian, M. (2002). *Colonial legacies in postcolonial contexts: A critical rhetorical examination of legal histories.* New York: Peter Lang.

Kaplan, C., & Grewal, I. (2002). Transnational practices and interdisciplinary feminist scholarship: Reconfiguring women's and gender studies. In R. Wiegman (Ed.), *Women's studies on its own* (pp. 66–81). Durham, NC: Duke University Press.

Kraidy, M. (1999). The global, local and the hybrid: A native ethnography of globalization. *Critical Studies in Mass Communication, 16,* 456–476.

Kraidy, M. (2002). Hybridity in cultural globalization. *Communication Theory, 12,* 316–339.

Lakshmi, V. (2004, February). Interview with Vijay Lakshmi. *Little India* [online]. Retrieved January 16, 2005 from www.LittleIndia.com/february2004/interview.htm

Lee, B. (1995). Critical internationalism. *Public Culture, 7*(3):559–592.

Lee, W. S. (1998). Patriotic breeders or colonized converts? A postcolonial feminist approach to antifootbinding discourse. In D. Tanno & A. Gonzalez (Eds.), *Communication and identity across cultures* (pp. 11–33). Thousand Oaks, CA: Sage.

Madison, S. (2005). *Critical ethnography: Media, ethics, performance.* Oakland, CA: Sage.

Malek, A., & Kavoori, A. (2000). *The global dynamics of news.* Stamford, CT: Ablex.

Marable, M. (2003). Racism in a time of terror. In S. Aronotwitz & H. Gautney (Eds.), *Implicating empire: Globalization and resistance in the 21st century world order* (pp. 3–14). New York: Basic Books.

McRobbie, A. (1996). Different, youthful, subjectivities. In I. Chambers & L. Curti (Eds.), *The postcolonial question* (pp. 30–46). New York: Routledge.

Miller, T., Govil, N., & McMurria, J. (2001). *Global Hollywood*. London: British Film Institute.

Mohanty, C. (2003). *Feminism without borders*. Durham, NC: Duke University Press.

Mongia, R. (1999). Race, nationality, mobility: A history of the passport. *Public Culture, 11*(3), 527–556.

Moore-Gilbert, B. (1997). *Postcolonial theory: Contexts, practices, politics*. New York: Verso.

Moreiras, A. (2001). *The exhaustion of difference*. Durham, NC: Duke University Press.

Parameswaran, R. (2001). Global media events in India: Contests over beauty, gender, and nation. *Journalism & Communication Monographs, 3*, 53–105.

Parameswaran, R. (2002). Local culture in global media. *Communication Theory, 12*, 287–315.

Parameswaran, R. (2004). Global queens, national celebrities. *Critical Studies in Media Communication, 21*, 346–370.

Parks, L., & Kumar, S. (2002). *Planet TV: A global television reader*. New York: New York University Press.

Radway, J. (1999). What's in a name? Presidential address to the American Studies Association, 20 November 1998. *American Quarterly, 51*, 1–32.

Rajagopal, A. (2000). *Politics after television: Hindu nationalism and the reshaping of the Indian public*. Cambridge, UK: Cambridge University Press.

Romero, L. (1997). Nationalism and internationalism: Domestic differences in a postcolonial world. In D. Kellner & A. Cvetkovich (Eds.), *Articulating the global and the local* (pp. 244–249). Boulder, CO: Westview.

Seshadri-Crooks, K. (2000). At the margins of postcolonial studies. In K. Cooks & F. Khan (Eds.), *The preoccupation of postcolonial studies* (pp. 3–23). Durham, NC: Duke University Press.

Shome, R. (1996). Postcolonial interventions in the rhetorical canon: An "other" view. *Communication Theory, 6*, 40–59.

Shome, R. (1998). Caught in the term 'postcolonial:' Why the 'postcolonial' still matters. *Critical Studies in Mass Communication, 15*, 203–212.

Shome, R., & Hegde, R. (2002a). Culture, communication and the challenge of globalization. *Critical Studies in Media Communication, 17*, 172–189.

Shome, R., & Hegde, R. (2002b). Postcolonial approaches to communication. *Communication Theory, 12*, 249–270.

Spivak, G. (1988). Can the subaltern speak? In L. Grossberg & C. Nelson (Eds.), *Marxism and the interpretation of culture* (pp. 271–313). Urbana: University of Illinois Press.

Stoler, A. (1995). *Race and the education of desire: Foucault's history of sexuality and the colonial order of things*. Durham, NC: Duke University Press.

Supriya, K. E. (2002). *Shame and recovery: Mapping identity in an Asian women's shelter*. New York: Peter Lang.

Supriya, K. E. (2004). *Remembering empire: Power, memory and place in postcolonial India*. New York: Peter Lang.

Valdivia, A. (Ed.). (1995). *Feminism, multiculturalism and the media: Global diversities*. Thousand Oaks, CA: Sage.

Wiegman, R. (2002). On location: An Introduction. In R. Wiegman (Ed.), *Women's studies on its own*, (pp. 1–44). Durham: Duke University Press.

Wiley, S. (2004). Rethinking nationality in the context of globalization. *Communication Theory, 14*, 78–86.

Zacharias, U. (2003). The smile of Mona Lisa: Postcolonial desires, nationalist families, and the birth of consumer television in India. *Critical Studies in Media Communication, 20*, 388–406.

7

A Knife of Fire: Social Justice, *Real Politick,* and "Foreign" Policy in a New World

Philip C. Wander
San Jose State University

We have, as a nation, lost sight of the great issue, the one most difficult to think through, talk about, and act on, involving the continuity of life on the planet. With this claim I make three assumptions:

1. The problem of continuity is global, a problem facing not only us but also the whole of humanity now and in the foreseeable future.
2. This problem grows out of the "miracles" of science in creating powerful, modern, military weapons.
3. The world of nation-states, as things now stand, cannot do much more than make the problem worse.

In addition, my argument presupposes a moral absolute, namely, that preventing the extermination of life on earth is a right, proper, and good thing to do. Obvious, I suppose. Maybe it does not need to be spelled out; in truth, I cannot conceive of it being objectionable, but I can imagine it being ignored, covered up, or given little weight in understanding the controversies of the day. This shows up in the silences of our public discourse and in the history of our foreign policies over the past half-century, which, far from

ensuring peaceful relations between and among nation-states, includes a
host of incursions and outright invasions (Zinn, 2003).

This chapter is divided into three parts. Part 1 offers my observation that
the erasure of the golden rule characterizes our polarized treatment of the
"foreign" in U.S. public discourse. Part 2 elaborates on the two meanings of
knife of fire in relation to 9/11 and the increase of global disaster because of
the U.S. doctrine of preemptive war. Part 3 argues for global well-being,
Ghaia, as a just and necessary principle to guide current and future U.S. foreign policies.

PART 1: U.S. PUBLIC DISCOURSE ABOUT THE FOREIGN IGNORES THE GOLDEN RULE

Public discourse surrounding foreign affairs is confusing, not only when politicians talk about the "foreign," but also when news broadcasters and commentators, administration critics, and even college professors discuss it.
Underlying some of this confusion is a simple distinction between the words
country and *nation*. They are often used interchangeably, becoming two
ways of saying the same thing. Yet there are distinctions that might help us
to understand why both words survive in common and in official usage.

Countries mark off their boundaries geographically. They have borders.
They lay claim to land within these borders, water inside and rubbing up
against these borders, and the skies overhead. Countries may be called
homelands, fatherlands, or motherlands. This is powerful stuff. I think of my
father and mother and do not want their memories to be desecrated; I feel I
owe them reverence. Without them, I would be nothing. Nor would I want
their land, our family home, overrun by enemies, foreigners, or thieves.
Countries often inspire songs, in which they are celebrated for the color of
their skies, fruitfulness of their plains, majesty of their mountains, and the
length and beauty of their rivers and lakes. These songs also affirm national
ideals, which can make them critical texts (Branhan, 1996). What makes
them so powerful is that we are nostalgic about the lands of our birth, often
irrationally so (Swartz, 2004), at least from the standpoint of the individual,
taken in isolation and freed from unexamined allegiances. However, from
the standpoint of the citizen, whose self-definition is bound up with home
and country, it is not only rational: It can be counted on during periods of
crisis.

Nations differ from countries. Some countries are nations (France is a
nation; America is a nation; China is a nation) and other countries are not
(Algeria is a country; Iraq is a country; Tibet is a country). It would be odd,

because of their size and their relative powerlessness, to call Algeria and Iraq nations. We would never say, for example, the nation of Guatemala, El Salvador, Nicaragua, or Cambodia. Citizens of these countries might refer to themselves this way, but for citizens of the United States, speaking in English, this would be an odd locution, in part because of unspoken assumptions about the hierarchical differences between nations and countries, one being natural and another inferior or nonthreatening.

Nations reach beyond the borders separating one country from another. Nations sometimes make colonies out of countries. At other times, they claim spheres of influence, joining together several countries into an area where their agents—secret service, military personnel, native collaborators, and such—are allowed to "assist" native populations. In the 19th century, nations, so the story goes, brought Christianity and civilization to "savage" peoples and "primitive" countries. In the 20th and 21st centuries, nations bring progress, freedom, and democracy to "backward" peoples and "underdeveloped" countries. Any country that does not aspire to our natural values and standard of living is backward and underdeveloped, in need of our help whether they want it or not, Iraq being the current beneficiary of our benevolence.

Countries seem fixed, but frozen and remote, whereas nations are dynamic, in motion, expanding and contracting. They "feed," in Owen and Ehrenhaus's (1993) sense, "upon those less well positioned in the world, and its perpetuation requires domination over those both within its boundaries and without" (p. 170). China is currently expanding; the United States, like her British ally, is economically contracting and militarily expanding, finding rough going in the Middle East. How rough it is too murky to tell, although I think the long-term implications of our actions are alarming. "We" cheer when our nation expands, finding in it evidence of our virtue and of God's approval. "We" despair when our nation contracts and begin looking about for evidence of foreign intrigue and foul play.

Nations and countries are also alike. Each draws a sharp distinction between domestic and foreign. Domestic affairs have to do with "us." They take place at home, inside our political unit. Foreign affairs have to do with "them." They take place abroad, outside our political unit. This, of course, is not entirely true. People on the inside sometimes find themselves on the outside, having become, with a change in the political wind, a foreign element. People outside sometimes find themselves on the inside, as with "colonials" who, by fiat, and, again, beneficence, of the former colonial powers, become citizens. A similar pattern can be seen with peoples brought in by force (slaves) or allowed to enter voluntarily (immigrants) to work on farms, in mines, factories, laundries, restaurants, and most recently high-tech companies. We blink and call this progress. During economic reversals, sometimes, we blink and call it an "invasion." Foreign peoples on the inside may or may not be citizens. Citizenship requires proper documentation. Even if foreigners manage to become citizens, they may, in moments of crisis, face laws passed with them in mind. Countries and nations are not above creating second-class citizens. Like foreign, second-class citizen means "other than." There is an unspoken "we" marking off a "them" who is other than "us." In our schools, we learn who "we" and who "they" are. If "they" go to our schools, read our books, and watch our movies and television, and play our video games, "they" also learn who they are. To students of rhetoric, this should sound all too familiar. It is called persuasion. Students of sociology, focusing on the creation of hierarchies, call it socialization.

If they are subject to "us," as with aborigines, slaves, or other kinds of second-class citizens, they may be required to perform what we know to be true about them. Abolitionist Wendell Philips once remarked that those who supported slavery accused slaves of being illiterate and made it a capital crime to teach them to read and write. Power is as power does. Thus, we and they come to know our place in the world and understand why we are who we are (educated, literate, filled with prospects) and why they are who they are (uneducated, illiterate, and fit only to be slaves, peasants, laborers, cannon fodder, or more recently the underclass).

Over time, "we" become skilled at identifying the mental, physical, esthetic, social, cultural, economic, political, ethical, and moral differences separating "us" from "them" and making them inferior. Our dialect, our standards become the norm. If such knowledge does not, in fact, keep us apart, if the veils begin to fall away, we may enact laws with the aim of keeping us apart or outlawing miscegenation between the races. In moments of crisis, we may reduce them to an "it," an object to be handled in any way we see fit. In such moments, we may wind up treating it in ways that would be monstrous were someone to do the same thing to us. Power is as power does.

Here, we reach an impasse; that is, if we dare to ask the question, For what do we stand? Because this question plunges us into questions about ethics and morality, we may avoid confusion here by refusing to ask ourselves what we stand for. Or we may get by asserting complete control over "them" and "it." Essentialism plays an important role here, and we may become trapped in our own language: "We are who we are. They are who they are. It is what it is. End of story." But what do we do when it becomes they and they begin to remind us of us? Or, at least, of something like us? Once again moral questions resurface.

Suppose I said "It made us do monstrous things!" Or, suppose I took some moral responsibility and said: "Yes, we did do monstrous things." In either case, whatever our motives, the act was admittedly monstrous—gassing, starving, bombing, raping, and so on. There is one sure-fire test for detecting an immoral or monstrous act: We would not let anyone do this to us and, this being the case, we should not do this to anyone else. Suddenly, we find ourselves at one with often ignored ancient moral teachings—the golden rule or variants of it: Do unto others what you would have others do unto you. Reversed, this is do not do unto others what you do not want others to do unto you. Love thy neighbor! Welcome strangers! The golden rule is found in many languages. When performed, the way of life it envisions makes love possible in this world. This principle stands at the heart of civility and, in a larger sense, civilization. The imperative transcends countries and nations, devastates distinctions between foreign and domestic, and obliterates lines drawn between "us" and "them." Such basic principles even children understand. Why do we, then, as adults, forget them? For my purpose in this chapter, the golden rule, the one that enjoins reciprocity, offers a basis for evaluating foreign policy in an anarchical world of nation-states. With this in mind, I now turn to 9/11 and evaluate the Bush Doctrine currently dominating U.S. foreign policy.

PART 2: FROM THE HORROR OF 9/11 TO TOTALIZING THE EVIL OTHER—BUSH'S PREEMPTIVE DOCTRINE

On September 11, 2001, a small number of people, mostly young and well-educated men from Saudi Arabia, hijacked four commercial airliners and crashed them into buildings in New York and Washington, DC, and a field in Pennsylvania. Shortly thereafter we were invading two countries. Our government, our public servants, 4 years later, have not offered any evidence proving that the governments of these two countries played any role in the 9/11 atrocities. What we do know is that the people who led Afghanistan and Iraq had been on the payroll of our Central Intelligence Agency; that the United States had armed, trained, and sent the Taliban into battle against the old Soviet Union; and, in the case of Iraq, that the United States had armed, trained, and encouraged Saddam Hussein to send Iraqi forces into battle against Iran, a country whose revolution in 1979 removed a brutal dictator that we had installed (Bunker, 2005).

Our public servants swore that Iraq had acquired all manner of weapons of mass destruction (WMD), that its leader was aiming them at us, and that he was on the verge of acquiring nuclear weapons. After the invasion and after an exhaustive search by U.S. experts, we did not find anything of the sort. No WMD, nuclear or biological, and no evidence that Iraq was acquiring yellowcake uranium or building nuclear weapons. With much fanfare we "won" the war in weeks, but we still, almost 3 years later, have troops under attack with a mounting death toll, including tens of thousands of Iraqi civilians, men, women, and children.

I think that U.S. foreign policy in the post-9/11 era, has not decreased but has actually increased the likelihood of global disaster, through the use of more powerful, modern weapons and through the newly articulated preemptive war doctrine of the Bush administration (Halper & Clarke, 2004). From a global standpoint, things are worse or potentially worse now than they ever were during the wars in Vietnam, Laos, and Cambodia. I write this as a veteran of the peace movement of the 1960s and 1970s. I do not think this way because our politicians are ignorant or stupid—in most cases they are neither. Making jokes about the president's verbal slippages is a diversion. Our foreign policy has taken a turn for the worse because 9/11 not only disabled the golden rule but also lent credence to preemption as the best way of solving foreign problems.

Preemption increases the potential magnitude of global disasters because evidence of aggression is replaced by our reading or sizing up a foreigner's intentions. Although evidence or proof cannot reduce uncertainty or risk completely, the reading of intentions, especially with an overwhelming presumption of evil in others, easily justifies ruthless, unprincipled use of weapons, big or small, conventional or nuclear. If all nations and tribes endorsed the preemptive doctrine, local communities and the world would be reduced to savage lawlessness. Such is social regression at its finest.

This administration's solution to 9/11, although familiar enough in U.S. history, is not uniquely American. Yuval Steinitz, a member of Prime Minister Ariel Sharon's Likud Party in Israel, and a parliamentary leader on security issues, has given a most succinct and memorable statement of the preemptive militarism I am critiquing in this chapter. Steinitz, speaking about the problem of terrorism facing Israel, said, "I'm confident that there is a military solution, and by brute force we can completely, or almost completely, eradicate terrorism" (quoted in Bennet, 2002, p. A3). Although I do not know Steinitz, nor am I an expert in the political and military context inspiring either his confidence or his decision to make a public declaration, I am troubled by his attitude—what is, in effect, our attitude.

I should tread carefully here. Much of the context and most of the relevant facts in the Palestinian–Israeli conflict depend on one's ability to speak and read Hebrew and Arabic. This is reason enough for me to remain cautious in my response. At the same time, what has shown up on my television and in my daily newspaper about Israel's predicament in the 3 years since Steinitz affirmed his faith in a military solution and brute force? A stream of stories about attacks and retaliations, suicide bombings and martyrdom operations, and ongoing human misery among Israelis and Palestinians alike (the disproportionate weight of this suffering, it is true, falls on the Palestinians).

Sadly, the position in which Steinitz and his government found itself was anticipated early in Israel's history and its implications were ignored. The founders of Israel had a choice in the mid-1940s between a monocultural and a bicultural state. The first, advocated by hard-line Zionists, was a state dominated by Jews dependent on the Great Powers for their safety. The second, advocated by Humanist Zionists, was a state in which Arab and Jew lived side by side and no one was a second-class citizen.

The Humanist Zionists at the time included Martin Buber, Albert Einstein, and a young Hannah Arendt. The leading figure, however, was Judah Magnes, an American rabbi and founder of the Hebrew University. Magnes wrote at the time about the bitter hatred being created by a zealous and self-righteous Zionism bent on domination. In a letter to a friend, written in 1947, Magnes summed up his despair: "Here is this magnificent work of upbuilding going on; old and young giving of their best strength and producing fine results, and all of this threatened by this moral decay on the one hand, and by the hatred we are arousing in the neighboring peoples on the other" (Magnes, 1982, p. 448). The United Nations sent for Magnes to broker a deal between Israeli and Palestinian leaders that would stave off a war between Israel and its neighbors. Magnes was the one figure who knew and enjoyed the trust of leaders in both camps. Although seriously ill, Magnes flew to New York where, with the help of his private secretary, Hannah Arendt, he did his best. He died trying to create a different future.

Whatever it does or does not tell us about the problems currently facing Israel, Steinitz's remark has one great merit: It gives voice to several assumptions underlying the rhetoric, if not the reality, of U.S. foreign policy. The United States, befitting its superpower status, is committed to military solutions to political problems. The Bush Doctrine laid out a few years ago in a 33-page document entitled the "National Security Strategy of the United States" declares that the United States would not hesitate to act alone and "pre-emptively" to thwart dangers from hostile states or terrorist groups armed with, or seeking, nuclear, biological or chemical weapons (Miller, 2002). The mere impression of such status, as in the case of Iraq, could trigger an attack by the United States against the wishes of the world community. The doctrine implies that because the United States is the world's greatest military power it is morally right—not merely self-serving—in dissuading "potential adversaries from pursuing a military buildup in hopes of surpassing, or equaling" our power (Miller, 2002, p. A19).

"The most surprising thing about the push for war [against Iraq]," writes Anatol Lieven, Senior Fellow at the Carnegie Endowment for Peace, was that it was so profoundly reckless. Lieven (2002) argued that the consequences of success or failure could likely be catastrophic: "A general Middle Eastern conflagration and the collapse of more pro-Western Arab states would lose us the war against terrorism, doom untold thousands of Western civilians to death in coming decades, and plunge the world economy into depression" (p. 8). This is, admittedly, a grim scenario; whether it pans out is beside the point—Lieven argued—correctly I believe—that the issue of Iraq had little to do with Saddam Hussian's tyranny and everything to do with the United States achieving its political goals. This made the gamble all the greater, because the Bush Doctrine envisions struggles—including nuclear war—against all rivals, including Iran, Syria, Cuba, China, and North Korea, to name only a few. If this is not an example of reckless arrogance, then I do not know what is (place the emphasis on reckless, though, because the doctrine of preemption places the lives of tens of millions, if not the future of life on the planet, at risk).

Just After 9/11, Who Supported or at Least Did Not Oppose the Invasion of Afghanistan?

Like perhaps many others in academia, I did not think to oppose the invasion of Afghanistan, at least not openly. Part of this was fear of reprisals from students, faculty, and administration, but only a part. Mostly, it was because of the events of 9/11 themselves. They were for me and, I suspect, many others, what Sharfstein (1980) has called an *axiomatic experience,* an experience that is so powerful, striking so deep, that it produces a new way of thinking that took time for me to digest. It could be called a metaphysical assumption but, in Sharfstein's view, "assumption" is too detached and impersonal for what he is describing. What he is pointing to is an experience that strikes so deep that it fuses thinking and feeling, reason and emotion, creating a unified sense of what now is and is not real, substantial, and important, providing an experiential foundation firm enough to serve as a basis for a new kind of reasoning. Such moments invite contemplation, which is something we scholars are particularly good at doing.

During 9/11, on the day and for days afterward, I found myself, as if in a dream, constantly referring back to the event, drawing insight from it, trying to understand it in relation to myself, as a citizen and a moral being. I also tried to understand it in terms of our collective future as a people; not as an academic project or as an effort to work out an intellectual puzzle, but to understand myself, my fellows, my people, my world in a way that would, in light of the great issue of human and planetary survival, make sense.

Knife of Fire: In the Now

The title of this chapter recalls the line of exploding fuel that burst into and out of the other side of the World Trade Center buildings in New York City. The explosion followed the shattered, titanium shells of the two planes as they cut through glass skin and boiled out the other side. I watched these images over and over, unable to take my eyes off the screen. During the days that followed, I began reading the *New York Times*. I renewed my subscription, which had lapsed for about 2 years, in the belief that, given its location, the *Times* would have an institutional stake and, in relation to its reporters and columnists, a personal stake in what was being printed.

I was not disappointed. Most moving in the *Times*, over the months that followed 9/11, were the photographs of those who perished in the collapse of the two towers. Day after day, as I looked at these photos and read the appended obituaries, I began to think of the victims not as part of a tragedy, but as people with names, jobs, sorrows, hopes, and loved ones; people who were once in that strangely satisfying moment of frantic calm when things somehow, almost magically, get done; people whose thoughts of death and destruction came, if at all, in the form of fictional Hollywood-esque popular entertainment. I also sensed in these people, apart from the horrible moment of their passing, a world absent not only in the *Times* but also in the whole of corporate media. The quiet realities and more, the poignancy of everyday life—the lives we lead and do not feel the need, even in reflective moments, to talk about, let alone, as academics are prone to do, theorize.

I was not, of course, thinking of theory at the time. The events, the suffering, and the outrage were in the air—immediate and beyond words. I could not in any real sense talk about all this. To talk about it in the here and now of 9/11 would include sounds and words calculated to refer to other than what was happening. The effort to put all that was happening into a stream of words was absurd, a project doomed by all that I did not know and all that stands beyond the capacity of language to express. Still, beyond the silent, seemingly transparent envelope of my everydayness was another "this" that I was overlooking: a "this" emerging in moments of crisis for people—police, firefighters, medics, doctors, and nurses—whose jobs place them not in a library or classroom or behind a desk but in the middle of things gone horribly wrong. In such contexts, the heroics of ordinary people reveal themselves. By this I mean the unpretentious, mostly ignored heroism of the get-up-and-do-the-job sort of folk; heroism lost in the humdrum; lost for (and probably to) people working in the middle of things; lost in the photo ops, glossed over in the glitter of the news, ads, and entertainment, where healthy, well-dressed, well-spoken actors star and where, in action scenes, well-paid stunt men and women take all the risks, and few get hurt.

What one finds beyond the images in such moments is a living, breathing affirmation of democracy through the capabilities of ordinary people. Beyond a question of rights, one encounters the wisdom of involving folks in decisions affecting their lives and the lives of their children. This discovery shakes up existing notions of power and authority. Because power and authority are rarely erected on democratic principles, government, corporations, churches, and the like are mostly top-down structures rooted in vague and questionable values.

In the midst of the experience of horror on 9/11 and learning about the heroic responses of ordinary people, many of whom perished doing their jobs, I began to grieve. I grieved for my country in a way quite different from the grief I felt during Vietnam, El Salvador, Nicaragua, and other places where the horrors of "our" policies crept out from behind the news. These were places where the ideals I had learned from my father (who had served) and my mother (who had faithfully waited at home for his return from the World War II) crashed into reality. I grieved for my countrymen and women who died and also for those who came from other parts of the world and found themselves in the wrong place at the wrong time. Above all, I grieved for the future.

Knife of Fire: In the Now of the Aftermath

The title of this chapter has another meaning, one that came to me long after placing the title at the top of my first working draft. This meaning grew out of my reflections on the changes 9/11 made in me and in what I once took for granted. This second-level meaning, the now in the aftermath, marks a line dividing the world I once knew from a world of which I am still trying to make sense. This was not a sharply drawn line, at least I could not make it so, but it was no less dangerous for being vague and hard to talk about. It was, I came to discover, a line dividing an Old World of Nations from a New World of Nations.

Since the collapse of the Soviet Union, the threat to the continental United States (in contrast to territories it claims through its "sphere of influence") from another nation has all but vanished in the sense of an attack involving a navy, troops, and airplanes in an effort to seize land and dominate our people. In the Old World, the one I grew up in after World War II, the great nations were pretty much secure from attack, except from other great nations equipped with troops, navies, air forces, and other conventional tools of conquest. This was especially true of the United States, which, since our Civil War, had never fought a battle or had a bomb fall on its soil (if we are willing to set aside the Indian Wars, border crossings during the Mexican Revolution, and few ineffective bomb-bearing balloons launched from Japanese submarines).

The New World given birth by the 9/11 knife of fire is filled with unimaginable and terrifying WMDs and the madness to use them. This is the world in which we, all of us, now find ourselves. This is a world in which even the great powers can be shaken by small bands of people: fanatics, prophets, messiahs, rebels, revolutionaries, insurrectionists, outside agitators, heretics, evildoers, and so on, whatever one cares to label them.

The most striking thing about our New World is that there are no safe havens. If terrorism is worldwide, the assumption is that we must face up to the globalization of evil. If terrorists gain access to powerful military weapons, then we now face the globalization of evil in the here and now dedicated to our destruction. If the object of terrorism is to induce terror (the gist of what the British Prime Minister said recently after the first bombings in London in July 2005), and if "they" succeed, then "we" are not in a position to understand what is happening. All we are left with is the experience of fear and the terrible political consequences of fear.

This effort at sense making is made even more difficult when who they are, what they do, and what we are doing in response in the world of nation-states remains a "state secret." Since 9/11, state secrets have begun to leak and official statements about what is real and what is not have turned out to be outright lies told knowingly to manipulate the public. The selling of the Iraq War, regardless of the facts, protests, or possible long-term consequences, may not be a one-shot affair; the enormously successful public relations campaign to sell this war calls our democratic processes into question. Chaim Kaufmann, a professor of international relations, carefully lays out the case for this concern. First, he describes the theory about how what he calls mature democracies are supposed to work:

Mature democracies such as the United States are generally believed to be better at making foreign policy than other regime types. Especially, the strong civic institutions and robust marketplaces of ideas in mature democracies are thought to substantially protect them from severe threat inflation and the "myths of empire" that could promote excessively risky foreign policy adventures and wars. The marketplace of ideas helps to weed out self-serving foreign policy arguments because their proponents cannot avoid wide-ranging debate in which their reasoning and evidence are subject to public scrutiny. (Kaufmann, 2004, p. 5)

Second, Kaufmann examined the official arguments justifying the invasion of Iraq, including the factual assumptions on which they relied. The problem, he concludes, was not merely that the facts were either manipulated, made up, or just plain wrong; rather, and most chillingly, they went unchallenged. Independent scholars rarely appeared before Congress or on television. Instead, many of the people we heard and the ones who sounded most authoritative were "think tank" employees. Often articulate and even gifted polemicists, most of these folks had done little objective, independent research.

Think tanks, unlike universities in their most ideal sense, depend on wealthy clients who want ideas to serve their interests. Since the 1970s, right-wing think tanks have been a growth industry, producing not only books, articles for think tank journals, and op-ed pieces for newspapers, but also providing well-spoken "experts" for television, whose claim to expertise comes from the fact that they appear on television—what Boorstin (1992) identifies as a form of "pseudo-event." These faux scholars were not independent and, predictably, did little more than echo administration arguments and promote administration policy (for a critique of think tanks and their threat to democracy, see Stefancic & Delgado, 1999).

For Kaufmann, the war in Iraq is one issue. Looming much larger are questions about the failure of our democratic processes to produce public criticism, encourage public debate, and have this debate aired. Our market place of ideas, Kaufmann (2004) concludes,

> failed to fulfill this [critical] function in the 2002–03 U.S. foreign policy debate over going to war with Iraq. By now there is broad agreement among U.S. foreign policy experts, as well as much of the American public and the international community, that the threat assessments that President George W. Bush and his administration used to justify the war against Iraq were greatly exaggerated and on some dimensions wholly baseless. (p. 5)

In the aftermath of 9/11, with a trumped-up war against an oil-rich country whose leader depended for years on economic and military support from the United States, there is reason for concern. When historical facts get lost and, in their place, we are given global evil, there is even more reason for concern. One assumption is that "they"—the terrorists—are psychopaths hyped up on religious fanaticism. They are people who live only to terrify others. Another corresponding assumption is that our job is to follow our leaders, support our troops, and ignore the "chattering classes" whose calls for free and open debate during times of crisis undermines morale.

Apart from official misrepresentations of the facts, the lack of any effective criticism about the way the war in Iraq was sold, and the endless chatter of "experts" on TV paid to push a particular brand of ideology, there is something about "War on Terror" that sounds awfully familiar to my ears. Terrorism, for me and many of the so-called baby boomers, recalls the word *communism* invoked during the Cold War. Like communism, communists, and fellow travelers, terrorism, terrorists, and potential terrorists are all around us, plotting the downfall of Western civilization, determined to destroy our way of life. Because we do not appreciate this threat, we depend on the "wisdom" of our elected officials to save us.

Unlike communism, however, terrorism does not have a well-defined political ideology. This makes it difficult to know what terrorists want in general, why they want it, and why we are being targeted. But this much is clear: Today's terrorists are quite different from past enemies, real or imagined. They do not, as yet, call themselves terrorists and do not, as a political faction, rule any nation-state. Former nonstate groups, prior to 9/11, were named according to their location and ideology (i.e., Peruvian, Colombian, Indonesian, Filipino "revolutionary" groups). After 9/11, they are now called terrorists. This nebulous naming inflates the number of national enemies so much that they, we have been told, operate in 80 countries and that it might take 100 years to win the war against terror.

Everyone—Democrats, Republicans, the President, CNN, Fox, and the *New York Times*—talks about terrorism. Differences between past worldwide enemies—the Axis Powers and the Communist menace—and our present worldwide enemy—terrorism—create practical problems for strategic planners. How can the United States preserve credibility or hope to win a victory if our adversaries and targets are unknown?

[T]he terrorist threat is difficult to deter because the United States so far has proven unable to find high-value targets to hold at risk. In this context how

can nuclear threats be adapted to the terrorists' calculus? Are the conduct
and direction of current conflicts contributing to the erosion of credibility?
(Gabel, 2004–2005, p. 195)

The terrorist threat is not like the Communist threat or the threat of the
Axis Powers. Nuclear threats, a staple during the Cold War, do not work, because we cannot locate "high-value" targets and because terrorists are not
responsible for protecting a country or its people.

Real women and men's heroic acts during and after 9/11 could have provided a fertile ground fostering a just global peace movement that honors
what I discussed earlier as the golden rule. Unfortunately, we did not take
advantage of this opportunity. Thus, we could be working to create a world
where no one is to go through the horrors of 9/11 again. We could be creating a world where everyone can enjoy basic human rights in sustainable
communities. But we took a different route—a war against global evil. The
cornerstone of this war lies in the preemptive war doctrine adopted after
9/11. If we affirm global life and equality, we must challenge, resist, and
replace this doctrine.

PART 3: FROM PREEMPTION TO *GHAIA*—ON A JUST RHETORIC OF U.S. FOREIGN POLICY

Twenty-one years ago, I published an article on the rhetoric of U.S. foreign
policy based on research I had done in the *Department of State Bulletin*
(Wander, 1984). I read everything that government officials in several ad-
ministrations, from Eisenhower, Kennedy, and Johnson, to Nixon, had said
about Vietnam. I wanted to know how they justified U.S. policy. The more I
read, the more I was struck that it had little or nothing to do with the facts of
the situation or what was happening abroad but everything to do with the
struggle for political power at home.

I argued that there were two ways of looking at the world (i.e., paradigms)
underlying official efforts to justify the Vietnam War. One I called *prophetic
dualism.* This mode posited a Manichean struggle between the forces of light
and the forces of darkness or between good and evil, holding that the struggle could only end with the destruction of one side or the other. The second
paradigm I called *technocratic realism.* This mode, which is closely associated
with the philosophy of *real politick,* tried to separate foreign policy from morality and, in particular, the brutal dualities of the Manicheans. Foreign policy was too complicated for moralizing; what it required was expertise,
people trained in the nuts and bolts of foreign affairs—the languages, areas,

cultures, and history of a region, and people willing and able to evaluate policies based on U.S. national interests, however defined.

There were reasons I resisted turning these paradigms into rival or mutually exclusive categories. First, they were big, leaky things. Second, these strategies could be and were often intentionally fused. Third, the practical application of these paradigms is always in flux, because they are useful not only in talking about foreign affairs, but also in reaching domestic constituencies cultivated by the two major political parties in the United States.

Prophetic dualism was favored by the Eisenhower administration. Eisenhower's Secretary of State, John Foster Dulles, frequently invoked God and talked about what he and others derided and exploited for political gain as "godless communism." An important domestic constituency of the Republican Party lay in Christian fundamentalists, Protestant mostly, but also Catholic, in the South and the Midwest. Official arguments spoke directly, although not exclusively, to the Republican base. Dulles noted the appeal to expertise but dismissed the principle he found in technocratic realism, calling it "calculated expediency." Dulles was the son of missionaries. Although he practiced "brinkmanship," threatening atomic war against the Soviet Union, he believed that foreign policy should never lose sight of moral principles that lay at the foundation of our civilization. He believed, along with the Republican Party, that political consensus in the United States and in the world had to be based on such principles—namely, freedom, democracy, and faith in God (presumably, atomic war does not violate any of these principles).

Technocratic realism, on the other hand, was favored by Presidents Kennedy and Johnson, who based their arguments on real-world complexities, expertise, and a practical, hardheaded look at our national interest. Kennedy looked at the Manichean element in foreign policy rhetoric and found it chilling, the sort of thing that, when the Russians used the same kind of rhetoric, reversing who was good and who was evil, made them sound paranoid to our ears. The Democratic constituency included university-educated, mobile, well-to-do people living in metropolitan areas, liberal Catholics and Protestants, members of labor unions, immigrants, and rural populists. It also included and counted on peoples brought together by the Civil Rights movement who, although often quite religious, put little faith in Protestant fundamentalism. The Civil Rights movement, it must be remembered, grew out of and had its base in Black Baptist churches. So, although technocratic realism might dismiss as foolish and dangerous an effort to understand foreign policy through a cosmic struggle between good and evil, there were other, less simplistic, and more inspiring ways to frame moral issues.

When Vietnam began to overwhelm and divide the country, during the Johnson administration, the official justification of the war began to change. The two paradigms were fused into one. God, morality, national interest, and signs of progress all came together to justify policy in an effort to strengthen and broaden the prowar coalition. This was a war against godless communists who threatened our most cherished institutions, and a war against poverty, ignorance, and disease that, under the direction of well-trained experts, could quicken the pace of development in underdeveloped countries and reduce the sum total of human misery in the world. The communists may be gone, but we are still waiting for the second part of this "war."

What struck me, listening to justifications for invading Iraq, was the second Bush administration's fusion rhetoric, merging the two paradigms, prophetic dualism and technocratic realism. So, after 9/11, although we once again found ourselves in a life-and-death struggle with evil, we were also making progress with our war efforts. "We" (Americans as the global good), working for peace and democracy, were pitted against "them" (Middle Eastern terrorists as the global evil), bent on war, dictatorship, and mass murder. Nazism and Communism were history. With terrorism, we once again encountered evil incarnate, but we also envision ourselves growing freedom, democracy, and progress in the war zones, as if these things sprouted up throughout much of the former Soviet Union.

Paradoxical fusion rhetoric creates the appearance of middle of the road or moderation. This broadens its domestic appeal. Fusion rhetoric may not enlist support from the liberal left, but it may, for a time, help neutralize liberal opposition to right-wing policy. Liberal-left opposition to wars based on God's will may still exist, but they can be moderated effectively if citizens can be made to believe that "shock and awe" can bring freedom, democracy, and prosperity to "primitive" or less fortunate peoples. Moreover, in terms of domestic politics, the values called on by an administration to justify its foreign policy, however unreasonable and barbaric the actions involved may be, it is quite reassuring to its domestic constituencies for whom respect for freedom and democracy and hope for increased prosperity are a secular version of old-time religion.

In the face of the Bush administration's fusion rhetoric, questions upholding the golden rule were rarely heard. Questions such as: "Do you think that democracy and freedom in the United States could, under any imaginable circumstance, be enhanced by having a 'foreign' country bombing our cities?' A lot, a little, not at all?" It is this question (i.e., the golden rule), that finally brings the moral dimension into both the evaluation and understanding of U.S. foreign policy: "What course of action would you consider if some other country bombed our cities claiming to enhance freedom and democracy in the United States?" Nuke them, bomb them with conventional bombs, kill their citizens whenever and wherever possible, or welcome them as liberators?

The golden rule—so important in evaluating our actions as individuals—is also important in evaluating the policies of nation-states. This argument becomes obvious when recalling historical instances of mass slaughter in the 19th and 20th centuries by nation-states in their colonies (Maier-Katkin & Maier-Katkin, 2004). The question becomes more important when we talk about human or planetary sustainability: How to break through the deadly and ultimately suicidal tribalization marking the way we understand and talk about foreign affairs? One answer lies in environmentalism with its concern with protecting ecosystems necessary for sustaining life on the planet. The Millennium Ecosystem Assessment Synthesis Report presented to the United Nations and made public March 23, 2005, identifies 24 ecosystems necessary for sustaining life on the planet. Of those, 60% (15 of 24) are being degraded or used unsustainably (Millennium Ecosystem Assessment Synthesis Report, 2005, p. 16). Clearly we need to pay attention to such facts; moreover, we need to do something about them.

Ecologic, however, brings with it two humilities. One has to do with space. Global warming and the poisons spreading into our land, air, and water do not respect national boundaries. There is no United States, no North Korea, no Iraq. Solving these problems requires global cooperation and global enforcement of laws, agreements, and projects. Existing political units are too limited for the task. Even the "greatest" of them, if they remain isolated, are helpless, when it comes to global projects designed to sustain life on the planet. Ecologic brings with it a second humility that has to do with time. Ecologic deals in 500-, 1,000-, 20,000-, and 1,000,000-year spans. Ecologic thinks in terms of eternity, not in quarterly reports and bottom lines measuring profit and loss in relation to personal portfolios or corporate accounting. Put in traditional, humanistic terms, ecologic considers the fate of our children's children's children's children (Wander & Jaehne, 1994, 2000).

Do we have any global organizations that might be able to respond to existing threats to life on the planet? For the generation that fought World War II, hope lay in the United Nations. Its charter envisions the protection of human rights; the elimination of genocide, both cultural and physical; and the moderation and eventual elimination of international conflict through ongoing, international deliberations and coordinated, cooperative interventions. In the nearly 60 years since the formation of the United Nations, however, conflicts between member states, and more recently, peculiar conflicts between the United Nations and its non-law-abiding member states, have blunted its authority, and thus its effectiveness to enforce treaties and world peace. Recall the U.S. invasion of Iraq, which was not supported by the United Nations in 2003. What this means cannot properly be understood until we appreciate the terrible danger introduced by preemptive military strikes, and until we move away from the hopeless and suicidal struggle against universal evil.

We need to transform this "war" into a struggle for the preservation and enhancement of global life or, what we may call *Ghaia*. The planet is not a thing for us to plunder. Rather it is a living, breathing organ on which all human beings depend for life support. From preemption to *Ghaia*, we cannot but feel humbled by the boundlessness of time and space. We feel the urgency to reach out, to cooperate. Once again, we become wise enough to appreciate the simplicity of the golden rule. The immensity of suffering felt at Ground Zero should not be inflicted on anyone else, now and in generations to come. For we and they share one thing, one fate: We want all of our children's children to survive and prosper on the planet. This necessarily includes the children's children of those we now call enemies.

CONCLUSION

In the modern world of nation-states, the issue is not whether morality, calculation of consequences, or a tiny, tribal God is being invoked; rather, it is whether or not we are prepared to evaluate our nation's policies in light of their contribution to the survival of life on the planet. This question deserves repetition: Are we prepared to evaluate our nation's policies in light of their contribution to the survival of life on the planet? Failure to answer this question is to forfeit the game. What we desperately need is a new orientation that leads to a different kind of religion and morality and to a different kind of *real politick*. This new kind of reasoning may use quite familiar language:

1. The golden rule: Do not do unto others what you would not want done to you! Love thy neighbor! Welcome strangers!

2. All life is sacred; it is all part of creation. The creator does not divide her or his creation between good and evil and urge destroying half of what she or he created.

3. National interest is served by the survival of life on the planet. Enlightened, hard-headed patriotism in our time must oppose whatever threatens the

continuity of life in the world, even if it is our own foreign policy, because it also threatens life in our country.

We live in an anarchical world of nation-states. This world has failed us because it has, over the last century, fallen into two World Wars and numerous colonial and—during the Cold War—proxy wars in different parts of the world. I offer this reasoning, hoping that over time it will become a new logic, a common sense that supports a *real politick* of global justice.

Some—we do not know how many—state and nonstate groups have, are seeking, or are manufacturing WMDs. Some states, such as those targeted by the United States, Iraq (before the invasion), Iran, Syria, and North Korea, for example, had or have good reason to establish a balance of terror (Gavin, 2004). States threatened by states other than the United States, such as India (whom the United States is now helping to produce nuclear power and weapons-grade plutonium) in relation to Pakistan and China, have reason to establish a balance of terror. Chemical and biological weapons are approaching the impact levels of the bombs dropped on Hiroshima and Nagasaki. Nation-states and nonstate groups may find in these less expensive, more easily produced, and more easily delivered weapons another way in which to achieve a balance of terror with other more powerful groups and states. In light of this, we need to radically reconsider the meaning of foreign, national interest, and national Gods and begin honoring what, for lack of a better term, I call the creator. We do not, I think, honor the creator through public displays of piety, but through concrete efforts to increase the likelihood that there will, in fact, be a future for our children's children.

Nations can and must commit themselves to working with each other toward some end greater than the interests envisioned by any one nation-state, an end that cannot be achieved by any one nation-state in isolation. It must, to have any hope of success, be an end that would serve the immediate and long-term interests of every nation-state, regardless of its power, ideals, religious institutions, sociopolitical or economic structure; an end spanning the spiritual and material, the practical and the ideal, the immediate and long-term hopes of humanity or, in the ancient language, the gods, God, or the creator.

What is this end? When spelled out, how does it avoid becoming one more strand in a web of failed idealism? Given our modern military weapons, continued evolution in their power, cost, and availability, and the annual increase in poisons released into land, air, and water all around the globe, the survival of life over both the short and long run is in doubt. If true, and I believe it to be so, it cries out for fashioning a new kind of *real politick* that calculates not merely bottom-line advantages and disadvantages for a fraction of humanity, but, rather, considers their implications for the continuity of life on the planet.

Where should we start? For students of rhetoric and public address, a good starting point is peace public address. A new field of research being conducted by my colleagues at San Jose State University, for example, focuses on rhetorical strategies used in the Nobel lectures (available online at www.nobelprize.org/peace) offered by all of the peace laureates since its founding in 1900. Another new direction is to examine world organizations that promote disarmament and world peace. The Stockholm International Peace Research Institute (SIPRI) is an example. In 1964, celebrating 150 years of unbroken peace, Tage Erlander, the Swedish Prime Minister at the time, initiated the idea of a peace research institute. In 1966, SIPRI was founded as an independent foundation. Its goal is "to conduct research on questions of conflict and cooperation of importance for international peace and security, with the aim of contributing to an understanding of the conditions for peaceful solutions of international conflicts and for a stable peace" (http://www.sipri.org).

Social justice in our time is not an abstract and unreachable ideal. It is better thought of as a tool working, as Aristotle suggests, to prevent civil war. Our weapons can put an end to life on the planet; therefore we can no longer tolerate war, the glorification of war, the conditions that lead to war, or any further development of weapons powerful enough to end creation once and for all. In our world, every war is a civil war. That this has to be said is a measure of the insanity in our time.

Much work needs to be done. I end my chapter, though, with an aspiration eloquently spoken by Maathai (2004), the most recent Nobel peace laureate and the first African woman to be awarded a Nobel Prize. She earned this honor for her leadership in the Green Belt Movement. Reflecting on her childhood experience with a stream next to her home, she said:

> I would drink water straight from the stream. Playing among the arrowroot leaves I tried in vain to pick up the strands of frogs' eggs, believing they were beads. But every time I put my little fingers under them they would break. Later, I saw thousands of tadpoles: black, energetic and wriggling through the clear water against the background of the brown earth. This is the world I inherited from my parents .... Today, over 50 years later, the stream has dried up, women walk long distances for water, which is not always clean, and children will never know what they have lost. The challenge is to restore the home of the tadpoles and give back to our children a world of beauty and wonder.

ACKNOWLEDGMENTS

I would like to thank Omar Swartz and especially Wenshu Lee for their assistance in revising this chapter, which I dedicate to the memory of Robert James Branhan, scholar, critic, and friend.

REFERENCES

Bennet, J. (2002, May 27). Israel is wresting security tasks from Palestinians. *The New York Times*, p. A3.

Boorstin, D. J. (1992). *The image: A guide to pseudo-events in America*. New York: Vintage.

Branhan, R. J. (1996). "Of thee I sing": Contesting "America." *American Quarterly, 48*, 623–652.

Bunker, J. (2005). Five faces of Saddam Hussein: A thematic analysis of *Foreign Affairs* 1979–2003. Unpublished master's thesis, San Jose State University, San Jose, CA.

Gabel, J. (2004–2005). The role of U.S. nuclear weapons after September 11. *The Washington Quarterly, 28*, 181–195.

Gavin, F. J. (2004). Blasts from the past: Proliferation lessons from the 1960s. *International Security, 29*, 100–135.

Halper, S. A., & Clarke, J. (2004). *America alone: The neo-conservatives and the global order.* Cambridge, UK: Cambridge University Press.

Kaufmann, C. (2004). Threat inflation and the failure of the marketplace of ideas: The selling of the Iraq war. *International Security, 29*, 5–48.

Lieven, A. (2002, October 3). The push for war. *London Review of Books, 24*, 8.

Maathai, W. (2004). *Nobel lecture.* Retrieved March 16, 2005, from http://nobelprize.org/peace/laureates/2004/maathai-lecture.html

Magnes, J. L. (1982). *Dissenter in Zion.* Cambridge, MA: Harvard University Press.

Maier-Katkin, B., & Maier-Katkin, D. (2004). At the heart of darkness: Crimes against humanity and the banality of evil. *Human Rights Quarterly, 26*, 584–604.

Millennium Ecosystem Assessment Synthesis Report. (2005, March 23). [Prepublication draft]. Retrieved April 2, 2005, from www.millenniumassessment.org

Miller, J. (2002, October 26). Keeping U.S. no.1: Is it wise? Is it new? *New York Times*, p. A19.

Owen, A. S., & Ehrenhaus, P. (1993). Animating a critical rhetoric: On the feeding habits of American empire. *Western Journal of Communication, 57*, 169–177.

Sharfstein, B. A. (1980). *The philosophers: Their lives and the nature of their thought.* New York: Oxford University Press.

Stefancic, J., & Delgado, R. (1999). *No mercy: How conservative think tanks and foundations changed America's social agenda.* Philadelphia: Temple University Press.

Swartz, O. (2004). Pride, patriotism, and social justice. *Mississippi Review, 32*, 195–199.

Wander, P. (1984). The rhetoric of American foreign policy. *Quarterly Journal of Speech, 70*, 339–361.

Wander, P., & Jaehne, D. (1994). From Cassandra to Ghaia: The limits of civic humanism in an ecologically unsound world. *Social Epistemology, 8*, 243–259.

Wander, P., & Jaehne, D. (2000). On the prospects for a "rhetoric of science." *Social Epistemology, 14*, 211–233.

Zinn, H. (2003). *A people's history of the United States.* New York: Harper Perennial.

8

Media Activism in a "Conservative" City: Modeling Citizenship

Tony Palmeri
University of Wisconsin Oshkosh

I am an academic by training and a socially committed citizen by inclination. The primary outlet for my creative and professional skills takes place in avenues that count for little in the academic reward system. Long ago I stopped being bothered by this—there are simply more interesting and important conversations for me to join. I am proud of the work that I have done, which I share with readers in this chapter. The larger point of this chapter transcends my experience. Substantial amounts of social justice work do not get accomplished in academia because many people cannot reasonably be expected to pursue such work if it does not conform with the rewards available on their respective campuses. If I succeed in sparking discussions of reform efforts in our society, one area of attention must be reevaluating the faculty reward system. Throughout my narrative, I illustrate and engage the tension that keeps many of us from doing our best and most useful work.

In this chapter, I assume that college professors play meaningful roles in local struggles for social justice. I base this assumption in the argument that the public intellectual role of academicians has been recognized in the West since the time of Socrates. The kinds of activist roles that college professors can play are unlimited, but the ones I discuss are related specifically to media activism. Specifically, I discuss the manner in which my local media activities have helped to create a space for progressive ideas in a community

149

that has historically been viewed as conservative. From my experience, it is clear that institutional, social, and community constraints prevent professors from being fully effective in such activist roles.

My purpose in writing this chapter is not to offer "how-to" advice for those seeking to become campus or community activists. Rather, it is designed to serve as a kind of autobiographical case study that may validate the experiences of like-minded professors and students. Social justice movements on our campuses and in our communities suffer from a lack of literature identifying the trials and tribulations—and success stories—of activists. Perhaps my experience can provoke others to write about their experiences; our collective notes might become a useful handbook for professors and students for whom truth seeking and social justice activism is more than a mere service activity on a vita.

The chapter proceeds as follows. First, I discuss two "big-picture" constraints that interfere with the practice of social justice from within the academy. I identify these as the decline of the public intellectual and as the tendency, however natural, to "preach to the choir," which causes much of our work to become insular and ineffective. After discussing these constraints, I turn to a specific discussion of my Oshkosh experience and detail the challenges and responses to my social activism in that community. I discuss four specific media activities in which I have been engaged since arriving in Oshkosh that exemplify my commitment to pragmatic social justice scholarly intervention. Two of the activities (public access television programming and an alternative student newspaper) are group oriented, whereas the other two (a Web site and monthly column) represent my own individual attempts at modeling critical citizenship.

TWO BIG-PICTURE CONSTRAINTS: PUBLIC INTELLECTUAL DECLINE AND CHOIR PREACHING

In the United States, activist professors find themselves saddled by a variety of constraints. In the big picture, the general decline of public intellectualism and the tendency of all activists (academic and nonacademic alike) to preach to the choir are formidable.

A scholar who has done important work to document the decline of public intellectualism in the United States and its effects on democratic culture is Jacoby (1987), whose celebrated *The Last Intellectuals: American Culture in the Age of Academe* set off a storm of debate when it first appeared. In his trenchant analysis of the disappearance of the non academic public intellectual in American life, Jacoby illustrates the demise of the Dwight

MacDonalds and Lewis Mumfords, whose writings were scholarly, at the same time connecting with a wider public. The growth of the American university system created the "professional" intellectual whose quest for tenure and acceptance on campus severely limited his or her ability or desire to address the wider public in any meaningful way. Although Farrell (1993) argues, correctly, I think, that Jacoby minimizes the fact of the academy itself as a site of political struggle, he reluctantly concedes the larger more important point: "that for a great many well-founded reasons, many of us have abdicated the responsibility that is as old as Socrates: to be a gadfly, 'thorn in the side,' irritant to the State" (pp. 147–148). Farrell urges a return to the oral tradition of rhetoric, grounded in the idea of public argument and controversy as positive social goods.

A similar position is taken by Dr. Clement Alexander Price (2002), Distinguished Public Service professor at Rutgers University. Price participated in civil rights activism in the 1960s. Like many academics of his generation, he is disappointed by the disappearance of the academic as community activist. He lamented professors' lack of engagement in the *Chronicle of Higher Education:*

> [F]ar too many faculty members who began their academic careers during the late 1960s now seem to prefer an institutional insularity that harks back to a more conservative era in higher education. Despite my belief that the scholars of my generation would answer the call, my generational cohort of university and college professors is now, officially, a part of the problem. We now have influence. Our voices, were we to raise them, would be heard—but too many of us have not raised our voices or pursued our early dreams of engagement.

These writings suggest that an academic public intellectual is operating ethically when he or she is engaged in a neo-Socratic process of engaging citizens in a conversation about vital issues affecting local communities, the nation, and the world.[1] The public intellectual might become an advocate for a particular side on a specific issue—as any citizen would be expected to do—but the public intellectual must do much more than that. Rather than tell citizens what to think, the public intellectual must show them a model of how to think. In a society where public discourse is often reduced to televised shouting matches between uncompromising bullies who have all the

---

[1]It is true that the growth of think thanks, most of which hire academicians to conduct research and communicate findings to the general public, does represent a form of public intellectualism. However, the "for hire" component is troubling. Soley (1995, 1998) and Washburn (2005) are replete with examples of scholarship being compromised by the needs of whomever is paying.

answers, the public intellectual's role is to raise questions, expose the falla- cies and shortcomings of accepted ideologies, and open up spaces for dis- sent. The late Edward Said's (1994) notion of the "amateur" intellectual is helpful here. For Said, the amateur is the antithesis of a careerist; thus he or she can engage ideas in a disinterested manner.

Acting as a public intellectual as I have described it is hindered by an- other big-picture constraint, and that is the tendency of politically engaged activists to preach to the choir. In many ways this is not the fault of the intel- lectuals. It is natural to speak in places where one has been invited and feels comfortable. Additionally, to interject oneself into a potentially hostile arena requires gumption that is unfair to expect from all who seek to influ- ence public discourse. Yet to understand why public intellectuals would be content to preach to the choir is not to excuse them for doing so. Clearly, there are some "dirty jobs" in society but "someone's got to do it." Taking the risk of communicating with the opposition is valuable and ethical for at least three reasons.

First, it is difficult to see how any society can develop in a positive direc- tion if the ideological barriers to change are not confronted openly. The complaints from liberal academicians about the intellectual condition of a "red-state" majority United States that elected George W. Bush are distress- ing when we consider the fact that few of these academics actually take the time to communicate meaningfully with red- or blue-state citizens. Yes, lib- eral academics often serve as expert commentators on broadcast public af- fairs programs, compose op-ed pieces, work in political campaigns, and perform a variety of additional useful services. However, these activities fre- quently fail to reach audiences at the grassroots level, especially those in disagreement.

Second, communicating with the so-called opposition is an important reality check for the intellectual. He or she begins to see the shortcomings in, and limitations of, his or her own thinking. He or she begins to recognize as myth the idea that the majority are set in their ways, resistant to challeng- ing their beliefs, and afraid of genuine dialogue. My experience, though anecdotal, suggests the kinds of transformation made possible through dia- logue with the so-called opposition.

Take for instance, the example of lifetime Oshkosh resident Paul Esslinger. Mr. Esslinger has been elected three times to the Oshkosh Com- mon Council. He is 41 years old, married with two young children, son of an Oshkosh firefighter, and works as a sales associate for a cable television firm. When I first met Paul in 1995, he struck me as extremely conservative and set in his ways, gravitating toward red-state political views merely due to self-interest. Paul became a regular viewer of *Commentary* and TonyPalmeri.com (two media activist projects that are discussed later). In preparation for this chapter I asked him to comment on how those projects have influenced him. He said:

> I would say that Dr. Palmeri had an influence on me and my votes on the City Council in general. I don't subscribe to any political party (I'm an independent thinker); however, I would say I'm more Conservative than Liberal. By viewing *Commentary* and TonyPalmeri.com, I have really come to learn and respect other peoples' opinions more. When I first started on the City Council [2000] I tended not to listen to other opinions, and felt that I was always right. Dr. Palmeri has a way to get me to understand other points of view, and through his show and website has taught me that I'm not always right. I don't feel that there is/was any specific thing that was on his show or website; I think it was a process that took years to develop. You might even say that through Dr. Palmeri's outlets, he taught me to mature! (personal communication, June 26, 2005)

In a move that shocked Oshkosh conservatives, Esslinger announced plans to introduce a resolution to place an Iraq War troop withdrawal resolution on the April 2006 ballot. Granted, my interaction with him is anecdotal and it is difficult to draw generalizations from it; however, it does illustrate the positive results that are possible when academics and working people take the time to communicate seriously about public issues.

Third, in an era of declining public support for higher education, it makes good practical sense to engage the population at large. Failure to engage makes it more difficult to contest the dominant (and false) perception of the "radical" universities teaming with Marxists and other establishment critics. Rather than have our ideas caricatured by Fox News and other media outlets, it is in our interest to take our ideas directly to the people.

THE OSHKOSH EXPERIENCE: CHALLENGES AND RESPONSE

In September 1989 I began employment in a tenure-track line as an assistant professor in the Department of Communication at the University of Wisconsin Oshkosh. My responsibilities were to teach four classes per semester (which included Fundamentals of Speech Communication, Rhetorical Criticism, Classical Rhetoric, and History of American Public Address), establish a record of professional and scholarly activity, and perform service activities appropriate to my position. As a native of Brooklyn,

New York, who had also spent 3 years at Wayne State University in Detroit pursuing a doctoral degree, Oshkosh presented me with somewhat of a culture shock. Descriptions of the city and the campus will help provide the necessary context for appreciating the media activist work I have performed since the early 1990s.

"Oshkosh on the Water" is located in Winnebago County in northeast Wisconsin where the Fox River enters Lake Winnebago. As of the 2000 census, the city's population is just under 63,000, which includes approximately 11,000 students at the University of Wisconsin Oshkosh campus and 5,000 in a variety of correctional facilities located throughout the city. Over 90% of the population are White, with the remainder consisting of African American (2%), Asian (3%), Hispanic (just under 2%), Native American (.05%), and "other" (05%). The city has a median household income of $37,636 and per-capita income of $18,964. The census reports that 10.2% of the population and 5.2% of families are below the poverty line ("Oshkosh, Wisconsin," 2005).

Oshkosh is a working-class community that, like many Midwestern cities in the era since the North American Free Trade Agreement (NAFTA), has steadily lost jobs in its manufacturing base while increasing employment in the service and retail sectors. For example, the Oshkosh B'Gosh corporation, famous for childrens' clothing, still maintains its corporate office in Oshkosh, but by 1995 it had moved all the manufacturing jobs out of the city. Most of the clothing is now produced outside of the country in places like Honduras and Saipan. Thousands of additional manufacturing jobs have left Winnebago County in the last 15 to 20 years ("Sustaining Wisconsin," 2002).

Once identified as "Sawdust City," Oshkosh in the 19th and early 20th centuries was known for its lumber processing.[2] In 1956 the citizens of Oshkosh via referendum changed their form of government from a strong mayor and aldermen elected from districts system to a professional manager and council appointed at-large system. This is important because dispute over the form of government has been a persistent source of local contro-

---

[2]A well-known woodworkers' strike in 1898 brought the famed Clarence Darrow to Oshkosh to defend the workers. Darrow's speech to the jury is a remarkable statement of outrage against the destructive forces of the industrial revolution. Darrow (1898/1976) referred to the trial as "but an episode in the great battle for human liberty, a battle which was commenced when the tyranny and oppression of man first caused him to impose upon his fellows and which will not end so long as the children of one father shall be compelled to toil to support the children of another in luxury and ease" (p. 35). In the trial, prosecutors serving the interest of the Paine Lumber Company attempted to define union activity as a "criminal conspiracy" to deny a corporation the right to make profits. Darrow's successful defense of the workers laid the groundwork establishing legal protections for unions (Crane, 1998).

versy, generating eight referendum campaigns since 1956 to change the form of government back to a strong mayoral system. Under the manager and council system, citizens elect seven council members at-large. The council is responsible for hiring a city manager to run the day-to-day affairs of the city. This "professional" government supposedly runs the city more efficiently than cities with directly elected, strong mayors, although data proving such an assertion are difficult to locate (Simmons, 1998). Since 1956, citizens have many times sponsored referenda to return to a strong mayoral form of government, yet each time the proponents have been dramatically outspent by the supporters of professional government. In 2005 the voters did approve a referendum question that allows for direct election of the mayor for the first time since the mid-1950s, although it is a weak mayoral system with limited powers ("City Will Elect Mayor in April," 2004).

The University of Wisconsin Oshkosh is the third-largest campus among the 13 four-year campuses in the University of Wisconsin System (behind University of Wisconsin Madison and Univeristy of Wisconsin Milwaukee). Known as Wisconsin State Teachers College until the 1960s, the campus experienced much enrollment growth when it expanded into a university and merged with other campuses to form the University of Wisconsin system in 1970. Today the campus houses colleges of Letters and Science, Business, Nursing, and Education. Students come primarily from the Fox Valley region (which stretches from Fond du Lac in the south to Green Bay in the north), with a significant number from the Milwaukee suburbs. Students of color comprise less than 10% of the campus population; faculty and staff are also predominantly White.

As with the majority of state campuses in the United States, University of Wisconsin Oshkosh had its prime activist period during the Vietnam and Civil Rights era. Probably the most well-known act of defiance on the campus was "Black Thursday" in 1968 ("Do Your Thing," 2002). Students, mostly African American, occupied the Dempsey Hall administration building and presented a list of demands that included the establishment of an African American cultural center; the hiring of more Black professors; the creation of courses in Black history, literature, and language; the financing of an African American Center; the sponsoring of Black speakers on campus; and calling for the termination of the director of financial aid, who was perceived by the students as being racist. The majority of the students were expelled and, although some of their demands were met, African American student enrollment on the campus never saw any significant increase. According to the campus Office of Institutional Research, in the spring of 2005 there were 100 African American students enrolled—1.15% of the total student population ("Headcount by Ethnic Status," 2005).

By the early 1990s it became clear that Oshkosh was suffering afflictions that plague all working-class cities in the post-NAFTA era: urban decay, job loss, and a decline in living standards (Scott, 2003). Another affliction—shared with all cities regardless of size or class status—was the breakdown of democratic culture. Symptoms included weak political parties, shrinking union membership, and corporate mainstream media. The local *Oshkosh Northwestern* (independently owned until 1998 and now part of the Gannett chain), the mostly right-wing talk radio, and television news originating from Appleton and Green Bay made few visible attempts to provoke critical discussions of conditions faced by the city. The existing media portrayed itself and the city as conservative, employing that term in the colloquial sense as meaning suspicious of change, antigovernment, and for big business.[3]

This was the situation I found myself facing in 1992 when I made a conscious decision to pursue media activist work designed to encourage Oshkosh citizens to become more engaged in the issues facing the city. Most of my activities centered on the production of a campus public affairs television show called *Commentary*. Later I developed an alternative student newspaper, a daily news Web site that I maintain today (TonyPalmeri.com), a monthly column for an alternative newspaper, two grassroots political campaigns, and a radio show. The purpose of each activity was to challenge the conservative ideology of the community and engage citizens in a conversation about alternatives.[4] In pursuing these activities I have had to deal with three major constraints: (a) occupational hazards, (b) local power elites, and (c) working-class suspicions.

Occupational Hazards

As is the case in most comprehensive public universities, University of Wisconsin Oshkosh requires faculty to meet teaching, research, and service re-

---

[3] In an essay for the *Wisconsin Political Scientist* (Palmeri, 2003), I referred to northeast Wisconsin's "Iron Triangle" of business, government, and corporate media. As is typical in most regions of the country, the Iron Triangle is prodevelopment, antitax, and generally hostile to dissent.

[4] In an April 2005 cover story for the northeast Wisconsin alternative newspaper *The Valley Scene*, I tried to define conservative, liberal, and radical as political orientations all grounded in opposition to reactionary politics. The reactionary argues from authority, holds that humans are essentially irrational, and consequently views government as the strong arm necessary to induce order in the out-of-control masses. Often the label conservative is attached to what should more appropriately be called reactionary. See "Fighting Reactionary Politics," http://www. tonypalmeri.com/frp.htm.

quirements to have their contracts renewed, and, ultimately attain tenure. Unfortunately, many of the most valuable actions of faculty do not comfortably fit in any of these categories. As Boyer (1990) noted, this problem has been exacerbated by the fact that even teaching-centered comprehensive campuses like University of Wisconsin Oshkosh mimic the research university in the way they evaluate faculty performance. Thus the "scholarship of discovery" (i.e., traditional peer-reviewed research) becomes the standard against which all other efforts are judged. Boyer proposed a broader, four-pronged model of professorial responsibility: scholarship of discovery, scholarship of integration, scholarship of application, and scholarship of teaching. As he argued:

> It is unacceptable ... to go on using research and publication as the primary criterion for tenure and promotion when other educational obligations are required. Further, it's administratively unwise to ignore the fact that a significant number of faculty are dissatisfied with the current system. Even more important, it is inappropriate to use evaluation procedures that restrict faculty, distort institutional priorities, and neglect the needs of students. (pp. 34–35)

Boyer's ideas sparked a significant amount of discussion when released, but actual methods of professorial assessment on most campuses have not changed dramatically. For comprehensive campuses like University of Wisconsin Oshkosh, peer-reviewed manuscripts remain the most important factor affecting renewal and tenure, along with teaching excellence.

I was tenured at University of Wisconsin Oshkosh in 1996, with the decision based largely on favorable evaluations of my teaching, a sufficient number of peer-reviewed essays in reputable journals, and service accomplishments that met the expectations of the department, college, and university. The work I am discussing in this chapter counted little toward my tenure and, in fact, hurt my case. Activism of all sorts—media, community, and others—is time consuming, inevitably creates enemies for the activist, and puzzles even friendly renewal and tenure file reviewers who are not equipped with a language to defend activist works as being vital to the academy and surrounding community. Consequently, senior faculty opposed to my renewal and tenure argued that my media activism did not fit the campus review criteria, allowing them to argue that I was spending too much time on work that had no scholarly value. Opposition to my tenure became so great that I was forced to invoke the University of Wisconsin System statutes that allowed my tenure hearing to be held in public. Many supportive students and faculty attended, making it more difficult for the department committee to vote "no."[5]

In short, the reward system on a campus is an occupational hazard that often becomes a powerful constraint against activism. Especially non-tenured faculty would be well advised to maintain open lines of communication with departmental colleagues and the campus hierarchy so as to attain as much clarity as possible about the career consequences of activist work.

Local Power Elites

The progressive era of the early 20th century may have done away with the blatant boss politics of that time, but it would be naive to think that cities are not still widely ruled by local power elites. The early progressives' hope that the creation of professional government would produce municipal leaders who would substitute problem solving for politics has turned out to be well intentioned but naive. So-called professional governments are just as likely to make decisions that benefit the wealth interests of a community, sometimes more aggressively than the less professional models they replaced (Page & Simmons, 2000; Simmons, 2001; Simmons & Hintz, 2002).

Working-Class Suspicions

In the early 20th century, the University of Wisconsin set the standard for a model higher education system conceived of as contributing to the general welfare. In place of an elitist, ivory tower model of the university, Wisconsin progressives proposed the Wisconsin Idea. Practical, applied scholarship was to be encouraged and valued. Doan (1947) outlined the key features of the Wisconsin Idea, calling it "democratic liberalism in practice ... [it was] the joint effort of the politician and the professor to serve the common interest of all the people rather than the special interest of particular groups. It was the application of intelligence, knowledge, and an open mind to the circumstances of each situation as it arose" (p. 15). The Social Security system, unemployment compensation, and the progressive income tax were all innovations pioneered by University of Wisconsin professors. At the height of

---

[5]I received a 6–5 vote at the department level, along with favorable reviews at each successive level and was granted tenure. The year before the tenure decision the department committee had actually voted to nonrenew my contract, but the provost at that time refused to accept the negative vote and asked the committee to reconsider, which they did.

the University's immersion in the Wisconsin Idea, working people knew that the university was on their side and generally held professors in high esteem.

This was not to last. The McCarthy period in late 1940s and early 1950s had dreadful effects on the universities, as reactionary politicians began red-baiting activist and politically liberal professors. Moreover, campus activism of the 1960s and 1970s failed to develop common bonds between universities and working people. The rhetoric of the New Left alienated many workers (Rorty, 1998). By the 1990s, Wisconsin's universities, like those throughout the nation, had become mostly servants of corporate power (Soley, 1995; Washburn, 2005). In such an environment, working people will naturally be suspicious of professors, sensing accurately that most academics are not willing or able to lend their knowledge and skills to the struggles of everyday people. The suspicion extends to those professors, like myself, who come from working-class backgrounds (my father was a shoemaker and mother a homemaker and McDonald's employee).

MEDIA ACTIVISM AND MODELING CITIZENSHIP

In the remainder of this chapter I discuss four specific media activities in which I have been engaged since arriving in Oshkosh. The four activities are cable access television, an alternative campus newspaper, a daily news Web site, and writing a monthly column. Each is a form of rhetoric designed to widen the community discourse. That is, each represents a conscious attempt to influence the attitudes and behaviors of their target audiences. In describing them I hope to show how consciousness of the constraints mentioned earlier influences the rhetorical choices made. When these activities work, it is because audiences perceive them as modeling democratic citizenship.[6] In other words, the activities are perceived as opening up a space for the discussion of a range of ideas not always welcomed into the mainstream press.

---

[6]University of Texas journalism professor and activist Robert Jensen has developed a citizens' pledge that captures the spirit of what I have been trying to accomplish via media activism:

I do solemnly pledge that I will faithfully execute the office of citizen of the United States, and that I will, to the best of my ability, help create a truly democratic world by (1) going beyond mainstream corporate news media to seek out information about important political, economic, and social issues; (2) engaging fellow citizens, including those who disagree with me, in serious discussion and debate about those issues; (3) committing as much time, energy, and money as possible to help build grassroots political organizations that can pressure politicians to put the interests of people over profit and power; and (4) connecting these efforts to global political and social movements fighting the U.S. empire abroad, where it does the most intense damage. And I will continue to resist corporate control of the world, resist militarism, resist the roll-back of civil rights, and resist illegitimate authority in all its forms. (See http://www.zmag.org/sustainers/ content/2005-01/20jensen.cfm)

Cable Access Television: *Commentary* and *Eye on Oshkosh*

At University of Wisconsin Oshkosh, the radio, television, and film program is housed in the Department of Communication. The program is
equipped with two professional television studios and a radio station. Original university programming is broadcast on a cable channel (reaching all
Oshkosh citizens with a basic Time-Warner cable package) from 7 p.m. to
midnight each night of the week during the fall and spring semesters. The
studios are managed by students with faculty and professional engineer
guidance. Much of the student program is derivative and heavily influenced
by mainstream network and cable programming. Because the majority of
the students entering the program see themselves—at least initially—as
working to obtain positions in mainstream media, it makes sense to them to
imitate the successful programs. For news programming, this has meant essentially copying the format of typical corporate, network news broadcasts
with more emphasis placed on local issues.

Even though I am in the speech communication area of the Department
of Communication and had no teaching responsibilities in the radio, television, and film program, in 1991 I found myself increasingly frustrated with
the campus television station. Having lived in Oshkosh for 2 years at that
point, I noticed that the mainstream local press (print and broadcast)
served mostly as cheerleaders for the status quo, especially big business. I
could not understand why the campus media did not make more of an effort
to provide alternative perspectives to the community.

In the fall of 1991 I disclosed my frustrations to Chris Lee, an active radio, television, and film student who had taken an elective class with me.
Much to my surprise, Chris challenged me to produce my own public affairs
program. "I'll direct it and get us a production crew," he said. We named the
program *Commentary*. The show was student directed from 1991 to 1996,
took a hiatus from 1996 to 1998, and then directed by Doug Freshner of
University of Wisconsin Oshkosh University Relations from 1998 to 2003.
In 1991 and 1992 we produced one half-hour program per week during the
fall and spring semesters (approximately 24 episodes per year). From 1993
to 1996 and 1998 to 2003 we moved to hour-long episodes. In the 1998 to
2003 edition we taped every week throughout the entire year. The format
was largely "talking heads" with occasional student-produced video pack-
ages embedded during the taping to complement the discussion taking
place.

From its earliest days, *Commentary* had three major goals: First, to provide a forum for a critical discussion of local, state, national, and interna-

tional issues; second, to engage the guests (most of whom were local opinion leaders from the worlds of politics, academia, journalism, business, and other fields) in a critical dialogue designed as a contrast to the shrill shouting matches found on most cable talk shows; and third, to provide student workers with the opportunity to experience a grassroots media alternative to the corporate model dominating most media programs including that at the University of Wisconsin Oshkosh.

As anyone involved in television production will know, producing a weekly program is extraordinarily time consuming. Developing program topics, booking guests, framing questions, and keeping a crew motivated is close to a full-time job. Being that the University of Wisconsin Oshkosh campus adheres to a traditional breakdown of teaching, scholarly, and service requirements for faculty, Commentary was never appreciated as more than a valuable public service activity. Nontenured faculty contemplating this kind of activity should be sure to understand the reward system of their campus, especially the renewal and tenure requirements. By 1994 I knew that producing Commentary was actually hurting my chances for tenure, but the clear need for it on the campus and in the community made it difficult for me to suspend my involvement.

Handling the local power elites proved equally challenging. To develop a connection to the local "establishment," I recruited former Oshkosh Mayor James Mather to cohost the program. Mather had served 14 years on the Oshkosh Common Council, worked for more than 30 years for the Wisconsin Department of Health and Social Services, was widely perceived as a political moderate, and was well known to opinion leaders and the community at large. Although he had no prior experience in broadcasting, Mather did a superb job. Largely due to his presence, we were able to get many local political leaders to be on the show, and Mather's "insider" type of questioning complemented perfectly my own tendency toward the "outsider" role. Unfortunately, even Mather's presence was not enough to shield the program from establishment attack.

In 1995 the Commentary student staff, inspired by the Rio Earth Summit of 1992, decided it would be a good idea to do a "toxic tour" of the city of Oshkosh. We took cameras to local toxic sites and interviewed local environmentalists at the sites. One of the sites was the production facilities of the Oshkosh Truck Corporation, a major defense contractor. The week the program aired, Oshkosh Truck sent a representative to my University office to demand that the show be taken off the air, claiming that we made them look like an irresponsible polluter. The representative could point to no inaccurate statements in the program, and did not respond to an invitation to appear on the program to face questioning. Instead, the company went to the chancellor of the campus and tried to get him to remove the program.

In 1996 I decided to run for state office. When I made the announcement in April of that year I suspended *Commentary* to avoid charges of using the campus airwaves to support a political campaign. When the campaign was over in November, I tried to restart the program but was met with resistance from the radio, television, and film staff who were feeling pressure from the chancellor's office. I was told that the chancellor had decided to start his own program, the *Chancellor's Report*, which was going to occupy the time slot formerly held by *Commentary* and that there would be no time to produce and broadcast *Commentary*.[7] Feeling somewhat defeated, I decided to put my energies into other areas. To my surprise, I received, through much of 1997 and 1998, numerous inquiries from members of the community asking when *Commentary* would return. Although I knew the program had a following, the extent to which people were willing to write letters or make phone calls to support the show was inspiring. Still, I decided to put my energies into department matters. In June 1998 I was approached by Doug Freshner, a longtime employee of the campus media relations bureau. He asked if I would be willing to restart *Commentary*. He claimed that *Commentary* had made a great contribution to the community, had influenced his own thinking about issues, and, as a production specialist, he saw it as good television. He said that Mr. Mather and I should not worry about the possible fallout from the chancellor. *Commentary* in 1998 proved to be wildly popular with the community at large. The format did not change, but now working with a seasoned professional like Freshner allowed for better reaction shots and an overall better "look" to the show. In addition, by 1998 I had developed a large e-mail list of the show's supporters, which allowed for multimedia connections.

Because the program continued to take a critical look at corporate power in the city, the chancellor in late 1998 called Mr. Mather (a person who had been awarded an honorary doctorate by the same chancellor) and myself to his office so he could tell us that we would not be able to continue production because, in his words, "Doug Freshner does not have the time to work with you." Shortly after, the chancellor's top aide called me on the phone to tell me explicitly that no more programs would be produced. I then immedi-

---

[7]The chancellor had received numerous complaints about *Commentary*, almost all from big business leaders who condemned the show's lack of "balance" on issues dealing with corporate power. These complaints were never put in writing, and were never communicated directly to me, but always through the chancellor's legal assistant.

ately contacted the local *Oshkosh Northwestern* newspaper and told them that the chancellor was attempting to censor a political program. The editorial page editor of the paper sent the chancellor's aide a list of pointed questions, explained that all responses would be on the record, and looked forward to his response. Probably wanting to avoid embarrassment, the chancellor backed off and the show continued until late 2003.

Commentary lasted as long as it did because of community support. The amount of e-mails and phone calls we received over the years from average, everyday people let me know that the program was succeeding in challenging the dominant worldviews coming out of the local mainstream press. I suspended the show again in late 2003 when I decided to make another run for office. When that campaign was over in November 2004, I was immediately invited to be a cohost of *Eye on Oshkosh*, a show founded by Melanie Bloechl and Cheryl Hentz, two lifelong Oshkosh residents, both from blue-collar, working-class backgrounds. Bloechl was elected to the Oshkosh Common Council in 1991 on the strength of support from the city's south side working-class community. She spent 2 years as mayor of the city. She did not attend college, has a reputation for speaking her mind, and is generally suspicious of broadcast news and opinion. Yet she saw value in *Commentary*:

> I watched the show because I felt this community was in dire NEED of another viewpoint, to hear others comments on the state of the community. I loved that Tony was unafraid to speak out and up, that he scheduled interesting guests that had a variety of viewpoints on numerous issues. (personal communication, June 27, 2005)

Moreover, the program influenced her thinking in a way that suggests some success at overcoming working-class suspicions of intellectual activists:

> *Commentary* affected my personal thinking on a number of levels. First, I have had great contempt for those intellectuals that busy themselves with the business of letting us all know how very superior they are, they offer very little to the quality of life overall in a community unless they too are willing to get their hands dirty with the real work of making things better, and not just talking endlessly about it. Debate is a wonderful tool, as are one's back, blood, and sweat. I have always believed that actions speak louder than mere words. This is only one of the reasons I have such great respect and admiration for Tony. Unlike his contemporaries, he not only speaks publicly and often about a variety of injustices, but has put himself up as a candidate for change in a number vicious political campaigns. He is willing to put himself

through this process to show us all that all things worth having are worth fighting for. He has changed my mind on a two-party system being the answer to our problems; I have seen more clearly that indeed, the two-party system is the problem! (personal communication, June 27, 2005)

Cheryl Hentz works as a freelance journalist and apartment building manager, and has held a variety of other jobs. Like Bloechl, she did not attend college and has a reputation for bluntness. She says:

I watched *Commentary* because, compared to the mainstream press, it provided me with more in-depth knowledge of the issues facing our community, not just in Oshkosh or Winnebago County, but on a more global basis (i.e., state, nation and world). During the political season the program also gave me more insight into the various candidates running for office and their positions on the issues. (personal communication, July 5, 2005)

Praxis: An Alternative Campus Newspaper

In October 1993 I was invited to speak to a group of 25 student leaders at a retreat sponsored by the Dean of Students office. The theme of the talk was "Communicating with HEART" (honesty, equality, accuracy, responsibility, and trust). Although designed as a 1-hour lecture and discussion, the event ended up going on for several hours, with the students spending most of the time struggling with the question, "Why isn't there more HEART on our campus?" The discussion revealed much cynicism about the campus bureaucracy; the lack of vision among faculty, students, and administration; and a variety of additional frustrations the students had never before discussed publicly.

The students concluded that it was important to do something. Off the cuff, I suggested that what was needed was a grassroots student movement on the campus, one that would make student interests visible to the faculty, administration, and community at large. Much to my surprise, the suggestion was taken seriously. One member of the student government announced that he would compose a press release for the student newspaper inviting all students to the campus union for the inaugural meeting of the grassroots movement. Signs were posted around campus, and announcements were made on the campus radio and television stations. Interested faculty promoted the meeting heavily in their classes.

As the meeting night approached, anxiety set in for the student organizers. There was no agenda, no recognized leader, and no formal presentations planned. What if no one attended? What if the event degenerated into a forum for fruitless whining? What if it were a complete waste of time?

Close to 100 people attended the meeting. Perhaps half of the students in attendance were current or former students of mine or of Dr. Mashoed Bailie of the University of Wisconsin Oshkosh radio, television, and film program. Another quarter were members of the student government, and the rest were people who became curious after hearing about the event. About a half-dozen faculty attended, and the assistant dean of students represented the administration.

Absent an agenda, a wide range of topics were covered. The tone was markedly different from what one may have heard at Berkeley or Columbia in the 1960s. The students were not so much concerned with justice or equality as they were with getting their money's worth from the institution. Some spoke passionately about poor advising on the campus, how wrong it was that they were not allowed to access student evaluations of professors, how terrible it was that mediocre professors taught some classes, and the rudeness of campus employees. Not exactly Port Huron circa 1962.

The campus newspaper reported that the inaugural meeting was mostly a gripe session, although it was more than that. For example, some attendees thought that critical conversation in and of itself was action. Others spoke against the tendency to personalize problems and argued instead that we should begin an examination of the ways in which institutional structures create "appropriate" models of behavior. Still others thought that the meeting itself was representative of the way that power relationships disrupt meaningful dialogue; they argued that some students were "playing up to" the faculty and administrator present.

The next several meetings were not as well attended. They became information-gathering sessions in which an administrator would show up and answer questions about advising and other student concerns. For a few weeks the dean of the College of Letters and Science attended; his goal seemed to be to get the students to rally behind his program for building diversity on campus. These meetings were somewhat the antithesis of grassroots action: Not only were most of the comments now being driven by faculty and administration, but also the goal of having a critical dialogue about issues was now almost entirely lost. What began as an effort to create a space in which individuals could engage in rational, critical discussion of campus issues and lay the groundwork for collective action became, instead, a forum for privileging powerful voices, legitimizing the participants' place on the institutional hierarchy. Equally troubling was the assumption that communication instructors in attendance were there to help individuals state their ideas more "effectively." Because everyone was already certain of what needed to be done, all that was needed was "communication skills" to bring about proper action. Critical communication theory (e.g., Schwoch, White, & Reilly, 1992; Splichal & Wasko, 1993), however, emphasizes the role of the communication instructor in democratizing communication; in judging effect not by an individual's success in persuading an audience to accept an already conceived platform, but by the collective ability to listen to and to take seriously all participant voices. The democratic communication model proved to be too disorienting for the majority of attendees. Perhaps it was unrealistic to think that unreflective attitudes toward communication and democratic involvement developed and reinforced over many years and in a variety of contexts could be transformed in the space of several meetings.

By January 1994 the meetings had almost died. Attendance had dwindled to less than a dozen, with little meaningful dialogue present. Then in February, two new students came to a grassroots meeting for the first time. Neither were communication students, campus leaders, or otherwise connected to the original group. Both had attended a larger campus and experienced problems with drugs and alcohol; in overcoming these problems they had discovered an appreciation for intellectual pursuits. Yet they found the University of Wisconsin Oshkosh campus hostile to critical thinkers. Seeking alternatives, they came to the grassroots meeting after seeing a bulletin board announcement.

Unlike the majority of students who had been attending the meetings, these two were interested in social justice, the environment, racism, homophobia, class, and other issues. They believed that the campus community suffered because of a lack of exposure to nonmainstream ideas. As they became more heavily involved, the character of the meetings began to change. Soon, those students who may have been there only to please the faculty began to disappear. The new group was antiauthority, prodemocracy, thoughtful and articulate young people who felt quite alienated on a conservative campus. Most important, the new grassroots group did not look to the faculty for any leadership. Their philosophy was that everyone attending the meetings was an equal who should be treated as such. The new group pleased us, because it appeared that we had finally managed, without engaging in any political maneuvering and propaganda, to get some activists out of the woodwork.

The new group changed its name to the Grassroots Collective and decided that what was needed was an alternative campus newspaper. The plan was to invite all members of the campus community to write for the paper, with the condition that potential authors would have to attend a Grassroots Collective meeting to read their work and participate in a critical discussion of it. The idea was that the written pieces would provoke the conversation that had been missing from the meetings. After much discussion, the group decided that the paper would be called *Praxis: Uniting Theory and Practice*. The mission statement stated:

> *Praxis* is dedicated to the promotion of a democratic space for the expression of alternative and historically marginalized voices. *Praxis* is a collective grass-roots student newspaper guided by a sense of social justice, standards of fairness and accuracy, and an ongoing critique of relations of power in society.

The plan was to publish primarily news articles, opinion pieces, prose, poetry, and illustrations. The criteria for publication were that the piece must in some way uphold the mission statement.

An initial obstacle to overcome was securing the funding necessary to produce the paper. On the University of Wisconsin Oshkosh campus the Student Allocations Committee (a large group whose membership includes students, faculty representatives, and administrative representatives) was initially hostile to the idea of supporting the paper with student funds. Grassroots Collective students remained persistent and repeatedly attended Allocations Committee meetings while communicating with the members informally outside of the committee hearings. The committee agreed to fund the first two issues of the paper on the condition that the Grassroots Collective solicit private funding sources thereafter. Significantly, the students made the case before the committee without faculty assistance, demonstrating the kind of independence that was the goal of the activity from its inception.

The first issue of *Praxis* was prepared over a several-week period in a highly primitive manner. Story and opinion piece ideas were brainstormed at the Grassroots Collective's weekly meetings in the campus union building. Management of the campus's official student newspaper (*The Advance-Titan*) would not allow any of their resources to be used for *Praxis*, so the paper was laid out in a makeshift editor's station consisting of several cafeteria tables joined together. The tensest moments were disagreements over whether to uphold the mission statement to publish virtually everything submitted. Proponents of the latter view took the position that to leave out any materials would be to engage in the same kind of censorship practiced by the corporate media. The other side argued that to publish everything would be to risk publishing the same types of materials found in the mainstream press, thus defeating the purpose of having an "alternative" paper.

The final product represented a compromise. The first issue featured articles critical of the campus administration's stalling on the establishment of a 24-hour computer lab, an analysis of the environmental factors that produce addictive behaviors on the campus, and a review of the Grassroots Collective sponsored presentation of the film *Manufacturing Consent: Noam Chomsky and the Media*. There was also a plea for more alternative literature in the library, an essay that identified the use of Prozac as a metaphor for the quick-fix mentality in contemporary America, a young feminist's explanation of why some married women choose to hyphenate their name, a satirical piece on being "pro-apathy," and a local artist's deconstruction of the "Joe Camel" cigarette ads.

Praxis and the Grassroots Collective survived in one form or another until around 2000. Although it is not uncommon for student organizations to fold as students graduate and others do not immediately step in to take leadership positions, *Praxis* and Grassroots Collective never overcame the institutional constraints in place to keep such activities down. Funding problems and reluctance of faculty to give students credit for working on an alternative publication were two powerful constraints. The group never developed a stable source of independent funding and eventually lost support from the Allocations Committee. The group failed to attract enough student writers at least in part because faculty did not encourage students to work for the paper. Consequently, a small group of core activists felt overburdened and eventually disbanded the project.

As with the *Commentary* program, faculty advisors to the Grassroots Collective and *Praxis* were put in a position of devoting a significant amount of time to a project that did not amount to more than a service activity in terms of the evaluative criteria used to judge faculty performance. Even though it was conceded by review committees that the paper had stimulated campuswide discussion of important issues, represented a quality educational experience for the students involved, and provoked engagement with the community at large, it still did not fit neatly into the traditional review categories. Moreover, the content of the paper placed advisors and students at significant odds with the campus administration and local elites threatened by its radicalism and brash style. Although shaking up the establishment was a goal of the paper, actually reforming power structures on campus never happened. The Grassroots Collective never materialized into the kind of grassroots movement needed to accomplish such change. Outreach to the working-class community suffered similar disappointments.

Students learned that simply placing a newspaper in someone's hands does not mean they will read it, and those who did read were often threatened by the militant tone. Getting actual citizens in the community to write for the paper became next to impossible, and by the late 1990s the newspaper had taken second place to other kinds of activism for the students involved.

Many of the students involved in the Grassroots Collective have become lifelong activists. The activity demonstrated clearly the transformative potential of extracurricular work rooted in issues of justice and social action. As noted by Giroux and McLaren (1992), "Central to the goal of critical pedagogy is the need to create a public sphere of citizens who are able to exercise power over their lives and especially over the conditions of knowledge production and acquisition". (pp. xxx–xxxi). Former Grassroots Collective activists are now engaged in classroom teaching, social work, journalism, public interest research, and socially conscious small business activities.

Commentary, Eye on Oshkosh, and *Praxis* were primarily group efforts. On the other hand, the Web site TonyPalmeri.com and the column "Media Rants" represent my own individual attempts to model critical citizenship in a conservative region. In some ways the occupational, power elite, and working-class suspicion constraints are easier to overcome when working as an individual. Further, the time and difficulties associated with recruitment, organization, and motivation of grassroots activists are not present. The downside, of course, is that one individual can be easier to marginalize.

TonyPalmeri.com: Independent News and Commentary

When *Commentary* returned in 1998, I decided to start a campus-based Web site to complement the program discussions. Originally a hobby (that I did not have time for!), the early site announced what programs would be airing, summarized the programs that had aired, and offered links to a variety of sites. As time went on, I experimented with placing headlines on the site in a simplistic manner that one might find on *The Drudge Report.* E-mails indicated to me that a substantial amount of viewers were accessing the site, which prodded me to create an e-mail distribution list. By the spring of 2001 I began e-mailing weekly updates to the distribution list. The updates included original reporting, links to stories, commentary, letters from readers, photos, and a variety of other items. Although the Web site homepage remained simple, daily updates to it became the norm.

As with the television shows, the Web site updating required much time. By 2002 the e-mail updates had become like online magazines, with editing, original writing, and responding to readers becoming very much like a full-time job. Today TonyPalmeri.com receives about 1,000 hits and 200 unique visitors each day, which is a pittance compared to mainstream news sources. Significantly, however, the readership is primarily local, activist, and represents a variety of perspectives. The site has helped readers to broaden their understanding of issues and provided them with a legitimate alternative to the mainstream press. Bill Wingren, a retired high school history teacher and an elected member of the Winnebago County Board of Supervisors, has this to say about the site:

> In this age of talking heads and 24/7 news, "civil discourse" is in danger of becoming an oxymoron. The threat is less ominous in our community because of Dr. Tony Palmeri's contributions both on his web site and television programs.
>
> On several occasions, Dr. Palmeri has posted the full and complete text of remarks I wanted to make but was unable to due to lack of interest or understanding on the part of my colleagues. Thus, the public has an opportunity to see my argument in full unlike the "sound bites" often used by the mainstream press which summarizes, often incorrectly, what they think is important.
>
> As a concerned citizen, I have often relied on Tony's web site and/or television interviews to pick candidates in local elections. He allows each person to explain their positions on a wide range of issues. Tony Palmeri makes people THINK!!! No greater service or compliment is needed.
>
> Because of Tony's involvement, civil discourse is alive and well here in our community. (personal communication, June 28, 2005)

Jody Thompson is a citizen activist in the small town of Chippewa Falls, Wisconsin. She became aware of TonyPalmeri.com while searching for information on an organization that she felt was exerting undue influence on the local government. She writes:

> Tonypalmeri.com is possibly the most authentic site on the net. The instinctive response to such authenticity is authenticity of your own, to whatever degree you can muster. It's probably inevitable that those who have enough of whatever it takes to stick around begin to think, "maybe I can do that too." Not to create a copy of his site, his style or his views but maybe to figure out exactly what I want to say and just say it. Maybe I can have the audacity to be myself too. Palmeri gives no example of "how to be," so naturally that becomes the best example of all. Palmeri's own involvement inspires involvement in others, the forms of which adapt and evolve to suit the individual

and their circumstance, making it impossible to track or quantify them. (personal communication, June 27, 2005)

TonyPalmeri.com was recently named Best News and Commentary site by the Oshkosh Public Library in its first annual Best Local Website contest ("Best Website Contest," 2005). As corporate media consolidation leaves citizens with fewer mainstream news options, a movement to develop alternatives takes on extreme importance. TonyPalmeri.com represents just one small step in that movement.

Media Rants: Traditional Format

In 2002 the editor of *The Valley Scene,* an alternative monthly newspaper in northeast Wisconsin, asked me write a monthly column of media criticism. The editor has been familiar with my media activist work and had been receiving my Web site updates. The column, "Media Rants," is written for a general audience and is essentially a critique of corporate media practices. Following the lead of Project Censored (http://www.projectcensored.org/), each year I devote two columns to highlighting the most censored local stories of the year. Following the lead of Multinational Monitor (http://multinationalmonitor.org/monitor.html), each year I also devote two columns to identifying the 10 worst northeast Wisconsin corporations of the year. The column has resulted in my getting many invitations to speak on public and commercial radio, before service clubs, political organizations, and others.

Because the "Media Rants" column is not peer reviewed, it too does not fare well in the academic reward system. However, in an age of media ownership consolidation, it provides concerned citizens with an independent voice. In Wisconsin's Fox Valley, the Gannett Corporation owns every daily newspaper (Palmeri, 2004). "Media Rants" performs somewhat of a watchdog role, and at its best it provokes average citizens to engage in their own kinds of media activism.[8]

CONCLUSION

Despite my efforts, Oshkosh is still a conservative area. Yet from the beginning it was never my hope that my efforts alone would transform the ideol-

---

[8]An archive of columns can be found at http://www.tonypalmeri.com/mediarantsarchive.htm.

ogy of the community. Rather, I have proceeded from a feeling that it is the responsibility of professors to push students and the community at large to explore the dialectical features of human communication. As noted by Giroux (1981), "the dialectic functions so as to help people analyze the world in which they live, to become aware of the constraints that prevent them from changing the world, and, finally, to help them collectively struggle to transform the world" (p. 116). In some ways what I have described in this chapter represents the key to overcoming the so-called red-state, blue-state divide that exists in the contemporary United States. A divide cannot be dismantled until well-meaning people on each side take the risk to cross over into enemy territory. To do so is to model citizenship.

REFERENCES

Best website contest. (2005). Retrieved June 21, 2005 from http://www. oshkoshpubliclibrary.org/pages/ internetguides/websitecontest.html
Boyer, E. L. (1990). *Scholarship reconsidered: Priorities of the professoriate*. Princeton, NJ: Carnegie Foundation for the Advancement of Teaching.
City will elect mayor in April. (2004). *Oshkosh Northwestern*. Retrieved June 21, 2005 from http://www.wisinfo. com/elections/osh/ele_18480299.shtml
Crane, V. (1998). *The Oshkosh woodworkers strike of 1898: A Wisconsin community in crisis*. Oshkosh: Wisconsin Sesquicentennial Commission.
Darrow, C. S. (1976). The great Oshkosh woodworkers strike trial. *Green Mountain Quarterly, 3*, 35–92. (Original work published 1898)
Doan, E. N. (1947). *The LaFollettes and the Wisconsin idea*. New York: Rinehart.
Do your thing. (2002). Retrieved June 21, 2005 from http://www.uwosh.edu/archives/bt/
Farrell, T. B. (1993). On the disappearance of the rhetorical aura. *Western Journal of Communication, 57*, 147–158.
Giroux, H. (1981). *Ideology, culture, and the process of schooling*. Philadelphia: Temple UP.
Giroux, H., & McLaren, P. L. (1992). Introduction: Media hegemony. Towards a critical pedagogy of representation. In J. Schwoch, M. White, & S. Reilly (Eds.), *Media knowledge: Readings in popular culture, pedagogy, and critical citizenship* (pp. xv–xxxiv). Albany: State University of New York Press.
Headcount by ethnic status. (2005). Retrieved July 1, 2005 from http://www.uwosh.edu/ oir/StudentStatsSpring2005/dFactSheetEthnicitySpr05.pdf
Jacoby, R. (1987). *The last intellectuals: American culture in the age of academe*. New York: Basic Books.
Oshkosh, Wisconsin. (2005). Retrieved May 1, 2005 from http://en.wikipedia. org/wiki/Oshkosh%2C_Wisconsin
Page, B., & Simmons, J. (2000). *What government can do: Dealing with poverty and inequality*. Chicago: University of Chicago Press.
Palmeri, A. (2003). Northwest Wisconsin's Iron Triangle. *Wisconsin Political Scientist, 9*, 16–17.
Palmeri, A. (2004, August). Northeast Wisconsin's media monopoly. *The Valley Scene, 12*, 5–6, 12. Retrieved from http://www.tonypalmeri.com/mediamonopoly.htm
Price, C. A. (2002, April 8). An academic life in the public sphere. *Chronicle of Higher Education. Online essay sponsored by the Woodrow Wilson National Fellowship Foundation on ca-*

reers for humanities Ph.D. Retrieved June 21, 2005 from http://
chronicle.com/jobs/2002/04/2002040801c.htm

Rorty, R. (1998). *Achieving our country: Leftist thought in twentieth-century America*. Cambridge, MA: Harvard University Press.

Said, E. (1994). *Representations of the intellectual*. New York: Pantheon.

Schwoch, J., White, M., & Reilly, S. (1992). *Media knowledge: Readings in popular culture, pedagogy, and critical citizenship*. Albany: State University of New York Press.

Scott, R. E. (2003). *The high price of "free" trade: NAFTA's failure has cost the United States jobs across the nation* (Economic Policy Institute Briefing Paper No. 147). Retrieved June 21, 2005 from http://www.epinet.org/content.cfm/briefingpapers_bp147

Simmons, J. (1998). Social conflict and political change in Oshkosh. *Voyageur, 14*, 22–38.

Simmons, J. (2001). Whither local government reform? The case of Wisconsin. *National Civic Review, 90*, 45–62.

Simmons, J., & Hintz, S. (2002). Exchange on municipal reform in Wisconsin: Form or substance? *Wisconsin Political Scientist, 8*, 11–12.

Soley, L. (1995). *Leasing the ivory tower: The corporate takeover of academia*. Boston: South End.

Soley, L. (1998). *Heritage clones in the heartland*. Retrieved May 1, 2005 from http://www.fair.org/index.php?page=1430)

Splichal, S., & Wasko, J. (Eds.). (1993). *Communication and democracy*. Norwood, NJ: Ablex.

Sustaining Wisconsin: Outagamie, Waupaca, and Winnebago Counties. (2002). Madison: Center on Wisconsin Strategy. Retrieved May 1, 2005 from http://www.cows.org/pdf/sw/ reg_rep/rp-sw-outagam.pdf

Washburn, J. (2005). *University, Inc.: The corporate corruption of American higher education*. New York: Basic Books.

9

Social Justice in Interpersonal and Family Relationships

Linda Potter Crumley
Southern Adventist University

Social justice is constituted and sustained through interpersonal communication. Communication creates the kinds of relating that could be termed socially just or unjust; in turn, the social justice or injustice of a relationship influences communication. This recursive process occurs because communication is both the cradle and the crucible of social justice. It is initially constructed through our earliest and closest relational communication, but it is tested and refined in a variety of interpersonal relationships. Scholars of interpersonal and family communication should consider questions of social justice as a crucial part of their research realm.

AN INTERPERSONAL DEFINITION OF SOCIAL JUSTICE

Before exploring how scholars of interpersonal communication relate to social justice, a review of the definition of social justice is in order. *Social justice* has been defined as "engagement with and advocacy for those in our society who are economically, socially, politically, and/or culturally under-resourced" (Frey, Pearce, Pollock, Artz, & Murphy, 1996, p. 110). This definition highlights the importance of inequity as a factor in social injustice. It also suggests that interpersonal communication is critical to social justice, both in the form of engagement (social interaction) with people who are underresourced and as advocacy (communicating with those who control the resources that are lacking) for these people. The term social justice consists of two parts: social and justice. The social portion of the term is closely linked to the interpersonal aspect of interpersonal communication. Both denote the importance of persons, people, or social groups in their constructs. *Social* comes from the Latin word *socialis*, "of companionship," from *socius*, "partner" (Agnes, 1999, p. 1360). This definition suggests the idea of people relating to one another on an interpersonal level—from being companions or partners to creating a community in which one associates with other people in a variety of ways. Indeed, companionship and community create and are created by interpersonal communication (Adelman & Frey 1997; Baxter, 2004).

Justice implies a moral imperative, a definite sense of right or wrong. Justice is the "principle or ideal of just dealing or right action" (Agnes, 1999, p. 777); it is by nature stern, impersonal, and solid. Justice notices and keeps account of boundaries—between morals, ideas, and institutions, as well as between people. The concepts of respect, equity, and fairness are foundational to a sense of justice. Justice, like social, is rife with meaning for scholars of interpersonal communication. Whereas social life is created in the interaction of many people and is never finished (Baxter, 2004), justice suggests that some interactive practices are more ideal than others. It implies a certain level of stability in assessing what is right-living, right-relating, perhaps even right-communicating.

As suggested by Frey et al. (1996), social justice becomes an issue when inequities exist between people. In relationships, inequities are ubiquitous and inescapable. What relationship does not involve differences? People differ in age, gender, attractiveness, intelligence, emotional stability, wealth, status, culture, viewpoints, health, and energy (among other things). These differences are a part of what makes relating interesting—and complicated. Erasing relational inequity is not possible or even desirable. Coping with inequity in a socially just manner, however, is a necessary skill for a quality relationship. A lack of social justice does not always destroy relational stability (e.g., see study of battering couples by Gottman et al., 1995, in which none of the wives of the most dangerous battering husbands left their relationships). However, social justice is an important consideration when the quality of a relationship is valued.

Social justice is of particular concern when inequities of power are considerable, such as in relationships between parent and child, employer and employee, teacher and student, or physician and patient. In these cases, the responsibility should rest on the powerful partner to ensure that social justice is maintained. Ideally, even in situations in which power is disparate, good interpersonal communication can help create and sustain socially just relationships that can be satisfactory and equitable to both partners.

In sum, social justice assesses the quality of an interpersonal relationship. A socially just relationship is one in which both commonalities and differences are valued, each relational partner's dignity is upheld, and the inequities inherent in any relationship are managed in respectful and caring ways. Because social justice is a salient dimension in relationships and is largely accomplished through interpersonal communication, scholars of interpersonal communication should address it in their scholarship.

CRADLE OF SOCIAL JUSTICE

A child huddles in bed and cries herself to sleep at night as her parents scream at each other in the next room. A woman forces a laugh and claims, "Oh, I fell down the stairs," when asked about the bruises on her face. A man stops attending classes because his ex-wife is stalking him. As these examples show, social justice or injustice often begins in relationships at home. In fact, the family is the cradle for social justice.

Our earliest communication experiences shape many of our later values and beliefs (Bandura, 1977). It is in our primary relationships, typically created with family members, that we learn what is "normal" in a relationship. These close interpersonal relationships are the setting in which we experience the essential elements of social justice or injustice. Family relationships not only show us what relating is about, but also set our expectations for the quality of relationships that we consider typical or ideal (Vangelisti, Crumley, & Baker, 1999). Our experience of social justice in early close relationships influences how we construct social justice in later relationships and impacts our ability to recognize and respond to later issues of social justice. If "normal" is socially unjust, our expectations for social justice may be blunted. On the other hand, if we live in ideal settings and never are exposed to social injustices, we may have difficulty believing that social injustice actually exists or we may not recognize its relevance and importance.

An understanding of fundamental relationship rules (e.g., Gottman & DeClaire, 2001) is needed to help people create relationships that are socially just. Scholars of interpersonal communication can help create a safer cradle for social justice in early relationships. There is still much to learn about the dynamics of dating, mating, and creating families, and we know relatively little about how people construct and sustain family relationships that support social justice for all family members. The remainder of this section examines social justice in a variety of familial relationships: couple, parent–child, sibling, and extended family. Although these groupings do not exhaust the types of family relationships that exist, they are convenient categories to highlight the need for social justice in all family relationships.

Couple Relationships

Social justice in couple relationships may be constructed in a variety of ways. People tend to assume that relational skills will be "caught" as individuals grow up, so they are rarely taught in any formal way. When a couple begins a relationship, they often have little or no education about what types of relational skills are more or less functional in creating healthy relationships. Instead, they are likely to pattern their communication after ways of relating that have been modeled for them in the past (e.g., Burleson, Delia, & Applegate, 1995). If their relational role models were successful in creating and sustaining satisfying and stable relationships with a high level of social justice, this can be positive. However, in an age in which unstable relationships and marital dissolution are pandemic, many couples have not had the opportunity to "catch" good relational skills through close-up observation of satisfying long-term relationships. Some couples recognize this problem and consciously try to create a healthier relationship than they have seen modeled. Unfortunately, deficits in knowledge or skills often sabotage their plans.

Basic relational rules are beginning to be discovered (e.g., Gottman & DeClaire, 2001) that suggest that the ways people respond to each other's attempts to communicate are critical factors in creating positive, stable relationships. It seems likely that these or similar relational rules might be used as a rough rubric to begin to identify social justice or its lack in personal relationships. As we learn more, it might be useful to require that couples planning to marry participate in some kind of premarital education that is based on sound relational research. Such training should develop specific skills sets known to relate to marital success (e.g., turning toward their partner [Gottman & DeClaire, 2001], constructive conflict styles [Gottman, 1994], and physiological soothing [Crumley, 2002; Gottman, 1994; Gottman, Coan, Carrére, & Swanson, 1998]). These skills would give couples a better chance of constructing relationships that are socially just and that can better support social justice in the broader society.

Research on a variety of levels is needed to assess how social justice functions in couple relationships. For example, the division of household labor is an important topic for many couples around the globe (Davis & Greenstein, 2004). Women still perform the majority of household labor (Bulanda et al.,

2004), even when they also work outside the home. Are there differences in relational quality for couples who support social justice in their everyday lives (e.g., by sharing household labor more equally) when compared to those who do not? Wives often view the division of household labor differently than do their husbands (Grote, Clark, & Moore, 2004; Kamo, 2000). It would be interesting to learn if wives' perceptions of the social justice of their relationships differed as well, and to know how this might influence other aspects of the relationships.

In addition to internal dynamics, such as household labor and conflict styles, pressures from the external world also affect the couple relationship (Baxter, 2004). Couples who struggle with economic hardship often are more hostile and less supportive in marital interaction (Conger et al., 1990). Relational problems associated with the lack of basic resources demonstrate that although social justice involves choice (i.e., how to relate to each other as a couple), it is also affected by the inequities and injustices of the larger society. Thus, social injustice must be attacked on multiple levels to effect change.

Parent–Child Relationships

The parent–child relationship is also a critical locus for social justice. Although family relationships should be the cradle of social justice, all too often they create and replicate social injustice instead. Ideally, parent–child interactions are supportive, responding to the child's changing needs in appropriate ways. Such communication also inculcates a keen sense of relational awareness so that children learn to recognize and reject interactions that are not appropriate.

Mutual respect and caring signify socially just parent–child relationships. With the inherent inequity of the parent–child bond, the parent must recognize the child's rights as an individual human being. At the same time, if the relationship is to fulfill its function in the development and socialization of the child, the parent must accept and act in the role of a parent rather than a peer. Child socialization is one of the major roles that the family is expected to assume (Stafford, 2004), and parental patterns of communication, especially in discipline, are critical to the child's development of self-control (Bradley & Corwyn, 2005). A study by Wilson, Morgan, Hayes, Bylund, and Herman (2004) linked the risk of child abuse to communication patterns. They found that mothers who were more likely to be abusive to their children used fewer affirming comments and were less open to their children's opinions than were mothers with a lower risk of being abusive. This pattern of nonaffirmation and one-way communication is reminiscent of many patterns of social injustice in which the people in control make demands, but do not seem to care for or to recognize the needs of the people who are under their power. Research by Davalos, Chavez, and Guardiola (2005) found that adolescents who perceived their parents' communication as supportive and interested were less likely to commit acts of delinquency than those with lower scores in family communication. Clearly, interpersonal communication is important to creating families that support social justice.

Familial abuse is the primary experience of social injustice. When a parent physically, verbally, sexually, or emotionally abuses a child, the parent not only practices social injustice at the moment of abuse, but he or she also teaches the child that such behavior is a prerogative of the powerful. Some children will undoubtedly rebel against this tyranny, but others will carry its effects into their own experiences and parenting expectations (e.g., Cicchetti, 2004; Locke & Newcomb, 2004; Milan et al., 2004). This is tragic.

One tragedy is the inherent injustice of child abuse in a relationship with a parent, whose role demands that they be trustworthy and supportive instead of neglectful and damaging. Another tragedy is the increased risk that abused children will grow up to repeat unjust behaviors in their own families (Swinford, DeMaris, Cernkovich, & Giordano, 2000; Widom, 1989), creating (or continuing) generational patterns of dysfunctional relationships and social injustice. Still another tragedy is that patterns of dysfunction endanger society as a whole when damaging relational practices are accepted as normal and promulgated as such in everyday life. These social norms extend into laws and policies when they are accepted as reflecting the will of the people, and eventually affect both current and future generations.

Societal norms affect the ease with which families engage in a daily experience of social justice. Parents who struggle day by day to meet basic survival needs for their families are more likely to subjugate children without consideration of social justice. This is partly a cultural norm for many lower class families, but it is rooted in the practical problem of scarcity of resources. The chronic stress of inadequate resources entangles the entire family in a web of dysfunction and poor health (McEwen, 2004). This is a family communication problem that could be positively influenced by responsible social policies that help families develop adequate resources. Families should be trained (e.g., Adams, 2001; Ireland, Sanders, & Markie-Dadds, 2003; Kosterman, Hawkins, Spoth, Haggerty, & Zhu, 1997) in how to modify generational dysfunctions to create a better life. Change is never easy, but changes in interpersonal communication habits can help people construct a reality that better fits their goals and needs and that supports social justice in the family unit.

Sibling Relationships

The sibling relationship is another area that plays an important role in constituting social justice. Children learn fundamentals of communication in relationships with brothers and sisters, as well as with peers (Stafford, 2004). These provide frameworks for normative social interaction in adulthood. "That's not fair!" is a complaint nearly every parent with more than one child has heard, yet when a sibling obviously needs extra parental care, children generally perceive this as acceptable (Kowal, Kramer, Krull, & Crick, 2002). This suggests that children are able to recognize issues of social justice (i.e., their sibling's well-being) even when they contradict their personal preferences, and can make choices that support social justice. On the other hand, much rivalry is engendered in children's struggles to negotiate with siblings their particular versions of social justice in moment-by-moment interaction. The active creation or negation of social justice among siblings can turn violent; sibling assault leads the list of forms of child victimization (Finkelhor & Dziuba-Leatherman, 1994). Patterns of fairness and justice (or the inverse) may cast long shadows; patterns created in sibling relationships often influence later marital relationships (Mones, 2001).

Extended Family Relationships

Extended family relationships, such as those with nonparenting relatives and close adult friends affect the child's experience and observation of social justice. Grandparents often assist parents in raising the children, and friends and relatives provide support that generally relates to positive outcomes for the child (Schmeeckle & Sprecher, 2004). This is one of the few areas in which underresourced people are the major focus of research; most research regarding the influence of social networks on children has focused on families with disadvantaged mothers (Schmeeckle & Sprecher, 2004). Still, little is known about how extended families practice and teach social justice in their interactions.

CRUCIBLE OF SOCIAL JUSTICE

Social justice, as defined earlier in this chapter, focuses on the quality of relationships between people, and particularly on an overall judgment of the way a relationship is or is not fair or just. Family relationships provide the first setting in which social justice is constructed. However, people communicate with others beyond their family members. Interpersonal communication is not only the cradle of social justice; it is also the crucible. In the heat of interpersonal interaction with a variety of people, we have the opportunity to test our impressions of social justice and learn their mettle. This section examines some of the major issues affecting social justice in interpersonal communication: the intersections between "we" and "they," language use, perception, and dialectical tensions.

We–They

Social justice is often perceived and interpreted along the intersections between people. These intersections, as described earlier, include inequities in almost every area of life (e.g., gender, power, status, race, role, social class, sexual orientation, religion, age, lifestyle, politics). It is difficult to construct socially just relationships with people whose lives and resources seem so different from those with which we are familiar. However, it is only in attempting the conversation that we may hope for success. As Baxter (2004) notes, "the construction of similarity and difference is a complex dialogic enterprise. Similarity and difference are ... not cast in concrete but instead are dynamic, interrelated constructions that are built through interaction" (p. 6). When we use stereotyped, scripted methods of interaction in dealing with people who are different from ourselves, it blinds us to the inventive interaction needed to construct similarity and create "we-ness."

The social construction of *they* versus *we* often subverts social justice. People who interact with each other as persons rather than as roles will construe and construct social justice differently. Ultimately, it is in getting to know each other, allowing each other into our worlds, being willing to risk our current understandings and perceptions, that we may change our minds and feelings. Together, communicators may join *we* and *they* into an all-inclusive *we* and change *other* into a much bigger, broader, and more vibrant *us*. However, the conversation is never finished, and because it frequently involves new participants, social justice will bubble to the surface over and over as a need, a goal, a priority, (hopefully) an achievement, and (again) a need. Long-term progress can be measured when the quality of the need changes toward less desperate disparities and more refined equities.

Language

"Language is the medium of expression we use to create our reality" (Bochner, 2002, p. 80). The ways language is used may need to change to facilitate the construction of social justice. Frey (1998) argues that communication scholars need to identify and reconstruct the "grammars" or uses of language that lead to social inequities. This is particularly true in the area of interpersonal communication, where millennia of traditional relationship habits from a variety of cultures influence views of social justice. One example of language change related to social justice is gender-neutral terminology. Although not perfect, gender-neutral language begins to recognize the essential unity of people (American Psychological Association, 2001). This is a step toward creating a society that is inclusive and allows many options for all members, rather than fragmenting us on the basis of the exclusive categorization of gender. More change may be needed in how we use language. As an example, tee box nomenclature used on golf scorecards suggests that women must tee off from the same location as junior golfers, whereas men are allowed to tee off from a location determined by their ability (Hundley, 2004). Golf may or may not be a microcosm of social justice, but such language-structured inequities are still common.

In interpersonal communication, it is not only the grammars, but also the glossaries of our relationships that need review. We not only need to change our words, but also our meanings. For example, politeness, in whatever words, is more likely to be displayed by the least powerful person in a relationship (Dillard, Wilson, Tusing, & Kinney, 1997). However, when people feel accepted and cared for, they often behave less politely (Miller, 1991). Why is this misuse of language and meanings acceptable? When appropriate words (i.e., politeness) can be used to reach inappropriate goals (i.e., dominance), the construction of social justice is subverted. Because of this mismatch, shared meaning may not be an immediately attainable goal as we seek social justice. When generations of differences and centuries of distrust and disdain are built into our vocabularies, the most for which we may hope immediately is a recognition and respect for shared personhood.

Scholars of interpersonal communication should examine how language and meaning impact (and are impacted by) common role and relationship practices. An interpersonally situated sense of social justice will require both respect and caring in the conversation. We create our worlds together, and we must dialogue with each other to enable the construction of social justice in ways that all of the participants perceive as just.

Perception

Social justice is, to a large extent, a judgment. Who makes the judgment? Who decides that social justice has or has not occurred? The participants in the relationship are typically the ones who assess their relationship as socially just or unjust, but their perceptions may differ. One may see the relationship as being perfectly just while the other views the relationship as fundamentally flawed. Furthermore, their perspectives may change over time and circumstances. Regularities in the behavior of communicators reflect implicit relationship rules and create the quality of their relationships. The perceived injustice of the communication in our "mundane interactions" (Gottman & DeClaire, 2001, p. 308) accumulates to become the overall injustice of the relationship. Long term, the perception of justice or injustice in interpersonal relationships may become one of the overarching qualities that define the relationship. People who (directly or indirectly) are benefited by social injustice may not fully recognize it as unjust, but those who are targets of injustice will notice and perceive it as negative. If a relationship is judged to be negative for a long time, negative sentiment override (Weiss, 1980) may develop, tainting the judgment of future behaviors (Grote et al., 2004) and poisoning the possibility of social justice.

Outsiders also influence relationships with their own perceptions of and visions for social justice. Baxter (2004) notes that "relationships are in dialogue with the social order that exists outside the immediate [relationship]" and "relationship parties are immersed in ongoing communication with outsiders to the relationship as they all go about the business of crafting an identity for that relationship" (pp. 6–7). Outsiders who perceive a relationship as socially unjust may not support or legitimate that relationship.

Whatever the perspectives of the participants or of outsiders, it is less important that assessments agree on the degree to which a particular relationship is socially just than that the issue be raised. If there is any question of social justice, it is important that we be willing to recognize each others' needs and views and act in ways that value and include others' perceptions.

Dialectics: Change Is the Constant

Social justice, like many relational qualities, is a part of the constant of change. As we communicate with each other (in socially just ways or not), we change each other (and our ideas of social justice), and are changed ourselves. Instead of expecting equilibrium, Baxter (2004) suggests that scholars consider change as the norm, and recognize that constant communication is required to survive. This seems an especially appropriate argument in the context of social justice. Social justice is constantly under construction and there is no "right" way to "do" social justice that will stay "correct" over time. Although the ideal of social justice changes slowly, the actual practice of social justice must be continually monitored and frequently adjusted. Social justice is constantly evolving with the inclusion of new people in the conversation and new nuances in the construct of its meaning. As mentioned earlier, new situations may demand novel responses.

In the context of interpersonal communication, Baxter and Montgomery (1996) list several dialectical tensions—simultaneous pulls in opposite directions—for relationships: autonomy versus connectedness, openness versus closedness, and predictability versus novelty. These dialectics are readily applicable to social justice and its communication. For example, the dialectic of autonomy versus connectedness is illustrated in the we–they construction discussed earlier. Does one stay separate (autonomous) or join in the bigger unity with *they* (connectedness)?

Openness versus closedness is also relevant to social justice. Openness implies vulnerability, whereas closedness implies security and stability in the face of change. For groups who are unwilling to be vulnerable, yet who desperately need change, this is a painful dialectic. Ethnographers (e.g., Basso, 1979; Geertz, 1973) who work with underresourced populations sometimes find that it is difficult, even as scholars, to allow a level of personal openness that permits them to move toward an understanding of people in unfamiliar and sometimes threatening situations. It takes time to be accepted and develop the level of trust necessary to begin to understand a group of people.

If being open is difficult for trained professionals, how much more tenuous is it for people whose ways of life are threatened when they are open? The problem is especially relevant for communities who have historically been deprived and disinherited by the system for maintaining their own values and patterns of communication (e.g., Native Americans in the northwest United States, Aborigines in Australia). Closedness may represent security, and openness an unnecessary threat when a dominant group has demonstrated its lack of understanding across many years. The resource holders, on the other hand, may not recognize their own closedness toward the underresourced group's culture or mores. They may see closedness in the disempowered as defiance or unwillingness to respond appropriately to their generosity. In this case, the dialectic is situated in the relationship itself, rather than in the individuals. Its tension is still intense, however, and makes the construction of social justice a daunting task for persons in both groups.

Other tensions that behave as dialectics, simultaneously pulling relationships (and social justice) in multiple ways, may include different values in working versus living (e.g., different social classes have different ideas about the amount of time and energy that should be spent in working vs. the amount of time and energy that should be reserved for living, as well as different constructions of the use of people vs. the use of things [Payne, 1995]). The point is that multiple tensions affect the construction of social justice in relationships. In the crucible of real-time interpersonal relationships, social justice is constantly being reinvented to meet the changing needs and visions of its participants.

THE CRUX OF THE MATTER

Because social justice and interpersonal communication are, by definition, integrally entwined, scholars of interpersonal communication have the responsibility to learn and communicate as we promote relational well-being and good interpersonal communication practices. The crux of the matter is learning how people interact with one another and using this knowledge wisely to support social justice. Interpersonal communication scholars need to learn and to communicate their findings to fulfill this mission.

To Learn

Scholars are taught to think, especially in terms of scholarly research. The drive to learn, discover, and contribute to the conversation of increasing knowledge is structurally supported by the publishing demands of many tenure committees, as well as the expectations of professional colleagues. This helps to generate a wide variety of research each year. The explosion of knowledge in recent years is due, in part, to such expectations and demands. Scholars, however, live not only in the world of ideas, but also in the world of people. Our academic skills and ways of thinking, when combined with a passion for people, open an amazingly diverse universe of opportunity. Interpersonal communication scholars need to invest thought and energy into imagining better ways to support social justice in the realm of interpersonal communication. Thinking deeply in this area will lead to a desire to learn—to investigate and discover as much as possible about our particular niche. If we connect with and help populations in need, we can offer both practical and theoretical help in recognizing and re-creating social justice in the many spheres in which we live.

Social justice is an important criterion to consider before committing to a project. It is important to choose research projects carefully—to consciously realize the limitations of our resources (e.g., time, money, energy) and to purposefully decide on the best use of these resources. Initially it may seem that learning should focus on immediately applicable research, but this is short-sighted. Some research that appears esoteric may prove its long-term applicability in ways that are yet unanticipated. Other research has immediate and obvious application, but all have potential value in the long-term support of social justice.

Although the majority of research in the area of interpersonal communication is still dedicated to the definition and explication of the various phenomena that comprise interpersonal communication, the discipline is beginning to develop further along several fronts. As basic definitions are created and tested, some researchers are moving on to map the linkages between various phenomena. Others are taking a deeper look at these linkages and creating theory to explain the bigger picture. Still others are reaching out to apply what we have learned and to meet problems in the broader world. In considering disciplinary development, it is important to note that defining and investigating phenomena are necessary to create a foundation of knowledge for a discipline. However, many scholars of interpersonal communication are becoming interested in the ways in which interpersonal research is applicable to the problems that people face in everyday life (Knapp, Miller, & Fudge, 1994). In the recursive interplay among research, theory, and application, both research and theory may help prepare the way for application. Practical application, in turn, offers additional motivation for research and tests theory in ways that primarily intellectual activity cannot. As we refine our own visions of social justice and become aware of the needs of the people around us, we will discover what fuels our passions and use it to add depth and meaning to our research (Bochner, 2002) and help connect our work with the people who need it most.

In seeking to apply our professional interests to the needs of the people around us, recognizing issues of social justice may add clarity to our purpose. If interpersonal communication scholars are to fulfill their roles as learners, they must connect with scholars of a variety of relevant disciplines to formulate theory. Many of the burning issues of social justice cannot reasonably be addressed from the perspective of a single researcher or even a single discipline. Although specific hypotheses may be testable within disciplinary walls, bigger issues need bigger thinking to frame a vision that recognizes the role of all in creating social justice. This interdisciplinary perspective should be heuristic, rather than limiting, and ideally will create connections that will serve a variety of learning tasks.

To Communicate

In addition to learning about social justice, scholars of interpersonal communication must communicate their findings with others. First, we must share our research findings with our colleagues. Not only does this contribute to the ongoing conversations of both theory and praxis that outlast any one scholar's lifetime, but it is essential in building the framework for under-standings that may facilitate important discoveries in the future. Scholarly communication, including the formal and informal advice and commentary of other scholars, helps ensure the quality and completeness of our work. The general public does not have the skills to judge most research, but it de-serves the best we can offer—a "best" we can achieve most effectively when we are encouraged and stimulated by communication with others in our field.

Scholars of interpersonal communication also need to communicate with helping professionals (e.g., counselors) who work daily with those suf-fering from social injustice. These professionals may be encouraged by in-formation about new research discoveries as well as by metatheoretical articles that articulate coherent pictures of collected discoveries. In turn, researchers may benefit from helping professionals' insights into what is happening in particular people groups and their understandings of the most vital current questions related to communication and social justice in various populations.

As professors we must incorporate the ideals of social justice into our teaching. We must find ways to talk about (and demonstrate) social justice in our classrooms and on our campuses. Students need to become aware of how interpersonal communication constitutes social justice and they need communication instruction that will empower them in constructing socially just lives.

In addition to research and teaching, it is important that we recognize and thoughtfully consider how society, government, and particular institu-tions support or sabotage sound principles of communication and justice. We should communicate our expertise to the decision makers who need quality information on which to base their decisions regarding policies and laws. Decision makers may create or exacerbate social injustice because of a lack of knowledge or understanding that scholars could provide if they were communicating with one another. Most "policy-oriented and regulatory bodies ... rely on research that already has been done" (Brown, 2002, p. 335), so scholars of interpersonal communication should be proactive in doing research that we consider necessary to influence policies that effec-tively support social justice. As Brown (2002) observes, "If we continue to talk only to ourselves, and do not look for opportunities to apply and show how our work is relevant, our intellectual contributions are correspondingly diminished." She recommends that we "broaden our perspectives, find al-lies and collaborators, and apply our knowledge in meaningful questions" (pp. 339–340). Although Brown's words were written for scholars of mass communication, they are quite appropriate for interpersonal and family scholars as well. The perspective of relational scholars is needed to help envision and put into place social structures that enhance the likelihood of people creating and sustaining healthy interpersonal relationships. We must let people know that we have something valuable to say and are willing to collaborate in creating social justice.

Social justice, defined in a broad sense, demands that the people who discover basic rules for relationship success must communicate these rules to the people who would like to know them but do not have the resources to discover them. It is a shame that people who want relationships that are right, good, ethical, and just have so little quality research information on which to draw when attempting to create such relationships. As any beginning student knows, reading academic research can be intimidating. Yet much of the research performed by interpersonal communication scholars directly or indirectly relates to the relationships conducted by all of us and may affect the quality of our lives. Many people are underresourced in the area of relational knowledge and skills. A few scholars (e.g., Gottman) are successfully bringing excellent-quality relational research to the general public, but much more needs to be accomplished in this area, particularly by scholars trained in interpersonal communication.

When communicating with populations at risk, it is important to offer information in a manner that is accessible. People are often confused and concerned about their relationships and interpersonal communication and would like to have better information on which to make their decisions. If this is offered in an appropriate and interesting way, they will grasp the concepts and try to apply them to their lives. For this purpose, scholars may need to use teaching tools that are not traditionally considered academic. Gottman, for example, has successfully engaged with the popular magazine market; summaries of his research findings appear in such venues as *Psychology Today* (Gottman & Carrére, 2000). But does research have to be written in only one way? Why not create novels or short relational stories (e.g., those in popular magazines) demonstrating effective principles of relating? Bochner (2002) suggests that stories are important vehicles for conveying information, and authors worldwide know that relationships make wonderful stories. For groups who cannot or do not read much, theatrical demonstrations of the most important findings in interpersonal communication research might be more effective. Principles of good relationships should be incorporated in television shows (including the old relational standby—soap operas), movies, and music. People gain information from modeling (Bandura, 1977; Stern, 2005), so why not present them with accurate information? Although such approaches are unusual, they are sorely needed to bridge the knowledge gap and create an awareness of both the need and some of the means for achieving social justice in interpersonal relationships.

Finally, interpersonal scholars must communicate their visions of social justice by the way they choose to live. When we try to construct social justice in our own relationships and lifestyles and to actively engage in helping people who are in need of social justice, those who know us will be influenced to do likewise. At a minimum, this means respecting and caring for our families, friends, colleagues, and community members. Becoming aware of and open to the needs of diverse people, groups, and individuals in our own neighborhoods, towns, or cities is a crucial first step toward becoming voices for social justice in our worlds of influence. Small acts of social justice—paying attention to our own interpersonal and relational communication—may teach us how to engage in the construction of social justice in the broader world, and to inspire others to join that conversation.

ACKNOWLEDGMENT

I thank Greta Martin for her research assistance on this chapter.

REFERENCES

Adams, J. F. (2001). Impact of parent training on family functioning. *Child and Family Behavior Therapy, 23,* 29–42.

Adelman, M., & Frey, L. (1997). *The fragile community: Living together with AIDS.* Mahwah, NJ: Lawrence Erlbaum Associates, Inc.

Agnes, M. (Ed.). (1999). *Webster's new world college dictionary* (4th ed.). New York: Macmillan.

American Psychological Association. (2001). *Publication manual of the American Psychological Association* (5th ed.). Washington, DC: APA.

Bandura, A. (1977). *Social learning theory.* Englewood Cliffs, NJ: Prentice-Hall.

Basso, K. H. (1979). *Linguistic play and cultural symbols among the Western Apache.* New York: Cambridge University Press.

Baxter, L. A. (2004). Relationships as dialogues. *Personal Relationships, 11,* 1–22.

Baxter, L. A., & Montgomery, B. M. (1996). *Relating: Dialogues and dialectics.* New York: Guilford.

Bochner, A. P. (2002). Perspectives on inquiry III: The moral of stories. In M. L. Knapp & J. A. Daly (Eds.), *Handbook of interpersonal communication* (pp. 73–101). Thousand Oaks, CA: Sage.

Bradley, R. H., & Corwyn, R. F. (2005). Productive activity and the prevention of behavior problems. *Developmental Psychology, 41,* 89–98.

Brown, J. D. (2002). Doing relevant funded mass media research. *Journal of Applied Communication Research, 30,* 334–340.

Bulanda, R. E., Bulanda, J. R., Colegrove, M. L., Crane, E. A., Deines, J. A., Osgood, A. K., et al. (2004). Guest editors' note. *Journal of Marriage and the Family, 66,* 1073–1075.

Burleson, B. R., Delia, J. G., & Applegate, J. L. (1995). The socialization of person-centered communication: Parents' contributions to their children's social-cognitive and communication skills. In M. A. Fitzpatrick & A. L. Vangelisti (Eds.), *Explaining family interactions* (pp. 34–76). Thousand Oaks, CA: Sage.

Cicchetti, D. (2004). An odyssey of discovery: Lessons learned through three decades of research on child maltreatment. *American Psychologist, 59,* 731–741.

Conger, R. D., Elder, G. H., Lorenz, F. O., Conger, K. J., Simons, R. L., Whitbeck, L. B., et al. (1990). Linking economic hardship to marital quality and instability. *Journal of Marriage and the Family, 52,* 643–656.

Crumley, L. P. (2002). Discourse of de-escalating arousal: How couples interact during problem-solving discussions when heart rate is decreasing. *Dissertation Abstracts International, 64*(07), 2310. (University Microfilms International No. 3099443)

Davalos, D. B., Chavez, E. L., & Guardiola, R. J. (2005). Effects of perceived parental school support and family communication on delinquent behaviors in Latinos and White non-Latinos. *Cultural Diversity and Ethnic Minority Psychology, 11,* 57–68.

Davis, S. N., & Greenstein, T. N. (2004). Cross-national variations in the division of household labor. *Journal of Marriage and the Family, 66,* 1260–1271.

Dillard, J. P., Wilson, S. R., Tusing, K. J., & Kinney, T. A. (1997). Politeness judgments in personal relationships. *Journal of Language and Social Psychology, 16,* 297–325.

Finkelhor, D., & Dziuba-Leatherman, J. (1994). Victimization of children. *American Psychologist, 49,* 173–183.

Frey, L. R. (1998). Communication and social justice research: Truth, justice, and the applied communication way. *Journal of Applied Communication Research, 47,* 155–164.

Frey, L. R., Pearce, W. B., Pollock, M. A., Artz, L., & Murphy, B. A. O. (1996). Looking for justice in all the wrong places: On a communication approach to social justice. *Communication Studies, 47,* 110–127.

Geertz, C. (1973). *The interpretation of cultures: Selected essays.* New York: Basic Books.

Gottman, J. M. (1994). *Why marriages succeed or fail.* New York: Simon & Schuster.

Gottman, J. M., & Carrére, S. (2000). Welcome to the love lab. *Psychology Today, 33,* 42–49.

Gottman, J. M., Coan, J., Carrére, S., & Swanson, C. (1998). Predicting marital happiness and stability from newlywed interactions. *Journal of Marriage and the Family, 60,* 5–22.

Gottman, J. M., & DeClaire, J. (2001). *The relationship cure: A 5 step guide for building better connections with family, friends, and lovers.* New York: Crown.

Gottman, J. M., Jacobson, N. S., Rushe, R. H., Shortt, J. W., Babcock, J., La Taillade, J. J., Waltz, J. (1995). The relationship between heart rate reactivity, emotionally aggressive behavior, and general violence in batterers. *Journal of Family Psychology, 9,* 227–248.

Grote, N. K., Clark, M. S., & Moore, A. (2004). Perceptions of injustice in family work: The role of psychological distress. *Journal of Family Psychology, 18,* 480–492.

Hundley, H. L. (2004). Keeping the score: The hegemonic everyday practices in golf. *Communication Reports, 17,* 39–48.

Ireland, J. L., Sanders, M. R., & Markie-Dadds, C. (2003). The impact of parenting training on marital functioning: A comparison of two group versions of the Triple P-positive parenting program for parents of children with early-onset conduct problems. *Behavioral & Cognitive Psychotherapy, 31,* 127–142.

Kamo, Y. (2000). "He said, she said": Assessing discrepancies in husbands' and wives' reports on the division of household labor. *Social Science Research, 29,* 459–476.

Knapp, M. L., Miller, G. R., & Fudge, K. (1994). Background and current trends in the study of interpersonal communication. In M. L. Knapp & G. R. Miller (Eds.), *Handbook of interpersonal communication* (2nd ed., pp. 3–20). Thousand Oaks, CA: Sage.

Kosterman, R., Hawkins, J. D., Spoth, R., Haggerty, K. P., & Zhu, K. (1997). Effects of a preventive parent-training intervention on observed family interactions: Proximal outcomes from Preparing for the Drug Free Years. *Journal of Community Psychology, 25,* 337–352.

Kowal, A., Kramer, L., Krull, J. L., & Crick, N. R. (2002). Children's perceptions of the fairness of parental preferential treatment and their socioemotional well-being. *Journal of Family Psychology, 16,* 297–306.

Locke, T. F., & Newcomb, N. D. (2004). Child maltreatment, parent alcohol- and drug-related problems, polydrug problems, and parenting practices: A test of gender differences and four theoretical perspectives. *Journal of Family Psychology, 18,* 120–134.

McEwen, B. S. (2004, October). *From molecules to mind: Stress, the individual and the social environment.* Keynote address at the annual convention of the Society for Psychophysiological Research, Santa Fe, NM.

Milan, S., Kershaw, T., Lewis, J., Ickovics, J. R., Meade, C., & Ethier, K. (2004). Prevalence, course, and predictors of emotional distress in pregnant and parenting adolescents. *Journal of Consulting and Clinical Psychology, 72,* 328–340.

Miller, R. S. (1991). On decorum in close relationships: Why aren't we polite to those we love? *Contemporary Social Psychology, 15,* 63–65.

Mones, A. G. (2001). Exploring themes of sibling experience to help resolve couples conflict. *The Family Journal, 9,* 455–460.

Payne, R. K. (1995). *A framework for understanding and working with students and adults from poverty.* Baytown, TX: RFT.

Schmeeckle, M., & Sprecher, S. (2004). Extended family and social networks. In A. L. Vangelisti (Ed.), *Handbook of family communication* (pp. 349–378). Mahwah, NJ: Lawrence Erlbaum Associates, Inc.

Stafford, L. (2004). Communication competencies and sociocultural priorities of middle childhood. In A. L. Vangelisti (Ed.), *Handbook of family communication* (pp. 311–332). Mahwah, NJ: Lawrence Erlbaum Associates, Inc.

Stern, S. R. (2005). Self-absorbed, dangerous, and disengaged: What popular films tell us about teenagers. *Mass Communication & Society, 8,* 23–38.

Swinford, S. P., DeMaris, A., Cernkovich, S. A., & Giordano, P. C. (2000). Harsh physical discipline in childhood and violence in later romantic involvements: The mediating role of problem behaviors. *Journal of Marriage and the Family, 62,* 508–519.

Vangelisti, A. L., Crumley, L. P., & Baker, J. L. (1999). Family portraits: Stories as standards for family relationships. *Journal of Social and Personal Relationships, 16,* 335–368.

Weiss, R. L. (1980). Strategic behavioral and marital therapy: Toward a model for assessment and intervention. In J. P. Vincent (Ed.), *Advances in family intervention, assessment and theory* (Vol. 1, pp. 229–271). Greenwich, CT: JAI.

Widom, C. S. (1989). Does violence beget violence? A critical examination of the literature. *Psychological Bulletin, 106,* 3–28.

Wilson, S. R., Morgan, W. M., Hayes, J., Bylund, C., & Herman, A. (2004). Mothers' child abuse potential as a predictor of maternal and child behaviors during play-time interactions. *Communication Monographs, 71,* 395–421.

10

The Desire to Know and to Love Is Never Too Small: My Musings on Teaching and Social Justice

Wenshu Lee
San Jose State University

For college professors in communication studies, the classroom is an important forum for bringing up, exploring, and debating socially important issues. Here, we try out new theories and assignments, and we reflect critically on their pedagogical implications for student learning. However, this process is often rocky, replete with our inability to grapple with many unasked and unanswered questions: Are there better ways to teach social justice and communication? How do we bring up difficult issues to stretch horizons? Whose horizons? How do we deal with students who do not accept the premises of social justice work? How do we deal with colleagues who do not share our commitment to social change? What are the implications for our career—salary increase, tenure, promotion, and retention? What are the implications for our conscience? How do we deal with the feelings of isolation, burnout, and cynicism?

Writing this chapter, I continue the search for theoretically informed ways of transforming college classrooms into social justice communities. I share in the first half of this chapter a pedagogical project I have enacted after my promotion to full professor at San Jose State University, an institution where no single racial group is the majority and most students come from working-class backgrounds with themselves being the first in their families to enter or graduate from college. In the second half of this chapter, I meditate on the implications my pedagogical efforts bear for social justice teaching.[1]

BEFORE 9/11: MY ITINERARIES

In my scholarly work, I consciously search for and study omissions that grow out of my upbringing, formal education, and border crossing in two different national contexts (Taiwan and the United States). Early in the process of pursuing my doctoral degree, I noted that, up to the late 1980s, interpersonal studies (an area of my emphases) used convenient samples, spotlighting college students who were enrolled at large universities in the Midwest. Coded critically, those who participated in interpersonal research were most likely White, middle-class, patriarchal, hetero-normative and American-centric. My relation with the scholarship available in graduate seminars thus was fraught with erasure and irrelevance, a state that ultimately propelled me in the 1990s into two new directions—critical intercultural studies and intersectionality scholarship in race, gender and, ultimately, sexuality.[2]

My scholarly career, in the early 1990s, made its break from a social justice unconscious paradigm to one that deems social justice as paramount for higher learning. My scholarly itinerary, in more concrete terms, has evolved over the past 15 years into critical intercultural communication, feminisms, womanisms, postcoloniality, and, ultimately, to queer theory. No longer invisible and unaccountable as a detached spectator, I read myself historically and institutionally as "a woman of color," and explore my own strengths and limits as a "colored womanist" living in the United States in a global con-

---

[1]A recent anthology edited by Clayton and Williams (2004) provides a strong overview of different philosophical approaches to social justice. More important, the third section of the volume provides chapters that apply and critique theories in concrete "sites of social justice," including family and gender, global poverty, environmental justice, and future generations. I find Anderson's (2004) advocacy of political egalitarian movements that address systematic forms of oppression more compelling than views articulated by Locke, Hume, Dworkin, and Rawls.

[2]My earlier work in critical intercultural communication advocates a sociohistorical approach (Lee, Chung, Wang, & Hertel, 1995), which argues against a context-free, ahistorical, and adaptation-oriented paradigm that had dominated intercultural studies in the 1970s and 1980s. I further theorized ways in which "strangers" from different linguistic and cultural communities can learn to build closer intercultural ties through the sharing of deep cultural codes; that is, humor and idioms (Lee, 1993, 1994). I became interested in the politics of memory and amnesia (Lee & Wander, 1998) and the trope of "Chinese women" in relation to feminisms. My deep discontent regarding the discourse emitted from White-centric, race, class, and sexuality unconscious second-wave feminists in women's studies and communication studies resulted in my retheorizing Chinese women's oppression and agency (Lee, 1998b), the rhetoric of the antifootbinding movement (Lee, 1998a), Whiteness and colorism as a gendered and racialized oppression (Lee, 1999), and Chinese lesbianism (Lee, 2003).

text. I believe it is politically urgent to forge stronger alliances between women of color in the United States and third-world women globally. Women of color should not be coded as a passive biological given. Rather, they are potential points of alliance building due to "a common context of struggles against specific exploitative structures and systems" (Mohanty, 2003, p. 49).

STUDENTS, WHY DON'T YOU GET IT!

However sophisticated and critical I try to be, I catch myself becoming enraged by "socially unjust remarks" from my students who come from privileged as well as oppressed communities. Over the years these episodes, big or small, accumulated to the point that I was compelled to deal with them seriously. The following are representative examples:

- A straight, White, former football player loudly declared his view one day in class: There is no racism in California, his Whiteness does not carry any privilege, and female sports reporters are all chosen because of their looks rather than brains and knowledge.
- An Iranian American student commented on her antifeminist desire to remain "girlie," her intense opposition to affirmative action, and her belief that increasing the minimum wage would cause inflation and would not benefit the poor.
- An Asian American student argued that homosexuality and abortion are sins and that God condemned both practices.
- Many students, women and men, complained that those who oppose spotlighting a professional title with gender specificity (e.g., a female doctor, a male secretary, a woman construction worker, and a male nurse) and identity-based profanity (e.g., bitch, nigger, fag) take things too seriously. People are too sensitive; they reason that people should not read too much into an other's intention.
- Many working-class students claimed that Americans have no business protesting against the World Trade Organization and International Monetary Fund because those who work in Nike's sweatshops in Indonesia are better off earning the low wages they do than prostituting themselves or starving themselves to death.

More generally, I became aware of the what I call "it does not bother me" mantra: It does not bother me if the federal government monitors my e-mails, because I have nothing to hide. It does not bother me if a man opens the door for me or pays for my dinner because I want to be treated like a "lady." It does not bother me if companies lay off people or cut health and retirement benefits because they need to remain competitive. It does not bother me if gays and lesbians cannot marry in the United States because marriage should be between a man and a woman.

Why don't students get it? My rage is near the level of explosion. Racism is still alive and well, even in California (remember Proposition 187 and the Rodney King incident). Whiteness carries with it undeniable privileges and violence (Roediger, 2002). Women can perform competently on any job, be it firefighting, construction, sports reporting, car fixing, and so on. Those who support equal rights took decades to establish affirmative action policies, which, unfortunately, have steadily been dismantled (on the other hand, what about the Ivy League's version of affirmative action: quotas for unqualified offspring of wealthy alumni and 40% of their students receive As?). Religion and the state should be separated and an individual's God should not dictate public policies. Mounting national deficits, artificially low interest rates, insane tax cuts for the wealthy, and money spent in maintaining the U.S. imperialistic presence in Iraq and other countries are bringing back the demon of "stagflation" (Krugman, 2005), which is far more detrimental to national and personal financial well-being than a minimum wage increase. Oppression and violence against the other in race, class, gender, religion, sexuality, and nationality are abhorrent and should be opposed collectively. Allowing government unrestricted access to our personal communication is to hand in a fundamental piece of our freedom and to allow an assault on our dignity.

FIVE METAPHORS FOR TEACHING IN A POST-9/11 CONTEXT

The changes in geopolitical contexts, especially after 9/11, have prompted a thorough reevaluation of my teaching and scholarship. However, it was not until my conversations with allies, well respected scholars in performance, intercultural communication, and gender and queer studies (including Gust Yep, John Elia, Mary Jane Collier, Bryant Alexander, Aimee Carillo Rowe, Sheena Malhorta, Dreama Moon, and Karen Lovaas) at a series of table talks on emotion, politics, and pedagogy at the conferences held by the Western States Communication Association and the National Communication Association that I began to explore the pain, disease, rage, and silence associated with the previous "why don't they get it" experiences in the classroom, and learn to teach differently.

My pedagogical experiment discussed here was initiated in Fall 2002. In 3.5 years, I used two basic assignment units—discussion leadership[3] and narrative performance[4]—in three upper division courses, including Interpersonal Communication, Communication and Culture, and Communication and Gender. In total, I taught roughly 220 students in six classes.

Similar to earlier days, I continued the use of inclusive and critical essays that follow Haraway's "situated knowledge" and womanist criticism's emphasis on "intersectionality" in race, class, gender, and sexuality (Crenshaw, 1994). My experiment, however, marked a dramatic break from my earlier practices in taking seriously five heuristic metaphors urged by scholars in critical theory: power, voicedness, contact zones, safe houses, and stage.

Power Relations

Power is not all evil or all benign. It is not something possessed by individuals. It lies in enacted relationships between people in so far as "one wishes to direct the behavior of another" (Foucault, 1988, p. 11). In my experiment, student-led discussions and student performances replace instructor lectures as main forms of classroom activities. In other words, student communication with me in terms of written assignments and oral discussion in my office remains "private and personal," but their communication with one another becomes "public." This is a radical change. Over time students reorient my role from a public advocate and judge to a supportive critic in the

---

[3]Each student leads her or his peers to discuss for 17 minutes a main issue constructed from an assigned reading. To perform as a discussion leader, a student is to turn in a two-page lesson plan that includes a summary of the reading, research about the authors, a personal story related to the overall theme of the course, an attention getter, and a leading question with a few prepared follow-up questions. The student leader should also demonstrate competent facilitation skills. In a class of 40, the discussion sessions run for 10 class periods (75 minutes each period) or 5 weeks. All other student participants who are not discussion leaders are graded based on reading checks (to assess if they have completed the reading) and the frequency and quality of their verbal comments.

[4]In the narrative performance unit, each student is to engage in a 12-minute performance in front of the entire class followed by a 3- to 4-minute question-and-answer session. Like the student-led discussion sessions, in a class of 40, the performance sessions run for 10 class periods (75 minutes each period) or 5 weeks. All students are required to meet with me face-to-face at least 1 week before their scheduled performance day. Each performer is to bring a performance proposal to the meeting. Students may revise the proposal as the result of our meetings. This assignment has a different focus in each class. In Interpersonal Communication, the performance assignment is about a relational turning point; in Communication and Culture it is about protest or disagreement against a chosen cultural hierarchy; and in Communication and Gender it is about gendered disease (e.g., trouble, sickness, harmful development, lack of freedom from pain, discomfort, injustice, difficulty, embarrassment, or constraint.). The student performer should be one of the protagonists in the story, use at least one interactive visual aid, conduct interviews, and incorporate class discussions, class readings, and additional scholarly research. The main goals of their narrative performance are to transform their peers and themselves as best as they can in unjust social hierarchies. However, they are not required to include any information against their will.

private space. Over time, they also reorient the roles played by their peers from strangers and competitors to friends and supportive critics in the public space. If power relationships are "changeable, reversible and unstable" (p. 12), that is, if both sides have a certain degree of liberty to mount a resistance or to direct the other, I want the main power relationships to be between students.[5]

Voicedness and Punctum

Voicedness is a concept that I borrow from Bakhtin (1986). It refers to words spoken in live speech communication rather than words gathering dust in a dictionary. It is embodied and expressive in concrete material contexts. It is saturated with a unique individual's aura, his or her intentions, personalities, and histories. That is, voicedness refers to uniqueness in the use of my word rather than "nobody's word" or "other's word:"

> [A]ny word exists for the speaker in three aspects: as a neutral word of a language, belonging to nobody; as an *other*'s word, which belongs to another person and is filled with echoes of the other's utterance; and, finally, as *my* word, for, since I am dealing with it in a particular situation, with a particular speech plan, it is already imbued with my expression. (Bakhtin, 1986, p. 88)

In my experiment, I structure assignments to facilitate students' cultivation of voicedness, or "my-word centered" communication. For example, after reading Love and Kohn (2001), I ask students to write reflexive essays on the cultures with which they identify, the ones with which they do not, and on a souvenir the sight of which gives them punctum. These essay assignments are based on studium and punctum, two copresent concepts Barthes (1981) theorized to explore layered meanings of photography. Culturally specific but quite average, *studium* means "a kind of general, enthusiastic commitment … but without special acuity" (p. 26). *Punctum*, on the other hand, in an unexpected manner, "is this element which rises from the scene, shoots out of it like an arrow, and pierces me … punctum is also: sting, speck, cut, little hole—and also a cast of the dice. A photography's punctum is that accident which pricks me (but also bruises me, is poignant to me)" (pp. 26–27).

---

[5]I am fully aware of the fact that, as long as I hold the authority to grade students, I cannot erase myself from classroom power relations. However, a student-centered power structure reflects my belief that they need to debate each other, treat each other's rejoinders seriously, and ultimately, when they finish the class with me, they will take the skill, knowledge, and love with them to create bigger and wider social justice spaces.

Barthes elaborates on these two copresent concepts. Studium is replete with docile interest, liking, voice of banality, and the nameable. Punctum involves intensity, detail, loving, voice of singularity, and the ineffable. The former may shout at us, but the latter makes us feel tender and wounded. However precise a meaning we hope to grasp, punctum and studium remain magically elusive. Derrida (2001) rightfully cautions against too literal a borrowing, "If one wishes to transpose them elsewhere, and this is possible, useful, and even necessary, one must proceed analogically, though the operation will not be successful unless the other opus, the other system of composition, itself also carries these motifs in an original and irreplaceable way" (p. 42). In my teaching, the emphasis on punctum, through students' reflections on a souvenir, is to provide a space for "my words," so that they can get closer to their being, and to feel touched afresh by what Susan Sontag calls "the delayed rays of a star" (Barthes, 1981, p. 81).

Contact Zones, Safe Houses, and Stage

In addition to power and voicedness, I also reenvision the classroom in terms of three other metaphors: contact zones, safe houses, and stage. The first two metaphors are proposed by Pratt (1997), a prominent scholar in feminist and postcolonial theory. She defines *contact zones* as "social spaces where cultures meet, clash, and grapple with each other, often in contexts of highly asymmetrical relations of power" (p. 63); and *safe houses* as "social and intellectual spaces where groups can constitute themselves as horizontal, homogeneous, sovereign communities with high degrees of trust, shared understandings, and temporary protection from legacies of oppression" (p. 71). In my earlier teaching, too much space was devoted to contact zones and insufficient attention was given to healing. A social justice pedagogy, in my view, needs to create safe houses in contact zones so that difficult issues can be raised, discussed, and argued over while support and healing are also made real and available.

The fifth metaphor, stage, grows out of scholarly work in performance pedagogy. In the past five decades, the return of performance in theater, literary studies, and communication studies reveals an antipathy toward language's erasure of our material existence. Transforming the classroom into a stage, in a sense, is to use the speaking material body as "a kinetic force of political resistance" and to "recover a lost sense of agency" (Walker, 2003, p. 171). The metaphor of stage heightens the importance of embodied work. In performing their own life stories, students act themselves into deeper meanings and alternative possibilities.

Professor's New Persona

Relationally as a professor, I perform in a less public and more privately dialogical manner as I cohere contact zones and safe houses on a student-centered stage, on which they foster each other's voicedness and work out their own power relations. In the discussion leadership assignment, I eavesdrop on the conversations among students on assigned readings. In the performance assignment, I become a confidant and devil's advocate, engaging in one-on-one conversations with a minimum of 30 minutes per appointment in my office. I no longer lecture except when I discuss the general parameter of each assignment and provide preliminary frameworks for the understanding of race, gender, and culture. I no longer give many examinations. Over half of the semester, I meet with students between 10 and 20 hours per week. I listen. I bite my tongue. I ask students simple questions in private. I hear them.

Teaching, for me, has become the hardest as well as the most exhilarating of occupations. It is hardest because I have to unlearn the tendency to make the point "for" students, correct "stupid" remarks, or confront socially unjust stories. Teaching becomes most exhilarating because, in the process, I begin to know my students' names effortlessly and, gradually, they become genuinely inspiring! Is it not exhilarating to find it unbearable to judge students in any hasty and simplistic way?

I provide here an extensive example to illustrate this point. Rainer's performance was celebrated by almost every one else in the class. Earlier in class discussions and through his journal entries, I found out about his anti-affirmative-action stance. Being a superb student, he could not get any financial assistance for his college education because his family was White and stood between poverty and lower middle class. In my written comments to his work, I challenged Rainer to look into the issue of "legacy quota" among the Ivy League schools (i.e., elite Whites' affirmative action) and the possibility of adding "class" to the existing affirmative action programs based on race and gender. Our private conversation made him aware of the important coalition between poor Whites and other racial minorities of different class background. However, I was aware of my own early judgment of him, if not too visceral and too indurated, as an unconscious White man, carrying with him an enormous sense of entitlement and newly found victimage.

Then came his performance on "Shortness/Stature, Manhood and Violence." Here Rainer talked about himself being 4 feet, 3 inches tall, when he was 13 years of age. Then he performed a traumatic episode. At a Boy Scout camp, he was "hogtied" by two bigger boys, one older and another of the same age. Rainer became a victim because he could not protect himself. Into adulthood, he faced the unjust impact of his smallness on people's perception of his lack of maturity, attractiveness, and leadership potential. Rainer made it clear that men are also affected by their physical appearances in a society that unconsciously endorses codes of masculinity. "My size," he said in closing, "has nothing to do with being able to stick up for myself and my friends. And most importantly, I am not a mistake."

A female peer commented on Rainer's performance:

> When he revealed this incident to class, I was speechless. Looking at the wonderful man, I couldn't fathom how he must have felt. I seriously wanted to break down and cry. People are so incredibly cruel .... His performance really impacted my life and truly hit home. I know how it feels to be judged by your outward appearance. It sucks. It makes you feel like shit. It is almost like you aren't saying anything on the outside, but you are screaming on the inside. I really think Rainer is an amazing person. He has so much going for him; he shouldn't worry about his height. It is easier said than done though, I know. I have told myself to accept me for me many times.

WHAT'S THE PEDAGOGICAL EXPERIMENT LIKE?

Issues of race, class, gender, and sexuality are, to different degrees, the core of all my classes. Throughout my years of teaching, I have come to realize that each critical vector, be it race, class, gender, or sexuality, needs more nuanced voices as well as embodied faces. During the first 5 weeks of discussion sessions, students become increasingly familiar with one another. Distant but amicable comments, little by little, evolve into thoughtful personal stories, witty remarks, and occasional volatile exchanges. In the first few sessions, whenever there is a difference in opinion, students tend to look toward me for arbitration. Soon, however, they learn that I intervene only if the discourse is too homogeneous or when a procedural issue demands clarification. Students may enjoy some sessions, and become frustrated and offended in others. They may not agree on many issues but it is undeniable that students get to know one another quite well—their personal stories, their university lives, and their views on important social issues. Without any doubt, a small learning community forms, but the engagement still remains on the surface. At this stage of the class, the discursive space is guarded enough to disallow transformation but civilized enough to give each other a small space to breathe.

Once we finish the first component, student-led discussions, and the second component, performance interviews begin, the class becomes potentially dangerous and extremely labor intensive for me. The performance interviews with students last between 30 minutes and 3 hours. Some students meet with me once, fulfilling the minimum requirement. Others have multiple meetings of different lengths. I follow the principles of circular questioning theorized by Bateson (1972) and later the Milan School of family therapy (Boscolo, Cecchin, Hoffman, & Penn, 1987). Students often come with topics that are safe and easily "inconsequential." Many preface the meeting with me as follows:

- "My life is kinda … I mean normal. I cannot think of a turning point in my life."
- "I cannot think of a disagreement or protest in cultural hierarchies."
- "I am unnoticeable. I have not experienced any gendered dis/ease."

The air in my office feels a bit rigid, if not entirely awkward. I label it the "end of the toothpaste tube" phase. They try very hard to squeeze it, but not much comes out of their mouth. Respecting their social ecology, I use a key word in their initial remarks, for example, "unnoticeable," and ask them circular questions: "Were there times that your life was too unnoticeable, and with whom? More unnoticeable, and with whom? Less unnoticeable, and with whom?" Focusing on perceived differences in degrees of noticeability rather than noticeability as an essence, the point of circular questioning is to get beyond ecological normativity constructed and preserved by the student's network of loyalty (e.g., with parents, with siblings, in the church) and facilitate their thinking in a double-descriptive way. This strategy often carries the power to transcend taboos and opens up transformative spaces for students to begin critical work on their inner self (Boscolo et al., 1987).

Instead of engaging social justice as a privileged, alienated, angry, or guilty student, they begin to name the names of incest, molestation, betrayal, date rape, intimate violence, pain and alienation, teasing and rejection, and other confusion or wound in multiracial and multisexual borderlands. A "normal" student brings up a childhood story of himself being ruthlessly attacked as a "nerd" on the playground. Or a beautiful young woman remembers herself as a 12-year-old girl who was teased as "beef thigh." One week after the interviews, students come to class to do their performances. Because they often take a greater risk in their performances than what they had proposed in our interviews, every class period has almost perfect attendance, even though it is toward the end of the semester.

As students finish their performance assignment, they are required to write a reflective essay to describe and evaluate their experiences. A thematic analysis of 40 student essays in my most recent Communication and

Culture course revealed that most students' initial perception of the performance assignment was far from positive. In their own words, they felt "clueless," or "a little sketchy," or "completely confused." Some others said that the assignment sheet was "intimidating," "overwhelming," or a "standard run-of-the-mill oral presentation."

Their confusion about the assignment was substantially clarified by two main factors. The first was meeting with me face-to-face, and the second was observing the other students' performances. Because I had assumed the role of a listener early in the semester, my observation of student-led discussion sessions enabled me to develop a good sense of their performative and intellectual competencies. I was able to replace weaker or less mature students with more competent or savvy ones for the first round of performances. As a result, the first four performers set the bar high enough for other students to understand the content and form of the assignment.

Many students commented on a decisive qualitative shift in their experiences:

- "Once these performances started to happen, the class took on a new life."
- "From the first day to the last has been a complete 180-degree turnaround in my perception of the communication department and this class in general."

Many students made the following final assessment of the assignment:

- "It is amazing that you can teach people something in just 15 short minutes."
- "One of the most eye-opening experiences I have ever had."
- "The most rewarding college work I have done."
- "One of the best and most important assignments that I have done in my entire college career."

Voluntary learning occurred in that self-initiation replaced imposition and enforcement. Students shared their observations:

- "I really enjoyed this performance, so it wasn't like it was something I had to do as it was something I couldn't wait to do."

The assignment proved to be effective in creating a safe house for students. They mentioned the following words: love, understanding, acceptance, comfort, support, friendship, and trust. The following comment is typical: "It was so wonderful to be a part of an environment where I felt that people wanted me to share my story and, in return, they gave me respect and understanding." In different ways, the assignment inspired personal courage, confidence, and healing:

- "For those of us who touched on something a little bit deeper we are taking the necessary steps in all of our own healing processes."
- "You have to take risks in order to grow."
- "Because of everyone's encouraging performances, I know it will help me break through my personal barriers for the future and believe in myself."
- "I realized first of all how powerful this type of speech could be, and second of all I realized that this helps bring closure to my situation. I am proud of both myself and all my peers for having this courage."
- "I was not alone in my experiences."

Students remarked on the changes of their peers from "strangers," to "familiar faces," to people with whom they feel close. In other words, a community was forming:

- "I feel that I am closer to this class as a whole than any other class I have been in."
- "I am so proud of all my peers for stepping up to the plate and being totally honest with the class about issues that most people would typically be embarrassed, insecure, or frightened about."
- "We all shared so much during our time together we became a pseudo family.... This family became the backbone, the comforting presence, and the eyes that fed and is still feeding myself and the other members of the family, as they stand in front of 40 people awaiting their personal story."
- "The most special thing I got out of this class was a personal connection to the rest of the students ... they became more than just fellow students ... after each performance, the small glimpse into a piece of their world created a new kind of respect and interest in each of the students."

Finally, the performance assignment carried deep implications for a new consciousness and personal or social change:

- "[The class] open[ed] my mind."
- "Our society views culture as either black or white, there are hardly any gray or in-between areas. Either someone is similar to me or they

are opposite of me; you're either black or white. However, that is anything but the truth. We have mixed backgrounds, beliefs, and traditions that link us together in many ways."
- "Thank you so much for the opportunity to inform and persuade the
  majority."
- "Any action can be the catalyst for another which can be the catalyst
  for another."
- "I realized that I had a tendency to stereotype people by the way they
  dress, talk or looked. This class has let me break out of my habit of ste-
  reotyping people by being able to get in touch with each student and
  create a community."

I feel differently about my students. I care about them. I respect them.
The fact that many of them can make it to class every day is itself a miracle.
They also take risks in front of a class. They still see people on campus after 2
years of taking a class together. There is a face to an injustice. There is a face
to courage and social change. Such progressive agency often goes beyond
their family and network of loyalty. They feel the darkness they live in is
shared by many of their peers, in different locations and different forms.
They have become "alive" and empowered to see social issues in a more embodied and personal way. Located in whatever intersectional positions they
find themselves, they have come to share a space of collective courage,
healing, and the power to speak out, speaking against racism, peer cruelty,
incest, physical and verbal violence, poverty, and professional rank ordering
due to gender, sexuality, physical appearance, and multiraciality.

THREE MEDITATIONS ON MY EXPERIMENT

My experiences in the six classes with roughly 220 students come back to
me from time to time. The totality of them, though, remains ineffable and
haunting. It is too delicate to allow rendering by a pen, dry and sword-like.
Meditation, thus, is a preferred path to visit old friends, who remain, to this
day, singularly palpable.[6]

Meditation I: Butterfly Emerging From the Cocoon

One early summer afternoon, I sat with my husband in the front yard
shaded by century-old elm trees, appreciating the new flower garden de-

---

[6]I attribute the formation of this expression "singularly palpable" to a late-night conversation on poetry with a close family friend, Charles Hasty, an American poet now living in San Miguel de Allende,
Mexico.

signed and planted by a dear friend. Unforewarned, we were pleasantly shocked by a sudden noise, a "thing" dashing toward the fountain. It was a hummingbird! Fluttering its wings, the shiny ruby green bird wiggled around, tossing water drops up and down into a minifountain within the big fountain. The bird in ecstasy, in a split of a second, dashed the water drops into the air to chase away another hummingbird who threatened to encroach. From afar, we saw a fluttering dot holding steady at a safe distance away from the fountain, waiting hopefully for its turn at the "bird bath," while the first bird oscillated between bathing in the fountain and fighter piloting in the air, defending its turf.

The pineapple fountain had been installed a short while before to provide a tranquil water sound in the corner of our front flower garden, soothing the souls of passers-by and those sitting in the yard. My husband and I talked about this fully engaged event, the desire and complexity displayed by two marvelous creatures, and our surprise at the speed with which they transformed an unobtrusive fountain into a bird bath and a turf war.

A theoretical notion, affordance, originally advanced by ecological psychologist J. J. Gibson (2002) and later elaborated by Michael and Still (1992), is relevant to this discussion of hummingbirds and social justice pedagogy. Simply defined, *affordance* means relational action possibilities between actor and object. To make this concept relevant to language communities, I enlarged the construct of affordance to include action possibilities between not just an actor but actors and their communities. This theoretical expansion allows the emergence of dyads, triads, and, ultimately, a community, in creative and unpredictable ways, to transform objects and to deal with important social justice issues such as poverty, human rights, misogyny, Whiteness, and antiracism.

Applied to the flower garden episode, affordance theory means the enacted possibilities between the object (fountain) and the two birds: the first hummingbird dashing in to bathe in the fountain, its dashing out to chase away the other hummingbird, and its vigilant dual acts—bathing and guarding at the same time. From my perspective, I witnessed what was afforded jointly by the object in my flower garden and two creatures. Affordances came with potential naming acts that transformed an object from a fountain into a bird bath, and ultimately a bath turf. What touched me deeply was not only the potential materialized by the hummingbird—its ability to engage in complex acts—but also its sheer devotion whether in the form of playfulness or aggressiveness.

Michael and Still (1992) merge Gibson's affordance with French poststructuralism. Affordance subverts what Foucault terms "histories of freezing," which "teased out the many discursive and practical forces that came together and froze the person as 'mad' or 'delinquent' or 'homosexual' and so on" (Michael & Still, 1992, p. 873) and becomes an effective tool for resistance. Michael and Still explain the link between unfreezing and affordance:

> Disciplinary power tells us that a chair is for sitting on, but ecological perception permits us to see that it affords standing upon, throwing, lying over, scratching against, and so on. There is latitude of affordances, that inheres in the ecology of the situation and that outstrips the more or less meager possibilities demarcated by power-knowledge. (p. 881)

Perhaps the classroom where we teach social justice issues is becoming a cliché (Moore, 2001), frozen in a cocoon of predictable reasoning and trite theory. Social justice, as a critical language, has become a mantra, a menace in the classroom. In other words, social justice pedagogy cannot tear open the cocoon and become a butterfly without more creative affordances unimagined by, in Foucault's words, disciplinary power.

How does social justice become alive again? This is a pressing question for professors, especially those of us who have experienced many students' effortless invocation of political correctness to dismiss our comments. This is also a pressing question for professors, especially those of us who sense deeply that students from historically oppressed groups may also get trapped in uncritically accepted identity politics that perpetuates reductionistic redemption. A viable social justice discourse, put differently, has to tap into the resources that lie in creative, unpredictable affordances between social agents and their environment. We should not freeze the fountain as a fountain. Students may see, instead, a bird bath, a turf war, and other ideas without using a prefabricated script. What we miss in a social justice classroom is the freshness and the eagerness to do something anew, something meaningful. To revitalize social justice in the classroom through potential affordances, a new musing on the language we use to communicate is useful. Toni Morrison helps me in my meditation on this process.

Meditation II: Word Work Is Sublime Because It Is Generative

In her Nobel lecture delivered in December 1993, Morrison used bird as a metaphor for language, a blind old woman for practiced writer, and children for younger minds (i.e., the generations to come). The story begins with the children coming to harass the blind old woman. They mock her old age and ridicule her wisdom. One child asks, "Is the bird in my hand living or dead?" This question is indeed unfair and impertinent given the fact that the old woman is blind and the children are young.

The woman first remains silent, which only intensifies the children's impatience and ridicule. Her refusal to make a judgment between life and death, which is designed to diminish her, is artfully replaced by her answer to a different question: Who is responsible for the bird, dead or alive? The old woman makes it plain and clear that the child is responsible for the bird's well-being. At this juncture using the bird as a metaphor, Morrison elaborates on two different kinds of language: dead and living.

Language, Morrison ruminates, is "susceptible to death, erasure; certainly imperiled and salvageable only by an effort of the will." Language is dead when it folds into the oblivion of the quotidian; that is, when it is no longer spoken and understood. Language, however, dies another kind of death when it is, in Morrison's words, "statist language":

> Ruthless in its policing duties, it has no desire or purpose other than maintaining the free range of its own narcotic narcissism, its own exclusivity and dominance. However moribund, it is not without effect for it actively thwarts the intellect, stalls conscience, suppresses human potential. Unreceptive to interrogation, it cannot form or tolerate new ideas, shape other thoughts, tell another story, fill baffling silences … . Yet there it is: dumb, predatory, sentimental. Exciting reverence in schoolchildren, providing shelter for despots, summoning false memories of stability, harmony among the public.

Morrison warns against tongue suicide and argues for a living language, marking its difference from death by its nuanced, complex, and midwifery properties:

> [L]anguage can never live up to life once and for all. Nor should it. Language can never 'pin down' slavery, genocide, war. Nor should it yearn for the arrogance to be able to do so. Its force, its felicity is in its reach toward the ineffable.

After Morrison marks the difference between a dead language and a living language, there is a sudden turn in the story line between the blind old woman and the children. Reacting to the old woman's silence and her refusal to answer the question posed to her, the children burst into unimagined word work. The story continues with the questions burst forward from the children to the old woman:

> We have no bird in our hands, living or dead. We have only you and our important question. Is the nothing in our hands something you could not bear

to contemplate, to even guess? Don't you remember being young when language was magic without meaning? When what you could say, could not mean? When the invisible was what imagination strove to see? When questions and demands for answers burned so brightly you trembled with fury at not knowing?

At this juncture, I, as a reader, gradually grasp the meaning of living language in Morrison's story. Language is alive when it reaches toward the ineffable, when it is generative but humbly aware of its inadequacy. There should be no bird, no language in children's hands. They need to have their own "language invented on the spot."

Teachers and professors are the old woman, whose job lies less in placing the bird, dead or living, in a child's hand than in participating jointly in the search for "magic without meaning," the invisible that haunts our imagination, and the burning desire to know. Their anger at us, their frustration with our inability to make effable our own experiences is generative because it tears our masks down. Tearing down our masks in everyday life is not easy. Tearing down our masks in the classroom may even be a professional suicide. But then, out of an uncontrollable vulnerability, we become young again, reaching far and beyond, when the desire to know and to love is never too small.

Morrison continues:

> You are an adult. The old one, the wise one. Stop thinking about saving your face. Think of our lives and tell us your particularized world … . We know you can never do it properly—once and for all. Passion is never enough; neither is skill. But try. For our sake and yours forget your name in the street; tell us what the world has been to you in the dark places and in the light. Don't tell us what to believe, what to fear … . Language alone protects us from the scariness of things with no names. Language alone is meditation.

Here is a profound realization for me. Morrison's children become my students. Her story helps me see my pedagogical experiment in a new light. It has to do with becoming young again, unobsessed with the arrogance to pin things down and courageous enough to strip one's mask that has almost turned into skin. To work with young people on social justice, I have to begin with myself, looking into the rawness of my face anew:

> It's quiet again when the children finish speaking, until the woman breaks into the silence. "Finally", she says, "I trust you now. I trust you with the bird that is not in your hands because you have truly caught it. Look. How lovely it is, this thing we have done—together."

A good classroom is for people of different generations and different life experiences to create magic. The bird, the language, is not something given to others, a creature to be had and killed. Language is a mutually generative process, and once again we dare embrace the ineffable, the untouchable, and the invisible. How to see without pictures. Meditation, a collective dream.

Meditation III: Mutual Transformation Into Parrhesiastes

Foucault, in failing health, taught his last seminar at the University of California, Berkeley in Fall 1983 (Foucault, 1983, 2001) and his last seminar at the College de France in Spring 1984 (Flynn, 1988). The subject of his last seminars was *parrhesia*, truth-telling or fearless speech. In a way, students' narrative performances and their preparatory conversations with me in my office constitute what Foucault (1983) terms *parrhesiastic utterances*, a speech activity that transforms students collectively into *parrhesiastes*.

A parrhesiaste is believed to know the truth and can tell others the truth. Succinctly, Foucault brings up two forms of parrhesiastic activity: political parrhesia and Socratic/ethical parrhesia. A political parrhesiastic activity is conducted in the agora and it is the right of a citizen, the loss of which is tantamount to enslavement.[7] A political parrhesiaste, in relation to his interlocutor, has less power. A king, therefore, cannot be a parrhesiaste because he risks nothing. A political parrhesiaste is virtuous because, in front of a political powerful (i.e., a sovereign), he demonstrates the courage to overcome the risk involved in truth telling, which may include the loss of friendship, popularity, or even one's life. However, as noted by Foucault, political parrhesia has its own problems:

> And now I think we can begin to see that the crisis regarding *parrhesia* ... is one of recognizing who is capable of speaking the truth within the limits of an institutional system where everyone is equally entitled to give his or her own opinion. Democracy by itself is not able to determine who has the specific qualities which enable him or her to speak the truth (and thus should possess the right to tell the truth). And *parrhesia*, as a verbal activity, as pure frankness in speaking, is also not sufficient to disclose truth since negative parrhesia, ignorant outspokenness, can also result. (p. 27)

---

[7]I use the third-person pronoun *he* exclusively in this portion of the chapter to refer to a parrhesiaste because in ancient Greece only males were granted citizenship status, which excluded slaves (both women and men) and women who were of nonslave status.

To address this dilemma, parrhesia gradually shifts from a public, political activity to a pedagogical and personal one, henceforth the rise of Socratic/ethical parrhesia and a more pronounced focus from parrhesia as an institutional right to a personal quality at the end of the 5th century BCE. Foucault delineates the second form, Socratic/ethical parrhesia, as follows:

> [T]he target of this new parrhesia is not to persuade the Assembly, but to convince someone that he must take care of himself and of others; and this means that he must change his life. This theme of changing one's life, of conversion, becomes very important from the Fourth Century BC[E] to the beginnings of Christianity. It is essential to philosophical parrhesiastic practices .... More precisely, I think that the decisive criterion which identifies the parrhesiastes is not to be found in his birth, nor in his citizenship, nor in his intellectual competence, but in the harmony which exists between his logos and his bios. (pp. 40–41)

What does the harmony between logos and bios mean? One of the ways to attain this status is through teaching offered by the Epicurean schools, where students attain "'the salvation by one another ... to save oneself—in the Epicurean tradition means to gain access to a good, beautiful, and happy life. It does not refer to any kind of afterlife or divine judgment" (p. 43).

Speaking truth in front of others takes courage. Courage, as I gradually come to understand, cannot be commanded. It grows mysteriously in witnessing others' truth-telling acts. It also grows brilliantly when there is an increasing harmony between one's words and one's life. In the private meetings with me, students grow into a space where they learn to engage in Socratic parrhesia—a safe house, no public humiliation, no immediate pressure to perform, just a conversation with a professor (who does not talk much) about "their life." It is up to them to find the harmony point between their private words, public performance, their old life, and a possible new life. When students perform in front of the class, in a way, they enact public parrhesia about themselves. They also serve as each other's witness and wish that each other's performance would go well. It is beautiful to see solidarity in action. A collective scaffolding grows bigger and stronger as each student goes to the front and finishes a performance that demands careful planning and, more important, much courage. After the storm, it is a warm but quiet coolness. Dark clouds, weighing heavy on so many young people's minds, are gone. There is no guarantee the weather will always be good. But each one of us, both students and myself, just know we can shoulder the next big one, any day, any time.

CODA

Critical acts are always interested and political, namely, partisan. Far from being a rant that reflects "unenlightened gestures of social interest" (Rodden, 1986, p. 103), critical acts can be creative and unpredictable. Recall the invocation of the water fountain, the bird in a child's hand, and truth telling. We learn to chisel away the dead skin of our souls, building a safe house, a community of social justice, which I term the *personal public sphere*, where individuals are empowered to explore the ineffable, tell the truth about their lives, in their own words, in creative and courageous ways.

My personal journey into the teaching of social justice is, hopefully, anticliché. It does not invoke the name of social justice in classroom discourse. However, it affirms the importance for putting a face on social injustice, personalizing the quotidian of sufferings, building spaces for collective risk taking and communal healing, inspiring transformation and social change, and accomplishing all of these through student-centered progressive advocacy.

Recall my earlier questions about teaching and social justice. Are there better ways to teach social justice and communication? How do we bring up difficult issues to stretch horizons? Whose horizons? How do we deal with students who reject the premises of social justice work? How do we deal with colleagues who do not share our commitment to social change? What are the implications for our career—salary increase, tenure, promotion, and retention? What are the implications for our conscience? How do we deal with the feelings of isolation, burnout, and cynicism? Readers of this chapter may pose different questions and find different answers. I have attempted my own answers, asked new questions, and am still searching for better ones. Good learning, even for professors, is analogical. In failing health, as demonstrated so well by Foucault, originality is still possible.

Each student has given me a gift, a spot of tenderness, through which I learn to look at myself without as much fear. Because I finally feel it—the desire to know and to love is never too small.

ACKNOWLEDGMENTS

I dedicate this chapter to all of my allies, students, and, specifically, Mr. Kristo Gobin, my coteacher in two Communication and Gender courses. His performance on queer politics and communication remains inspiring.

REFERENCES

Anderson, E. S. (2004). Against luck egalitarianism: What's the point of equality? In M. Clayton & A. Williams (Eds.), *Social justice* (pp. 154–185). Oxford, UK: Blackwell.

Bakhtin, M. M. (1986). *Speech genres and other late essays.* Austin: University of Texas Press.

Barthes, R. (1981). *Camera lucida: Reflections on photography.* New York: Noonday Press.

Bateson, G. (1972). *Steps to an ecology of the mind.* New York: Ballantine.

Boscolo, L., Cecchin, G., Hoffman, L., & Penn, P. (1987). *Milan systemic family therapy.* New York: Basic Books.

Clayton, M., & Williams, A. (Eds.). (2004). *Social justice.* Oxford, UK: Blackwell.

Crenshaw, K. (1994). Mapping the margins: Intersectionality, identity politics, and violence against women of color. In M. A. Fineman & R. Mykitiuk (Eds.), *The public nature of private violence* (pp. 93–118). New York: Routledge.

Derrida, J. (2001). *The work of mourning.* Chicago: University of Chicago Press.

Flynn, T. (1988). Foucault as parrhesiast: His last course at the College de France (1984). In J. Bernauer & D. Rasmussen (Eds.), *The final Foucault* (pp. 102–118). Cambridge, MA: MIT Press.

Foucault, M. (1983). *Discourse and truth: The problematization of parrhesia.* Retrieved June 11, 2005, from http://foucault.info/documents/parrhesia/

Foucault, M. (1988). The ethic of care for the self as a practice of freedom. In J. Bernauer & D. Rasmussen (Eds.), *The final Foucault* (pp. 1–20). Cambridge, MA: MIT Press.

Foucault, M. (2001). *Fearless speech* (J. Pearson, Ed.). Los Angeles: Semiotext(e).

Gibson, E. J. (2002). *Perceiving the affordances: Portrait of two psychologists.* Mahwah, NJ: Lawrence Erlbaum Associates, Inc.

Krugman, P. (2005, April 25). A whiff of stagflation. *New York Times.* Retrieved April 18, 2005, from http://www.nytimes.com/2005/04/18/opinion/18krugman.html?hp=&pagewanted=print&position

Lee, W. (1993). Communication about humor as procedural competence in intercultural encounters. In L. A. Samovar & R. E. Porter (Eds.), *Intercultural communication: A reader* (7th ed., pp. 373–382). Belmont, CA: Wadsworth.

Lee, W. (1994). On not missing the boat: A processual method for inter/cultural understanding of idioms and lifeworld. *Journal of Applied Communication Research, 22,* 141–161.

Lee, W. (1998a). In the names of Chinese women. *Quarterly Journal of Speech, 84,* 283–302.

Lee, W. (1998b). Patriotic breeders or colonized converts? A postcolonial feminist approach to antifootbinding discourse in China. In D. Tanno & A. Gonzalez (Eds.), *Communication and identity across cultures* (pp. 11–33). Thousand Oaks, CA: Sage.

Lee, W. (1999). One whiteness veils three uglinesses: From border-crossing to a womanist interrogation of colorism. In T. Nakayama & J. Martin (Eds.), *Whiteness: The communication of social identity* (pp. 279–298). Thousand Oaks, CA: Sage.

Lee, W. (2003). Kuaring queer theory: Autocritography and my race-conscious womanist and transnational turn. *Journal of Homosexuality, 45,* 147–170.

Lee, W., Chung, J., Wang, J., & Hertel, E. (1995). A sociohistorical approach to intercultural communication. *The Howard Journal of Communications, 4,* 262–291.

Lee, W., & Wander, P. C. (1998). On discursive amnesia: Reinventing the possibilities for democracy through discursive amnesty. In M. Salvador & P. Sias (Eds.), *The public voice in a democracy at risk: Citizenship for the 21st century* (pp. 151–172). Westport, CT: Praeger.

Love, L., & Kohn, N. (2001). This, that, and the other: Fraught possibilities of the souvenir. *Text and Performance Quarterly, 21,* 47–63.

Michael, M., & Still, A. (1992). A resource for resistance: Power-knowledge and affordance. *Theory and Society, 21,* 869–888.

Mohanty, C. T. (2003). *Feminism without borders: Decolonizing theory, practicing solidarity.* Durham, NC: Duke University Press.

Moore, N. (2001). The politics of cliché: Sex, class, and abortion in Australian realism. *Modern Fiction Studies, 47,* 69–91.

Morrison, T. (1993). Nobel lecture. Retrieved April 2, 2004, from http://nobelprize.org/literature/laureates/1993/morison-lecture.html

Pratt, M. L. (1997). Arts of the contact zone. In P. Gibian (Ed.), *Mass culture and everyday life* (pp. 61–72). London: Routledge.

Rodden, J. (1986). Book review of Terry Eagleton's *The spectator to post-structuralism. Quarterly Journal of Speech, 72,* 103–106.

Roediger, D. R. (2002). *Colored white.* Berkeley: University of California Press.

Walker, J. A. (2003). Why performance? Why now? Textuality and the rearticulation of human presence. *Yale Journal of Criticism, 16,* 149–175.

11

Reflections on a Project to Promote Social Justice in Communication Education and Research

W. Barnett Pearce
Fielding Institute

In the early 1990s, the Department of Communication at Loyola University Chicago revised its curriculum. The revision was initiated by a decision to promote social justice; consequently, a social justice concentration was included in the new curriculum. Although the project was successfully implemented, the number and the intensity of efforts to block or constrain it surprised me. My assumption that all well-intentioned people would be for—or at least not against—social justice was proven naive. As we were implementing the project, I found myself opposing the opponents rather than trying to understand them. I was less able than I would have liked to resist the seductions of confrontational, power-based patterns of interaction.

Since leaving Loyola, I have moved on to other projects that continue the emphasis on social justice in the form of participatory democracy in public settings. In part because of the experiences described in this chapter, these projects explicitly foreground the quality of communication (see Spano, 2001; www.publicdialogue.org; www.pearceassociates.com). However, Olson and Olson's (2003) sharp attack on what they called "the Loyola group"—they characterized our calls for social justice scholarship as "unhelpful, even counter-productive" (p. 438)—shocked me so much that I revisited old wounds and accomplishments.

215

I begin this chapter with two stories of our project. Both are true but emphasize different things: accomplishments and controversies. Taken together, they amount to something of a cautionary tale for those who would undertake similar adventures.

THE PROJECT AND ITS ACCOMPLISHMENTS

In 1991, I was appointed Chair of the Department of Communication at Loyola University Chicago. Bringing in a chair from outside the University was unusual, part of a determined effort by university administrators to make some constructive changes in the department. Among the tasks assigned me by the dean and senior vice president were to reduce the total number of courses offered by the department, increase the average enrollment per course, reduce the dependence on part-time faculty, increase the research productivity of the faculty, conduct three national searches to fill open faculty positions, and integrate three senior faculty members who were added as a result of Loyola's merger with Mundelein College.

At the same time, my instructions continued, I was to take unspecified steps to increase the full-time faculty members' ability to work together in harmony. My initial introduction to this challenge came during my first week as chair. Three faculty members comprised a search committee for a full-time non-tenure-track position. After intensive discussions of the candidates' qualifications, each member of the committee ranked the five finalists, achieving the statistically improbable feat of producing a perfect five-way tie. I remain convinced that this accomplishment reflected genuine differences in professional orientations and judgments.

I benefitted from some extramural coaching about how to act in this situation, and came up with the not surprising idea of establishing a transcending project for the department that would make past differences irrelevant and create contexts for shared commitment. While participating in a weekend retreat offered by the Vice President for Ministry as opportunities for non-Jesuit faculty and staff to learn about the religious order that sponsored the University, I found what seemed to be an appropriate topic: social justice.

The department's curriculum committee, chaired by Larry Frey, conducted an inclusive, 2-year process. These were among the constraints under which that process operated: different visions of what "communication and social justice" would look like in a curriculum; dysfunctional interpersonal relationships and lack of models for productive collaboration; and the requirements imposed by the dean that the curriculum have fewer, more highly enrolled courses taught by fewer part-time faculty (for a fuller account and a detailed description of the curriculum that we developed, see Frey, Pollock, Artz, & Pearce, 1996).

We were stalled until we began systematically applying the question "Whose interests are being served?" We immediately realized that the structure of our curriculum served the interests—or at least the mental habits—of the faculty rather than that of the students. Like most comparable departments, our curriculum had been organized by the medium or context in which communication occurs: in our case, radio, television, and film; organizational, interpersonal, and public communication; and journalism. When we shifted to the perspective of our students, already accustomed to the multimedia environment that developed long after our disciplinary structures were inscribed, this structure seemed quaint at best.

We developed a new curriculum focused on *praxis* and process, treating communication as something that people do (praxis) and striving for *phronesis* (prudence or good judgment) toward achieving specific ends. We were careful not to prejudge what those ends should be; rather, our learning objectives included teaching students to think about the constitutive role played by communication and to develop the habits and abilities for reflecting critically about what ends and whose interests are being served by various communication processes.

Perhaps the key moment in the development of the curriculum occurred when we reread, with the question "Whose interests are being served?" in mind, the materials used in our introductory and research methods courses. We were astonished by how little we found in our professional journals about individuals and groups who were harmed or marginalized by the social system in which they live, and, among the studies about these individuals and groups, how few included any explicit way for the research project itself or the published account of it to be used by or for them. We were also surprised to find such a small percentage of research projects using any of the rapidly expanding categories of collaborative, participatory, or action research methods in which those doing the research and those being studied work together in mutually beneficial and transparent ways.

Within this curriculum, we developed a social justice concentration that presupposed a more specific set of goals:

> This special program helps students understand existing cultural practices that foster injustice, examines the role played by communication in helping to solve contemporary social problems, and provides opportunities for students to put into practice their communication knowledge for ethical action.

(retrieved from http://www.luc.edu/communication/programs.html on November 26, 2004)

To participate in this concentration, students select 18 semester-hours of designated courses. The courses designated for this concentration:

> (1) have an explicitly critical perspective that encourages active engagement with and advocacy on behalf of the under-represented in society; (2) explicitly challenge norms, practices, relations, and structures that underwrite inequality and injustice; (3) foster perspectives that promote increased access to public discourse and the media, improve participatory democratic decision making, and challenge existing structures that produce and reproduce unequal resource allocation; (4) allow students to challenge the problematic structures in the classroom; and (5) in liberation-theology terms, advocate unequivocally a "preferential option for the poor," including the economically, socially, politically, and culturally under-resourced (Frey, Pollock, et al., 1996, pp. 86–87)

We recognized that the university radio station had enormous potential for giving voice to targeted groups not usually represented in public broadcasts, and created opportunities for students to work with community groups in producing useful programs. We resonated with the service learning initiative (see the essays by Murphy, Pollock, and Keller, Harder, and Kois in Droge & Murphy, 1999) and used (not uncritically; see Artz, 2001) the infrastructure it provided to connect students with the groups we had in view as part of their formal education.

The new curriculum, including the social justice concentration, is in place (see http://www.luc.edu/communication/programs.html). This project succeeded in stimulating collaborative activities among the faculty, including professional writing and presentations. A large number of students have been involved in classroom and community projects in which they have been sensitized to the unwanted consequences of the social system in which they live, have learned the role of communication in that system and some of the potentials for using communication to redress its problems, and have had opportunities for first-person experiences as social justice activists.

The attempt to build in a block of community and alternative programs within the schedule of the campus radio station, WLUW, was the single most controversial issue. As of this writing, WLUW is officially described as "a community oriented, pro-social radio station, committed to the Jesuit philosophy of ethical action, whose broadcasts fulfill the social justice and service learning initiatives at Loyola University and the Department of Communication" (http://www.luc.edu/communication/orgs.html#wluw).

It has evolved from a campus station to an independent community station supported primarily by donations. It has the largest audience of any noncommercial, non-National Public Radio (NPR) station in Chicago, and has a partnership with NPR station WBEZ (M. A. Pollock, personal communication, December 11, 2004). Its schedule includes programs specific to the community to which it broadcasts as well as news and other programming not available in mainstream media (see http://www.wluw.org).

THE CONTROVERSIES ELICITED BY THE PROJECT

The story of the accomplishments of the project is true, but incomplete. An equally true story, with quite a different affective tone, focuses on the conflict and opposition elicited at every step.

Conflict and Opposition in the Department

The department had a well-earned reputation for being unable to reconcile professional differences among the faculty. We were all surprised and elated when the full-time faculty members approved the new curriculum unanimously. However, as some members of the faculty were quick to point out, the "aye" votes were cast with different levels of enthusiasm.

The explicit commitment to social justice in the concentration and cocurricular activities was the most controversial aspect of the new curriculum. Some faculty members felt that a departmental commitment to social justice imposed a static description of social relationships as conflicted while they preferred to explore and work toward creating alternative social patterns. Others said that the criteria for social justice courses were divisive, taking sides in the conflict between beneficiaries and victims of the social order, thus alienating us from important and legitimate clients for consulting work and employers for our graduates. We sought to acknowledge and respect these opinions by making our commitment to social justice a concentration within the curriculum rather than an aspect of the whole curriculum.

Our attempts to create a block of prosocial programming at WLUW were strenuously resisted. Some faculty in the department told us that we were jeopardizing the chances of our students to find jobs in broadcasting if they were associated with "leftist" programming. The director of the radio station—a staff member—consistently neglected to implement the programming changes mandated by the department while reporting that he had done so; I ultimately had to replace him.

Even those who strongly supported social justice disagreed with each other about what it means. Well aware of these differences, we made a considered and, as it turned out, fateful decision not to strive for a departmental orthodoxy. Instead, we acknowledged that our emphasis on social justice "weaves together several strands of intellectual, moral, and social traditions" and articulated a "sensibility" (rather than a definition or theoretical exposition) that "(1) foregrounds ethical concerns; (2) commits to a structural analysis of ethical problems; (3) adopts an activist orientation; and (4) seeks identification with others" (Frey, Pearce, Pollock, Artz, & Murphy, 1996).

The process by which we revised the curriculum included all (approximately) 15 full-time faculty members and was in itself an achievement of which we were proud. However, as soon as we announced the new curriculum, other stakeholders publicly opposed it. Some of the response was based on genuine concerns: Parents inquired about the quality of education in the new curriculum; many part-time faculty members correctly saw that their teaching opportunities would end; and students were concerned about the impact on their ability to graduate in a timely fashion. But as I answered what seemed an inordinate number of parental phone calls and met with various groups of students, I began to recognize a recurring agenda. The questions were worded in the same way and not in terms I would expect students or parents to use; the questions presumed negative answers and were based on a set of assumptions about communication education from which we had clearly distanced ourselves. We soon realized that some individual or group was orchestrating the opposition to our proposals and later discovered that this in fact was the case. A part-time instructor who was a graduate of the department, had been closely connected to the radio station, and was currently a special assistant to the chief administrator was either the leader or spokesperson for this group. Using his position and at least sometimes the letterhead of the person whose assistant he was, he challenged the intellectual soundness and motivation of the new curriculum in conversations with students, members of the college curriculum committee, and the administration.

Conflict and Opposition in the University

When we brought our work to the College of Arts and Sciences curriculum committee for approval, we encountered opposition that seemed to me not based on the merits of the proposal. After answering normal questions about resources and impact, the whole conceptual basis of the curriculum was challenged. The proposal was tabled and we were required to submit it for peer review by the chairs of all the departments of communication at other Jesuit colleges and universities. I found this requirement professionally insulting and unprecedented in my experience in university administration. The responses from other chairs were positive about the curriculum and curious about the need for peer review.

The social justice concentration elicited a great deal of opposition. The college curriculum committee sent it back to the department with the explanation that they thought it inappropriate for one department to "monopolize" social justice.

In informal conversations among university leaders, the department was frequently characterized as strident and a source of contention despite the fact that we were working together better than we had in years. When reported to me through official channels, the message was that I should do something about it. This put me in an interesting bind, given the tasks assigned me when I was hired, and made me feel that my administrative supervisors were at most neutral rather than supporting my efforts.

It is hard to document an attack that uses rumor as its tool, but one instance became public. A senior academic administrator publicly and frequently accused a newly hired assistant professor, a central person in the social justice concentration, of verbally attacking a senior faculty member in another department. My dean asked me to investigate and to instruct this faculty member about appropriate behavior. My investigation included a conversation with the allegedly abused senior faculty member, who told me that he had in fact met with the person accused of disrespectful and uncivil behavior, but that the encounter was very different than the description circulating among administrators. To the contrary, he recalled the meeting with pleasure and described their conversation as unusually interesting and productive. When I reported that the attack "never happened," I asked that a public apology be issued to my untenured faculty member commensurate with the publicity given to the unsubstantiated rumor. No such apology was forthcoming.

After we had implemented a block of "alternative" and prosocial programming at WLUW, two vice-president-level officials—including the person who had led the "Jesuit weekend" that I attended—summoned me to a meeting. By now a bit suspicious, I invited Larry Frey, chair of the department's curriculum committee, to accompany me. We were told to cease broadcasting one of these programs—*Labor News*, a weekly half-hour program geared to members of labor unions. When we inquired about the reason, we were told that the University was attempting to prevent unionization of its staff and believed that this program was inconsistent with the University's position with respect to organized labor. When we pointed out the inconsistency between this action and the content of what we were teaching our students majoring in journalism and broadcasting about ethics and professional responsibility, we were told to put the corporate interests first. In a deliberate act of noncompliance, we continued to broadcast *Labor News* in its usual place on the schedule.

Conflict and Opposition in the Communication Discipline

Transparency and reflexivity were important goals in this project. We published descriptions of our curricular reform (Frey, Pollock, et al., 1996) and our emphasis on social justice (Artz, 1998; Frey, Pearce, et al., 1996; Pollock, Artz, Frey, Pearce, & Murphy, 1996). We invited others to join us in a commitment to social justice. Noting that "some of our colleagues in the communication discipline have channeled their energies and resources toward challenging the norms, practices, relations, and structures that underwrite inequality and injustice," we called "for our discipline to give serious consideration to the work of those pioneers who have begun exploring the value of what we do for social justice, in the hope of extending and complementing the mainstream activities in the discipline." We described the ways the discipline might change, at least as we imagined it, "if its practitioners were to take a more coherent and systematic approach to theory, research, and pedagogy about social justice" (Frey, Pearce, et al., 1996, p. 110).

These efforts drew sharply contrasting results. Our initial article on social justice in the curriculum (Frey, Pearce, et al., 1996) received the Distinguished Article Award from the Applied Communication Division of the National Communication Association, but also was the subject of criticism from other researchers. Wood (1996b) found fault with our considered decision not to define social justice and disagreed with our claim that there is a relative dearth of social justice scholarship in our discipline; Wood (1996b) and Makau (1996) criticized our focus on structural issues to the neglect of interpersonal moral issues, and Olson and Olson (2003) found our emphasis on knowledge that benefits excluded, underresourced, or oppressed groups to be exclusive and dysfunctionally limiting. What they characterized as our insistence on useable knowledge as the sole criterion of social justice research, they argued, performs five disservices to the field:

- Only "manageable" social injustices would be addressed by research-ers.
- Dependency relationships between lay people interested in social jus-tice and communication researchers would be encouraged, disadvan-taging those lay people.
- Short-term recommendations, which might be to the detriment of underresourced persons in the long term, would be favored.
- Responsible scholarly "discovery" would be impeded by the simulta-neous search for scholarly "application."
- Academic isolationism and territorialism would be fostered, restricting the range of research methodologies employed in the discipline. (pp. 446–449)

THREE LEARNINGS FROM MY REFLECTIONS ON THE PROJECT

Remembering, rereading, and conversing with my colleagues about this project has been helpful to me. I am very proud of what we accomplished, have a better understanding of the consequences of the choices we made, have developed greater appreciation for those who opposed the project, and have drawn some conclusions—although surely not the same as would be drawn by others.

The Wisdom of Avoiding Orthodoxy About Social Justice, and the Value of Making Perspicacious Distinctions Among Social Justice Projects

We made a considered decision not to develop an abstract definition or the-oretical explanation or justification of social justice. We actually made the decision twice. The first time was when we began the process of revising the curriculum. We could have framed the issue in either of two ways: as a scholarly debate about which of our differing opinions was right or as a col-lective decision about what to include in the courses we offered to students. We chose the latter and found that despite our different theoretical vocabu-laries and personal learning histories, we were able to work together com-fortably. We revisited the decision after reading reviews of Frey, Pearce, et al. (1996) by Wood (1996b) and Makau (1996), both of which faulted us for being insufficiently precise. Characterizing the dangers as "Scylla and Charybdis," we said,

If we are too specific about what we mean by social justice, we may be misunderstood to be suggesting that we have the only path to justice, leaving us open to being branded with the dreaded label of "politically correct." If we strive for flexibility in our use of the term, then we are subject to charges that we have not given the matter sufficient thought. (Pollock et al., 1996, p. 142)

I still believe that the decision to avoid orthodoxy about social justice was the right one. As pragmatists Dewey (1929) and Rorty (1979) argue, there are important differences between projects based on making declarative propositions about things and those involving actions to be taken. These differences involve the nature of knowledge (spectator vs. participant as Dewey, 1929, p. 196, put it) and the actions taken to achieve it. Had we engaged in debate about what social justice is, we would have moved our project, and the students for whom it was intended, from the realm of action to the realm of contemplation, and in so doing rendered it much less likely to accomplish the goals we had for it.

However, as noted earlier, this decision had unfortunate consequences. In retrospect, I think we would have done better if we had coupled our deliberate decision not to define social justice with a more well-developed way of making perspicacious distinctions among what we and others meant about it. The following are some bases for making these distinctions.

Abstract Generalizations or Situated Judgments?   One of the unintended virtues of our project (and one that caused problems and for which we have been openly chastised) is that it is part of an emerging and not yet fully articulated new paradigm about ethical decision making. For practical reasons, we chose to avoid what Levine (1998) described as moral philosophy:

> In its purest form, [moral philosophy] is *an effort to develop general normative principles or procedures that can be defended with arguments and then used to settle at least some concrete cases.* (By "cases," I mean acts, choices, situations, characters, habits, institutions, or plans of life that require moral assessment.) (p. 4, italics in original)

Drawing on Wittgenstein, Ryle, and MacIntyre, Levine champions an alternative paradigm in which

> judgment, rather than abstract reasoning, is the crucial process that we use to make moral decisions. By "judgment," I do not mean, with Kant, the application of laws to particular cases. Instead, I mean an act of interpretation that

describes something *as* something else, without relying (even covertly or implicitly) upon clear, general definitions. (p. 50)

This distinction mirrors Dewey's (1929) argument that "intelligence in operation" rather than knowledge of abstract laws about an allegedly immutable reality, "becomes the thing most worth winning" (p. 204).

Our disciplinary colleagues were correct that we did not offer a theoretically satisfactory definition of social justice, but I interpret this more as evidence of the seductiveness of the old paradigm of moral philosophy than as an indictment of what we did. Let me display the two paradigms with reference to another situation. Bellah et al.'s (1985) *Habits of the Heart* was a major study of the moral languages of ordinary Americans. The researchers used "active, Socratic" interviewing to "uncover assumptions, to make explicit what the person we were talking to might rather have left implicit" (p. 304). Although they "did not seek to impose our ideas on those with whom we talked" (p. 304), they did presume that moral judgments should and did take the form of articulatable general principles and pushed their respondents to supply them.

In his critique of this method, Stout (1988) noted that the persistent attempt to push people to supply philosophically sound justifications for their actions can be seen as bullying and the person interviewed "either becomes confused or starts sounding suspiciously like a philosopher" (p. 35). Working from a perspective influenced by Wittgenstein, Stout does not assume that the real reasons are "implicit" or "behind" what people actually say and do. Rather, he warned:

> There are many propositions that we are justified in believing but wouldn't know how to justify. Anything we could say on behalf of such a proposition seems less certain than the proposition itself. By now, it is hard to debate with flat-earthers. What real doubt do they have that can be addressed with justifying reasons? .... [W]e ought to be suspicious of people who want reasons even when they can't supply reasonable doubts. (p. 36)

In a close reading of the interview with Brian Palmer, one of the participants in the study, Stout found him to use a vocabulary of reciprocity, involvement, shared goals, and mutual respect grounded in personal experience. However, the official interpretation found Palmer's moral language deficient: "His new goal—devotion to marriage and children—seems as arbitrary and unexamined as his earlier pursuit of material success. Both are *justified as idiosyncratic preferences rather than as representing a larger sense of the purpose of life*" (Bellah et al., 1985, p. 6; italics added).

Although we did not discuss it in these terms, and I am not at all sure that we would have agreed about it if we had, I think our project was exemplifying the situated judgment side of the distinction I am proposing here. Despite our conceptual differences, we found that we had no difficulty in agreeing "that justice has been denied in certain instances (e.g., when students are silenced in classrooms, when a group is systematically denigrated in the media, when domestic workers are consistently exploited, when 40,000 children die of starvation each day)" (Pollock et al., 1996, p. 143).

Although this will not satisfy those seeking abstract generalizations, I suggest that this calls for further elaboration of the alternative paradigm rather than increased attempts to satisfy the criteria of the old paradigm.

The Method of Handling the Tension Between Responding to Immediate Needs and Intervening in the Larger System That Creates Those Needs.   Confronted with the reality of injustice or oppression, noble motives impel us to take action as advocates, partisans, or champions. One of the cruelest ironies is that these well-intended actions often have the unintended consequences of perpetuating the system that produces the injustices or oppression that we intended to eliminate. For example, giving a monetary handout to homeless persons might ease their immediate needs, but paradoxically reduce the pressure to change the system that produces and condones homelessness. The term *enabling* is used to describe attempts to protect persons and groups from the severest consequences of their own actions (e.g., substance abuse) or social situations (e.g., homelessness) while reducing the opportunity for changing those actions or situations.

I can think of three categories of responses to this tension: (a) feeling that one can do nothing, (b) taking direct action based on the assumption that one knows best (often guided by an abstract principle about what constitutes the good, as described in the previous section), and (c) enhanced attentiveness to the question of what is being made in the patterns of interaction. The latter is consistent with the American pragmatists, who caution against any sense of certainty and call for a continued reflection about the relationship of intentions and effects. In my own working out of these ideas, I suggest that the primary question to be posed is "What are we making together?" (Pearce, 2004).

This basis for making perspicacious distinctions is not an either–or. Rather, it calls attention to the ways in which people handle the tensions between seeking to intervene in the specific moment and seeking to transform the social system that gives rise to such moments. As I move in memory and imagination between righting wrongs and being deliberately mindful of what we are making together, I hear strident voices from each position denouncing those at the other. Those who focus on righting wrongs might well see the more inclusive, longer view as inimical with their genuine feelings of outrage, as paralyzing action by engaging in excessive analysis (e.g., asking "What will we become if we win this struggle?"), and as a betrayal of sorts because one is not "against" the oppressive other. On the other hand, those who focus on what is being made might well be short-tempered with those who rush to right wrongs because their actions either perpetuate the type of system that is going to exclude or oppress someone, even if the oppressors and oppressed change position. Or they might wish that the righters of wrongs would take cognizance of the third- and fourth-level consequences of their actions, some of which might be to reinforce the social structure that they are trying to change, or to call into being a worse problem than the one they are addressing.

What Are the Relationships Among Those Involved in the Project?   Whatever else might be involved, social justice is about relationships, and prepositions are the vocabulary of relationships. In the various descriptions of the project, we used, not always consistently, three prepositions—about, for, and with—to describe the relationship between educator or researcher and the groups we had in view for research or teaching.

About.   Most of the research and teaching in our field is about "samples who are European American, middle-class, heterosexual, able-bodied, and educated. As important as this group of people may be, it is not the only group ... nor is it representative of even Western society" (Wood, 1996a, p. 106). Curricula and research that merits the designation of social justice should at least also be about groups and individuals who are systematically excluded from participation in and the enjoyment of the benefits of the social order. For example, Wood (1996a) identified these groups: "individuals who are gay, working class, physically challenged, lesbian, not college educated, African American, Native American, Asian American, or of other ethnicities" (p. 106).

For.   As part of the Enlightenment tradition, objective knowledge is often held as the standard to be achieved. As scientists struggled against the theocratic domination of learning, this was an effective alternative. However, as Toulmin (1990) points out, current intellectual trends are both rediscovering some of the humanist heritage within Western intellectual traditions and moving beyond the limitations of what he called the project of modernism. The issue is clear: Should one be objectively neutral or be explicitly "for" the people one is studying?

By inviting our students to inquire about whose interests were served by communication policies and practices, we sought to address both the strengths and limitations of the idea of neutral scholarship. In the social justice concentration that was a part of the curriculum, we invited students to take a different relationship, unabashedly "for" those they studied.

With.   Our group was very excited about the potential of research and education that was not only about and for, but also with the groups that we had in view. We believed that our discipline had underutilized participatory and action research methods, and we developed new research methods courses focusing on these collaborative approaches.

Part of my learning about the importance of relationships with subjects came from work that I was doing with people who are blind or visually impaired. McCulloh and I were invited to offer a course in nonverbal communication at Chicago's Blind Services Association. In preparing materials for this training, we found some—although not much—research about the nonverbal communication behaviors of blind persons, but virtually none that was explicitly for them or with them—that is, projects that included in the design any way of employing the knowledge gained for the benefit of the blind persons themselves (instead of, e.g., those who provide service to them), or including the blind persons being studied as coresearchers in projects guided by their own interests. I discovered the importance of collaborative research when I learned, from the blind and visually impaired persons themselves, that they have profound political differences with important implications for what counts as useful information. These differences were invisible in both research literature and textbook and training materials.

In our enthusiasm for promoting social justice that is with groups who have been treated unjustly, I think we blurred the distinction between being for and with the groups we have in view. This blurring is one way of understanding the criticisms brought by Olson and Olson (2003). Using this vocabulary of relationships, their position might be paraphrased as saying that sometimes there are good reasons why it is impossible or undesirable to be with the group we have in view, and that research and education that is both about and for them should be recognized as legitimate ways of promoting social justice. Said this way, of course, they are right.

Had we used something like this analysis of relationships to describe our work in social justice, I think that I would have understood better the reasons why well-intentioned people have found our work disturbing or worth opposing. Without making any judgment about which is better, even though both may be about, for example, the poor, work for them differs from work with them. For example, work with people who are homeless, blind, ethnic minorities, or poor requires the researcher or teacher to use a differ-ent vocabulary and grammar than that is equally for but not with them. In these different vocabularies and languages, different selves are called forth, with different rights and responsibilities, and different methods of acting seem appropriate.

Examples of Making Perspicacious Distinctions.   Those of us concerned with social justice have many ways of working available to us. For example, we can describe and expose the effects of oppression, explain the causes of oppression, and join with oppressed people to identify and work to address their interests. We can attack the oppressors, taking power from the haves and giving it to the have nots, or join with the oppressed to teach or collaborate. If the distinctions I have already made are useful, they will per-mit us to describe various projects, appreciating what they have in common while differentiating them in useful ways. Here are some examples and test cases, all of which I consider to promote social justice.

Talking Poverty: Power Arrangements in Poverty Discourse (Myers, 2005) is a study of how power relations are constructed within the public sphere, not about "poor people." Using critical discourse analysis, Myers found that edi-torials in the *New York Times* and the general academic and political litera-ture on the topic construct poverty as a personal, rather than a structural, problem in which the causes and solutions to poverty are ascribed to indi-viduals, rather than the political or economic system. In this discourse, poor persons are cast as "clients" and depicted as passive. The editorials in the *Wall Street Journal*, on the other hand, depict poor persons as capable and in-dustrious, victimized mainly by governmental policies and programs. In terms of the questions posed here, the study focuses on abstract things (power relations), is about poverty but neither about nor with poor people (the voices of the poor do not appear, although what scholars and politi-cians say about them does), and is primarily concerned with what is being made in the discourse about poverty (again, power relations).

Humiliation and the Poor: A Study of the Management of Meaning (Sayler, 2004) is not only about and for, but also with the group in view. His method was a narrative analysis of a series of interviews with specific people, whose voices he brought into settings in which they would otherwise not be heard. In the interview, he directed their storytelling, enabling them to tell a richer set of stories than they otherwise would. Although he drew implications for larger social policy, I view his study as focused on specific situations rather than looking toward abstract generalizations. His work was designed to learn from homeless people how all of us can better handle humiliating experiences: This suggests to me that he was less interested in intervening in specific situations then in developing resources for being mindful of what we are making together when we interact with each other.

The Media Research and Action Project (Ryan, Carragee, & Schwerner, 1998) is not very well described as about the "over 200 social movement organizations, community groups, and non-profit organizations" (p. 169) with whom they work, but is clearly for and with them. The Project's method is to engage in partnerships, short-term consultancies, and introductory trainings to help organizations "employ news as a political resource" (p. 169). Although they are dealing with a pervasive social structure that disproportionately favors organizations with access, resources, and know-how, they are helping specific organizations to accomplish their purposes, so I describe them as holding the tension between intervening in specific situations and being concerned with what they are making.

Crabtree (1998) described two cross-cultural participatory development and service learning projects (involving students from the United States and communities in El Salvador and Nicaragua). The goal was "mutual empowerment" of all concerned, both service providers and recipients:

> Participatory development is expected to empower the disenfranchised poor; cross-cultural experience is expected to induce substantial personal growth and intercultural awareness; and service learning attempts to empower students within the learning environment and (in a more generalized way) as citizens. When practiced together, the three components can be expected to produce evidence of "mutual empowerment" for both the so-called disadvantaged and advantaged participants. (p. 188)

The notion of mutual empowerment transforms the meaning of the with relationship; it becomes genuinely collaborative rather than a one-way service delivery. I see her project as not very much about, but clearly for and, in an enriched way, with the groups she has in view. In fact, the groups in view become not only those with the "problem" but also those ostensibly providing the service. I would locate her project as simultaneously intervening in specific situations and being mindful of what is being made in the situation.

Discursive Processes That Foster Dialogic Moments: Transformation in the Engagement of Social Identity Group Differences in Dialogue (Wasserman,

2004) used a participatory action research design that simultaneously was about dialogue groups struggling with social identity groups and with them to help them achieve their goals. Although the researcher brought certain resources to the group in the form of her expertise and willingness to play the roles of observer, interpreter, and interlocutor with the group, in all important ways, the groups studied themselves and took actions based on their findings.

THE VALUE OF DIALOGIC COMMUNICATION AND THE HARD WORK THAT IT TAKES TO MAKE IT HAPPEN

Even those of us who were the most visible supporters of the social justice project disagreed about the form of communication in which it could best be developed and presented. Should it be advocacy or dialogue? Partisan or inclusive? My initial assumption was that Loyola's Jesuit heritage was a powerful context prefiguring dialogic communication. Some of my colleagues were less sanguine. Reflecting on an early draft of this chapter, Artz (personal communication, December 2, 2004) said that he would

> want to continue the discussion about how communication can overcome seriously conflicting social/material interests. I believe dialogue could at very least make those conditions clear, and in some circumstances clarify appeals to our joint humanity. I also believe dialogue models the appropriate form of communication for a more human social order. History, however, suggests that it will be highly unlikely for certain individuals who benefit from inequality will willingly give up their privilege: "Power concedes nothing without demand ... " wrote Frederick Douglass.

Reflecting a more conventional understanding of representative democracy, on the eve of the Faculty Senate's vote on our curriculum, my dean, assuming that I had canvassed (and struck deals with?) all the senators, asked what the vote would be. Somewhat embarrassed, I reported that I assumed that each senator would vote on the merits of the proposal (it passed with only a few dissenting votes).

In retrospect, it is clear that my assumptions that dialogic communication would naturally occur were naive and unrealistic. My considered judgment is that dialogic communication should be the preferred form of interaction in projects like these, that we engage in confrontational communication too soon (as the first rather than the last choice, or by anticipating it create a self-fulfilling prophecy that it will occur), and that (at least at the current state of the development of we as persons and us as a culture) dialogic communication requires both wisdom and work. In the project to promote social justice, we did not do enough of the work required to achieve dialogic communication. Since leaving this project, I have learned much about the work required to make dialogic communication possible. There is no way to know whether we could have conducted the process more dialogically; I now know that there are things we could have done that none of us knew how to do at the time, and I am convinced that the project would have been better if it had been more dialogic.

We did better in achieving dialogic communication among the faculty in the department than we did with certain, highly visible others in the university. The confrontational communication pattern between "us" and "them" deleteriously affected the whole project. At least some of the opposition was based on unnecessary misunderstandings of what we were about. For example, when we alluded to liberation theology, we were thinking of its commitment to a preferential option for the poor and we were not sufficiently mindful that liberation theology was also a highly controversial political movement within the Catholic Church involving power relations between bishops and the Pope. We inadvertently signaled our participation in political processes about which most of us had little knowledge or interest. We were also insufficiently sensitive to the preexisting meanings (and value-laden responses) to the term social justice in the communities in which we were working. Although I have no proof, I am convinced that many people heard the term, assumed that we meant what they would mean by it, and opposed us because they opposed what they understood the term to mean, even if it was quite different from the specific proposals we were advancing. Had we been in patterns of dialogic communication, these and similar concerns could have been articulated, heard, and responded to in a way that might well have reduced a good bit of the opposition to our project.

With the benefit of distance in time and space, I now understand that it is possible for good people to oppose our project for good reasons. Some of these included the following:

- Genuine compassion and care for others; for example, students whose career prospects might be compromised.
- Genuine concern for the "positioning" of the department and the university within complex social systems of economics and power.
- Personal discomfort with bringing into our classes and our research the tensions between the "haves" and "have nots."

- Having different systems in view (e.g., individuals, interpersonal systems, society-wide systems) and different concepts of the dynamics involved (e.g., the differences between personal ethics and social justice).
- A considered rejection of the worldview and social analyses that lay behind our commitments.
- Legitimate differences in conceptualization of social justice.
- Genuine feelings of wanting to be on the moral high ground but feeling that we had, in various ways, worked to appropriate it for ourselves.

Had the dominant pattern of communication been dialogic, we would have engaged these concerns at the point of trying to make sure that they enriched and improved our project. Instead, the engagement was at the confrontational point of deciding whether the project should be implemented as is or blocked. By getting into zero-sum conflicts and all-or-nothing proposals, we lost the opportunity that dialogic communication offers for learning, creativity, and evolution of ideas.

After leaving Loyola, my research and practice has focused on ways to create the preconditions for dialogic communication in public settings about highly charged issues (see Pearce, 2002; Pearce & Littlejohn, 1997; Spano, 2001). These experiences have increased my appreciation for the values of dialogic communication as well as enriching my appreciation for the wisdom, skill, and hard work involved in bringing it about.

GETTING THE PROCESS RIGHT IS THE SINGLE BEST GUARANTEE THAT THE BEST POSSIBLE THINGS WILL HAPPEN

For 30 years, I have been a central part of the development of the theory of the coordinated management of meaning (Barge & Pearce, 2004); for the past 10 years, I have also been engaged in a number of projects designed to improve the quality of public communication in cities and other communities (Pearce, Spano, & Pearce, in press). These experiences as a scholar-practitioner (see Pearce & Pearce, 2000) have shaped my belief in the centrality of process.

All of us seeking to promote social justice are trying to make better social worlds. The question is not whether we should act to accomplish those goals, but how we can do so most effectively. One idea is to start with some vision of the desired outcome and to reason backward to the means by which it can be achieved. In my opinion, no matter what goal is envisioned, this procedure gives undue importance to abstract, generalized ideas. However, there are at least two distinct ways in which we can affirm the other option—focusing on specific situations. One is to take sides; being for one group and at the same time against others. Another is to focus on what we are making together in that specific situation. If we focus on what we are making together, we should and can be for everyone in the situation, even if those people and groups are against each other. That is, we are neither partisans nor neutral; we are passionately committed to the question of what game is being played, and, that determined, how it is being played. Less metaphorically, we seek to bring about a second-order change in the relationships among the people involved to create patterns of relationship in which better things can happen. For examples of how this works, see Pearce (2002) and Spano (2001).

Note that this commitment to getting the process right does not mean that a perfect outcome will occur. In the spirit of Dewey's (1929) critique of the unintended and unwanted consequences of the quest for certainty, I believe that the world is too uncertain and complex to impose any notion of perfection or any person or group's idea of the right way of being. Rather, this lesson says that if the process is right then the best possible outcomes (which might be rather far from anybody's notion of the ideal outcomes) are most likely to be achieved.

To act according to this lesson involves taking a not-knowing position in relation to the outcome of the process. This position is warranted by the belief that any determined effort to steer any process to a predetermined outcome is guaranteed to come into conflict with the ideas of other people and the unpredictability described by chaos theory. At the same time, this rationale compels intense attention to the qualities of the process, whether that process is the interaction between teacher and student in the classroom or between researcher and the subject population (or coresearchers) in the field.

In *Communication and the Human Condition* (Pearce, 1989), I made the bold claim that all persons, everywhere, in all societies, must work toward coordination in actions with their fellows, coherence in their meanings about themselves and the world around them, and mystery in recognition of the gap between the potential and what they are able to achieve in coordination and coherence. The form of communication is the way in which these universal tasks are accomplished.

One description of the right process is the concept of cosmopolitan communication that contrasts with monocultural, ethnocentric, and modernistic forms of communication:

> Cosmopolitan communication results from a commitment to find ways of achieving coordination without (1) denying the existence or humanity of "other" ways of achieving coherence and mystery, as monocultural communication does; (2) deprecating or opposing "other" ways of achieving coherence and mystery, as ethnocentric communication does; or (3) being committed to a perpetual process of changing one's own way of achieving coherence and mystery, as modernistic communication does. When performed well—with high levels of social eloquence—cosmopolitan communication enables coordination among groups with different, even incommensurate, social realities. Unlike other forms of communication, it is particularly sensitive to the unintended consequences of practices and to the nonsummative nature of the logic of interaction. (Pearce, 1989, p. 169)

This definition of cosmopolitan communication depends much more on comparisons and negations than on forthright statements of what it looks like in practice. I have started to use the term *dialogue* as a positive statement, defined as remaining in the tension between standing your ground and being profoundly open to the other (Pearce & Pearce, 2004).

The primary salutary effect of engaging in dialogic communication or cosmopolitan communication (for these purposes, the same thing) is that they transform practices and ideas in ways that promote social justice. For example, one cannot engage in dialogue with another person without transforming the relationship such that power is redefined in a more mutual, equitable manner. When we engage in dialogue, we have to take a certain (and, in the present political context, increasingly rare) perspective to our own truths: to see them as partial, incomplete, provisional. Dialogic communication both requires and enables us to take a magnanimous approach to our social position and culture by seeing ourselves, as Geertz (1983) put it, "amongst others; as a local example of the forms human life has locally taken, a case among cases, a world among worlds. Without this largeness of mind," he concluded, "objectivity is self-congratulation and tolerance is a sham" (p. 16).

The models and concepts of the theory of the coordinated management of meaning may be seen as prostheses for the series of transformations involved in cosmopolitan communication. These transformations include seeing one's self in patterns of interactions with others (the serpentine model), as caught up in patterns of reciprocally defining stories about the world in which we live (the hierarchy model), of living in densely textured clusters of relationships with others (the daisy model) that are shaped by the stories we live and tell as well as by those that we do not tell, do not hear, and do not know (the LUUUTT model).

For example, there are several ways in which one can be for others. One sense (in the absence of being with them) is to advocate or do good things for them from a distance. Another sense (involving being with them) involves joining them as allies, making their enemies our enemies. The cosmopolitan perspective advocated here would suggest a third way: committing ourselves to be the custodian or curator of a fair, open-ended process. In doing so, we are for everyone, including those people who (currently) see themselves opposed to others. There are several ways of being with others, among them one-way service delivery (taking an expert role, bringing charity) as opposed to full collaboration. The cosmopolitan communication process inevitably involves full collaboration.

There are substantial tensions involved in being simultaneously for and with others. Some of these tensions are addressed in Pearce's (2002) *Making Better Social Worlds: Engaging in and Facilitating Dialogic Communication*, but this remains a topic deserving continuing attention.

CONCLUSION

I am proud of the project in which my colleagues in the Department of Communication at Loyola University Chicago and I engaged. I am well aware of ways in which it could have been conducted better. I hope my reflections on the project and the lessons I have drawn from it will be useful to others who promote social justice.

REFERENCES

Artz, L. (1998). African-Americans and higher education: An exigence in need of applied communication. *Journal of Applied Communication Research, 26*, 210–321.

Artz, L. (2001). Critical analysis and praxis in service learning. *Southern Communication Journal, 66*, 239–250.

Barge, J. K., & Pearce, W. B. (2004). A reconnaissance of CMM research. *Human Systems, 15*, 13–32.

Bellah, R., Madsen, R., Sullivan, W. M., Swidler, A., & Tipton, S. M. (1985). *Habits of the heart: Individualism and commitment in American life.* Berkeley: University of California Press.

Crabtree, R. D. (1998). Mutual empowerment in cross-cultural participatory development and service learning: Lessons in communication and social justice from projects in El Salvador and Nicaragua. *Journal of Applied Communication Research, 26*, 182–209.

Dewey, J. (1929). *The quest for certainty.* New York: Putnam.

Droge, D., & Murphy, B. O. (Eds.). (1999). *Voices of strong democracy: Concepts and models for service-learning in communication studies.* Washington, DC: American Association for Higher Education.

Frey, L. R., Pearce, W. B., Pollock, M. A., Artz, L., & Murphy, B. A. O. (1996). Looking for justice in all the wrong places: On a communication approach to social justice. *Communication Studies, 47,* 110–127.

Frey, L. R., Pollock, M. A., Artz, L., & Pearce, W. B. (1996). From medium to context to *praxis* and process: Transforming the undergraduate communication curriculum. *World Communication, 25,* 79–89.

Geertz, C. (1983). *Local knowledge.* New York: Basic Books.

Levine, P. (1998). *Living without philosophy: On narrative, rhetoric, and morality.* Albany: State University of New York Press.

Makau, J. M. (1996). Notes on communication education and social justice. *Communication Studies, 47,* 131–141.

Myers, C. L. (2005, January). *Talking poverty: Power arrangements in poverty discourse.* Unpublished doctoral dissertation, Fielding Graduate University, Santa Barbara, CA.

Olson, K. M., & Olson, C. D. (2003). Problems of exclusionary research criteria: The case against the "usable knowledge' litmus test for social justice communication research. *Communication Studies, 54,* 438–450.

Pearce, K. A. (2002). *Making better social worlds: Engaging in and facilitating dialogic communication.* Redwood City, CA: Pearce Associates.

Pearce, K. A., Spano, C., & Pearce, W. B. (in press). The multiple faces of the Public Dialogue Consortium: Scholars, practitioners, and dreamers of better social worlds. In L. R. Frey & K. N. Cissna (Eds.), *Handbook of applied communication.* Mahwah, NJ: Lawrence Erlbaum Associates, Inc.

Pearce, W. B. (1989). *Communication and the human condition.* Carbondale: Southern Illinois University Press.

Pearce, W. B. (1998). On putting social justice in the discipline of communication and putting enriched concepts of communication in social justice research and practice. *Journal of Applied Communication Research, 26,* 272–278.

Pearce, W. B. (2004). The coordinated management of meaning. In W. Gudykunst (Ed.), *Theorizing communication and culture* (pp. 35–54). Thousand Oaks, CA: Sage.

Pearce, W. B., & Littlejohn, S. W. (1997). *Moral conflict: When social worlds collide.* Thousand Oaks, CA: Sage.

Pearce, W. B., & Pearce, K. A. (2000). Extending the theory of the coordinated management of meaning ("CMM") through a community dialogue process. *Communication Theory, 10,* 405–423.

Pearce, W. B., & Pearce, K. A. (2004). Taking a communication approach to dialogue. In R. Anderson, L. Baxter, & K. Cissna (Eds.), *Dialogue: Theorizing difference in communication* (pp. 39–56). Thousand Oaks, CA: Sage.

Pollock, M. A., Artz, L., Frey, L. R., Pearce, W. B., & Murphy, B. A. O. (1996). Navigating between Scylla and Charybdis: Continuing the dialogue on communication and social justice. *Communication Studies, 47,* 142–151.

Rorty, R. (1979). *Philosophy and the mirror of nature.* Princeton, NJ: Princeton University Press.

Ryan, C., Carragee, K. M., & Schwerner, C. (1998). Media, movements and the quest for social justice. *Journal of Applied Communication Research, 26,* 165–181.

Sayler, M. D. (2004, July). *Humiliation and the poor: A study in the management of meaning.* Unpublished doctoral dissertation, Fielding Graduate University, Santa Barbara, CA.

Spano, S. (2001). *Public dialogue and participatory democracy: The Cupertino Community Project.* Cresskill, NJ: Hampton.

Stout, J. (1988). *Ethics after Babel: The languages of morals and their discontents.* Boston: Beacon Press.

Toulmin, S. (1990). *Cosmopolis: The hidden agenda of modernity.* Chicago: University of Chicago Press.

Wasserman, I. C. (2004, January). *Discursive processes that foster dialogic moments: Transformation in the engagement of social identity group differences in dialogue.* Unpublished doctoral dissertation, Fielding Graduate University, Santa Babara, CA.

Wood, J. T. (1996a). [Review of the book *Communication of social support: Messages, interactions, relationships, and community*]. *Quarterly Journal of Speech, 82,* 105–107.

Wood, J. T. (1996b). Social justice: Alive and well in the field of communication. *Communication Studies, 47,* 128–134.

12

Conclusion:
On the Material
Consequence
of Defining Social Justice

Lee Artz
Purdue University Calumet

This collection of chapters reflects dramatically two important conditions of contemporary social justice scholarship. First, its publication underscores the increased concern with social justice within communication studies and indicates an emerging acceptance of its scholarship claims. In less than a decade, social justice communication studies has become vital and vibrant, as indicated by an increase in published books, journal articles, conference presentations, and curriculum development (e.g., Droge & Murphy, 1999; Frey, 1998; Frey & Carragee, 2005; Swartz, 2005; Wood, 1996). We now have a lively community of self-identified social justice scholars passionate about using their skills, understandings, and academic positions to improve the human condition. In the tradition of understanding communication as both a reflector and creator of social relations and social practices, the authors in this edited collection represent a commitment to recognizing and adjusting communication processes for a greater social good, understood in a myriad of ways.

This myriad of understandings, however, is the second notable assessment triggered by this book: Any accepted definition of social justice remains elusive, but urgently needed. Most of the authors in this volume reference the Loyola University Chicago scholars' definition of social justice as an "engagement with and advocacy for those in our society who are economically, socially, politically, and/or culturally under resourced" (Frey, Pearce, Pollock, Artz, & Murphy, 1996, p. 110). Contributors proceed to modify, challenge, extend, or subsume that initial suggestion within some rubric other than social justice, such as voice (Simpson & Adelman, chap. 5, this volume), global multiculturalism (Shome, chap. 6, this volume), interpersonal communication (Crumley, chap. 9, this volume), ontology (Rodriguez, chap. 2, this volume), performative affordance (Lee, chap. 10, this volume), or partisan criticism (Swartz, chap. 1, this volume). Thus, despite the stated shared spirit for communities of justice with what Swartz calls a "radically democratic social agenda," the authors assembled here champion widely disparate banners of social justice.

On the surface, the differences seem to be those of emphasis or research site. After closer observation, however, it appears more fundamental: Underlying tensions among perspectives on what constitutes social justice and its priorities influence the research arena, teaching, and action of social justice communication studies. More important, the uneasy alliance of ambiguity undermines fulfillment of the social justice charge. Perhaps this text calls forth a watershed moment inadvertently asking this question: What is the future for social justice and communication studies? To proceed we desperately need clarity in definition to help identify agency and objectives. In this final brief chapter, I do not intend to summarize or attempt to have the final word. Instead, I dearly want to challenge professed social justice researchers and advocates to consider the material reality of injustice and its naked call for on-the-ground resolution.

THE SOCIAL JUSTICE IMPERATIVE

Many do not share my resolute concern for defining social justice and its scholarly obligation, because it seems stark and strident, challenging all to bring their "street cred" (e.g., Olson & Olson, 2003; Wood, 1996). In his reflection on the backlash against the social justice project at Loyola Chicago, for instance, Pearce (chap. 11, this volume) recognizes the consequences of being "insufficiently precise" in defining social justice, yet still prefers the pragmatic avoidance of "abstract generalizations" in the "moral philosophy" tradition. Pearce favors "further elaboration of the alternative paradigm," loosely described as "making perspicacious distinctions" of interpretation of instances of justice and injustice. Admittedly, abstractions do not always help resolve concrete cases. Nonetheless, making any distinction always requires some evaluative criteria. Meanwhile, maintaining unlimited tolerance for ambiguity not only disguises significant disagreement, it also inadvertently weakens the appeal for justice. If we are unable or unwilling to recognize justice or injustice, how are we to achieve social relations and practices necessary for a just world (certainly not by accident or goodwill)? I suggest that even case-by-case interpretations of conditions or practices as instances of social justice or injustice requires some shared vocabulary—as Pearce himself notes—which essentially comprises a definition of social justice disguised as situated judgments.

Granted, entire historic movements have made revolutionary changes without waiting for theoretical purity or definitional clarity. In Nicaragua in 1979, for example, the dictatorship of Anastasio Somoza was overthrown by a coalition of workers, peasants, mothers of martyrs, Christian lay workers, students, and middle-class professionals under the leadership of a politically eclectic and organizationally divided radical-nationalist liberation front, the *Frente Sandinista Liberacíon Nacional* (FSLN). As Pearce would note, none needed "abstract generalizations" about dictatorships, nor, despite the largely Catholic tendencies of the population, did many need an extended logic in "moral philosophy." Rather, the material experience of injustice and the possibility of collective action securing some semblance of justice prompted thousands into revolutionary action (Artz, 1997)—with the leadership of the FSLN coordinating actions that ended the injustices of the dictatorship. In the course of a few months of collective, organized, and conscious human action, an unjust social order was dismantled and the foundations were laid for a new society dedicated to equality, freedom, and justice (Melrose, 1985). Although U.S. intervention soon destroyed physically the potential of the Nicaragua revolution (Walker, 1982), the 10-year experiment in transformation from dictatorship to democracy illustrates several requirements for social change: conscious leadership, clarity of purpose, and engaged public dialogue and communication. Nicaraguans were not unique in their oppression—Salvadorans, Guatemalans, Hondurans, and others throughout Central and Latin America continue to live under similar conditions—but their good example underscores how a shared community of dedicated intellectual activists (in the Gramscian sense) might dialogue with citizens to construct a program of action (see Gramsci, 1971).

Of course, academics can survive considerable ambiguity: A complex of concepts and actions that have an affinity of temperament can even proceed and grow as an identifiable and recognizable subdiscipline. This leads to an obvious question: If social justice is unidentified or so ambiguous as to permit any research using the buzzword, how will the resultant legitimacy and collegiality of that inclusive interest group be effective in promoting social justice? As many contributors to this volume assume, intellectuals have an obligation to engage in scholarship and public presentation that advances understanding and, ultimately, the human condition. Accepting ambiguity about social justice solely for the sake of civility and collegial relations only aids and abets injustice. Consider: Does the "Healthy Forests" initiative protect trees? Does the "Clear Skies" program improve air quality? Does "social justice" phrasing empower any scholarship or application? Ambiguity about justice seems naive at its idealistic best and obstructionist in actual practice. To paraphrase Dr. Martin Luther King, Jr., justice undefined is justice undelivered. Although Pearce fears "strident voices from each position denouncing those" with other positions, I believe those motivated to promote social justice can dialogue civilly and productively, even in the midst of harsh critique (e.g., Olson & Olson, 2003). More important, whatever controversy arises, the best means for improving our knowledge and hence our realization of social justice is to engage continually the "methods of debate and discussion" (Dewey, 1927, p. 208). Besides, given the conditions of social injustice in this world, including slavery, starvation, imprisonment, war and occupation, and oppressive exploitation, we should be able to tolerate some discomfort or disruption within our discipline as we seek to contribute to a just world. I am not advocating harangues or polemic excesses. I am suggesting that we need to emulate the contributions in this volume by Swartz, Frey, Pearce, and others: to move our conversations forward, as cordially as possible, recognizing the good intentions of all, yet willing to accept disagreement and sharp challenges in the ongoing participatory pursuit of improved methods, clearer theories, and more powerful applications of our insights for changing the world.

This collection of essays provides examples of the kind of reciprocal communication needed within a community of social justice scholars, including multiple instances of style and form that encourage engaged, open conversation, from public task forces (Tompkins, chap. 4, this volume) and classroom activities (Rodriguez, chap. 2, this volume) to enacted public performances (Lee, chap. 10, this volume; Simpson & Adelman, chap. 5, this volume). Certainly the skills and sensibilities of our collective experience should enable us to construct the means and methods for participatory, reciprocal communication in the dialogic tradition, accepting that although we have no Socrates, we all have perspectives to share as we resolve our disparities (or not) and identify our complementary understandings. This means that from whatever definition of social justice we begin, whether the initial Loyola Chicago contribution or some other formulation, we can identify deficiencies, strengths, and possibilities for definitions and characteristics of social justice in communication studies. The result of this process should help identify priorities for where and when we can contribute to understandings and actions that will have some material consequence and move us closer to a just world.

As a closing contribution to this challenge, I offer a series of assumptive observations presented as a series of questions intended to spur response, critique, and modification.

1. *Is justice and injustice a human construction that can be identified in concrete, identifiable practices?* In contemporary society, are these practices institutionally structured? Do existing institutions and practices secure and advance material privileges for identifiable social groups? Do existing institutions and practices reflect and represent the power to name, to decide, and to benefit? In other words, does social justice have a material consequence for organizing social relations that influence our quality of life? Further, if social justice and injustice are the result of particular social relations, material practices, and institutions, can we observe and identify those relations, practices, and institutions that advance social justice? Given that all social and cultural processes are complex and contradictory, can we identify any apparent features or material manifestations of global social justice and injustice?

2. *Does social position, experience, or interest influence the perception of justice and injustice?* Is it possible that those benefitting from inequality might not recognize or be willing to acknowledge the injustice of existing arrangements? Do contradictions among experiences and perceptions of diverse social groups change the material consequence of justice or injustice? In other words, do those with power and privilege have the right to deny the existence of injustice, or determine actions intended to win justice?

3. *Is social justice different from justice?* Is there a difference between the injustice of an individual wrongly accused due to the testimony of an impaired eyewitness and the social injustice of groups of individuals wrongly imprisoned due to de facto racism; economic inequality; or class, gender, or religious policy that intentionally privileges an elite group? Is the energy and commitment of John McHale's defense of a wrongly accused prisoner an example for activism (cited in this volume by Frey, chap. 3, this volume), or does it also address the social injustice of disproportionate convictions, sentences, and executions of Black youth? What difference does it make for scholarship, advocacy, and application if social justice can be differentiated from justice more narrowly, individually, or legally defined? Is there a level of justice to be valued beyond fairness and equity in individual relations?

4. *What is the relationship among individual consciousness, interpersonal relations, and the cultural fabric of social relations that create social justice or injustice?* How is the individual experience of interpersonal relations and practices connected to culturally normalized and ritualized relations of power and institutionally organized practices? What is the material significance of individual students being tolerant of difference while the social injustices of poverty, homelessness, unemployment, illiteracy, and institutional discrimination increase? Can one address social justice without recognizing social relations, without some intentional action for change? Is social justice simply the outcome of good intention?

5. *Does social justice include rights?* Do those suffering injustice, inequality, and oppression need permission from those benefitting, participating, or practicing injustice? Do slaves have a right to freedom? Do hungry children have a right to eat? Do the homeless have a right to shelter? Or do they each need permission from the established power and its social order? Is tolerance of the homeless, the indigent, or the outcast sufficiently just? Do alms release the charitable from responsibility? Must the powerful and ignorant be persuaded before justice is granted or achieved? In other words, if beneficiaries of injustice fail to recognize or respond, should the inequities be accepted until such time as enlightenment comes—or should the right to justice be privileged over inequality in realizable actions?

6. *If we accept that all humans have the right to life, to eat, to peace, to human resources, and to human dignity, at what point must we consider global institutions and practices that impact the lives of millions?* Should we bracket the material consequence of trade and profit and power? Should we deny the material existence of those institutions (e.g., the International Monetary Fund, the World Bank, the U.S. military, and a legion of transnational corporations) and practices (from outsourcing, sweatshops, child labor, and the sex trade, to military occupations and government-sanctioned torture) that are features of our capitalist world? How can we meaningfully champion social justice and ignore capitalism, its institutions, and its practices? How can we discuss social justice in the early 21st century without confronting the market economy and global structures of the free market? In every country, on every continent, mass movements for social justice have arisen that challenge the injustices of policies and practices organized by institutions of power (e.g., Assies, 2003; Beinin, 2005; Parenti, 2005; http://www.asia-pacific-action.org/; http://www.zmag.org/weluser.htm). Even a cursory look at the World Social Forum or other more regional sites of conversation and organizing by the oppressed and impoverished of the world suggests the real existence of movements for social justice. Are they mistaken and mis-

guided? Water rights, health care, land rights, national resources, the right to a job, security and safety, and a sustainable environment are but a few of the predominant issues of these campaigns for social justice. Moreover, as noted in a John Berger quote on the inside cover of the program booklet for the World Tribunal on Iraq, "The new tyrants, incomparably over armed, can win every war—both military and economic. Yet they are losing the war of communication. They are not winning the support of world public opinion. More and more people are saying no. Finally this will be the tyranny's undoing. But after how many more tragedies, invasions, and collateral disasters?" (quoted in Reinart, 2005, p. 3). We know that thousands of communication strategists are working for injustice in this war; so, how can social justice communication scholars contribute to democracy and equality in this war of communication to stop the injustice and suffering?

7. *Even confining social justice research and advocacy more locally, how can we seriously challenge injustice without admitting the societal dimensions?* For instance, how can we understand homelessness without implicating the material consequences of real estate, insurance, and banking practices? At what point does the human right to shelter submit to the right to a decent return on investment? What then is the kind of social justice advocated if the rights of banks, realtors, investors, and slum lords must be "balanced" with the right of all citizens to shelter? Perhaps ambiguity on the meaning of social justice has a material benefit after all. Consider this: At what point is the right to life, the right to health care, the right to nutrition, and even the right to water, superseded by cleverly worded laws, protected corporate profits, and agency practices that obstruct the realization of these human rights? Granted we understand the efficacy of good public relations and well-constructed persuasive arguments, but still, should we counsel the oppressed to be careful about offending the comfortable? Does the right to education require the less educated to be more literate, more refined, more convincing, less offensive, less obnoxious, and less demanding? Should we instruct the impoverished, the unwashed, the illiterate, and the socially outcast to improve their persuasive skills as a prerequisite to defending their rights? Must civility precede justice?

8. *Is it possible that injustice is more recognizable, more experiential for the subordinate than for those who benefit or tolerate injustice?* Is it possible that discrimination occurs without the awareness and intent of people of good will? Must the oppressor recognize inequality before the oppressed has the right to resist? Must the slave convince the master of his or her humanity before fleeing or refusing the lash, the shackle, the prison? Before justice may be demanded, granted, or wrested, must the beneficiaries and practitioners of

injustice be persuaded of the error of their ways? Does ignorance of injustice excuse support for and benefit from injustice? In short, what rights belong to the beneficiaries of an unjust social order? Which unjust practice should be privileged or tolerated over social justice?

9. *Is social justice negotiable?* If rights are situated within conditions constructed by human agents, intentionally or inadvertently, and justice is morally superior to injustice, does the securing of human and civil rights include the right to change the practices, institutions, and relations of an unjust social order or condition? Must the other wait for recognition? What if we are the other? How can one be nonpartisan on actual issues of social justice? Should one be impartial on torture, slavery, and hunger? Well-financed elite death squads in Brazil regularly assassinated street children in the 1980s as a means of ridding polite society of criminal elements and social refuse. Would urban teens in Rio be immoral in defending themselves by any means necessary?

10. *What if the material realization of social justice begins with the actions of those having none?* What if social justice is defined and enacted by those denied equality of benefits and burdens by contemporary social relations? What if the working masses and their allies are the determining audiences, agents, and enactors of social justice? What if they do not need the approval of the officials of an unjust society? What happens when the right to human dignity is greater than any existing legal norm or privilege? What happens when the right of human dignity seems reasonable, desired, and required by world citizens who recognize the other as that minority that benefits from injustice? Although social disruption will occur and the results may be contradictory and messy, it is possible to realize changes for social justice, peacefully and democratically. Even the uneven action of the Venezuelan revolution indicates as much: Land reform has benefitted small farmers, education is now free to the university level, popular food markets have stanched hunger, and worker cooperatives have turned waste dumps into shoe and shirt factories and found employment for thousands (Parenti, 2005). The point is not simply to urge solidarity for democracy in Venezuela and to insist on resistance to U.S. intervention—that would require answering the public relations slanders engineered by the Venezuelan elite, their media monopoly, and their U.S. advisors—which can easily be done. Rather, the example of Venezuela (or Nicaragua in the 1980s) is mentioned only to illustrate how debates on social justice necessarily entail discussion and debate over conditions, practices, and possible actions to achieve social justice.

It is not a little troubling that in a book on social justice, few contributors (Wander, chap. 7, being the obvious exception) focused on the U.S. occupation of Afghanistan and Iraq, the U.S. political and military offensives against Latin America, the catastrophic destruction of the environment, or the consolidation of wealth and power in manufacturing, trade, and media. Nonetheless, these urgent crises and active social movements struggling for social justice around the world indicate that these should be among our priorities. Of course, participation in conversations about these conditions and actions to overcome these conditions is fraught with disagreement over evaluations and prescriptions—but social justice demands no less. We seek to include all, but that inclusion must be predicated on social justice for all. Unity can never mean inequality. Social justice means the end of advantage. Elite critics of Chavez in Venezuela fear that they may lose their privileges, and rightly so, for their privilege is contingent on the poverty and injustice of millions. However, "far from ruining the country," there are "good things happening" (Parenti, 2005, p. 8), despite orchestrated elite condemnations that sound eerily familiar to the criticisms launched by critics of social justice scholarship (Fish, 2004; Kuypers, 2000) that always defend the vagaries of the status quo.

If social justice means securing for humanity the right to all the burdens and benefits of humanity, then working for social justice must also mean we have a responsibility to advocate, advance, and secure those rights as democratically, persuasively, and effectively as possible, as soon as possible, in opposition to all existing obstacles. In the words of Reinart (2005), who witnessed testimony at the World Tribunal on Iraq, "solidarity is not a sentimental nicety, but a huge, transforming reality" (p. 4). To transform our reality to one of social justice, we must be vigilant in our solidarity with those in struggle.

Tantum possumus, tantum scimus
(We do what we know)

REFERENCES

Artz, L. (1997). Social power and the inflation of discourse: The failure of popular hegemony in Nicaragua. *Latin American Perspectives, 24*, 92–113.

Assies, W. (2003). David versus Goliath in Cochabamba: Water rights, neoliberalism, and the revival of social protest in Bolivia. *Latin American Perspectives, 30*, 14–36.

Beinin, J. (2005, March 10). Popular social movements and the future of Egyptian politics. *Middle East Report and Information Project*. Retrieved June 10, 2005, from http://www.merip.org/mero/mero031005.html

Dewey, J. (1927). *The public and its problems*. New York: Holt.

Droge, D., & Murphy, B. O. (Eds.). (1999). *Voices of strong democracy: Concepts and models for service-learning in communication studies*. Washington, DC: American Association for Higher Education.

Fish, S. (2004, May 21). Why we built the ivory tower. *New York Times*, p. A23.

Frey, L. R. (Ed.). (1998). Communication and social justice research [Special issue]. *Journal of Applied Communication Research, 26*.

Frey, L. R., & Carragee, K. M. (Eds.). (2005). *Communication activism* (2 vols.). Cresskill, NJ: Hampton.

Frey, L. R., Pearce, W. B., Pollock, M., Artz, L., & Murphy, B. (1996). Looking for justice in all the wrong places: On a communication approach to social justice. *Communication Studies, 47,* 110–127.

Gramsci, A. (1971). *Selections from the prison notebooks.* New York: International Publishers.

Kuypers, J. A. (2000). Must we all be political activists? *American Communication Journal, 4*(1), 1–13.

Melrose, D. (1985). *Nicaragua: The threat of a good example.* London: Oxfam.

Olson, K. M., & Olson, C. D. (2003). Problems of exclusionary research criteria: The case against the "usable knowledge" litmus test for social justice communication research. *Communication Studies, 54,* 438–450.

Parenti, M. (2005, July–August). Good things happening in Venezuela. *Z Magazine,* pp. 8–10.

Reinart, U. B. (2005, July–August). World tribunal on Iraq. *Z Magazine,* pp. 3–7.

Swartz, O. (2005). *In defense of partisan criticism.* New York: Peter Lang.

Walker, T. W. (1982). *Revolution and counterrevolution in Nicaragua.* Boulder, CO: Westview.

Wood, J. T. (1996). Social justice: Alive and well in the field of communication. *Communication Studies, 47,* 128–234.

Author Index

Subject Index